MASTERS

OF THE AIR

MASTERS
OF THE AIR

The Great War Pilots
McLeod, McKeever, and MacLaren

ROGER GUNN

DUNDURN
TORONTO

Publisher: Scott Fraser | Acquiring editor: Kathryn Lane | Editor: Dominic Farrell
Designer: Laura Boyle
Cover images (left to right): McLeod, © Imperial War Museum, Q 067601
McKeever, Library and Archives Canada, PA- 006026
MacLaren, Directorate of History and Heritage, 2015-06-28-0-32650

Printer: Webcom, a division of Marquis Book Printing Inc.

Library and Archives Canada Cataloguing in Publication

Title: Masters of the air : the Great War pilots McLeod, McKeever, and MacLaren / Roger Gunn.
Names: Gunn, Roger, author.
Description: Includes bibliographical references and index.
Identifiers: Canadiana (print) 20190181354 | Canadiana (ebook) 20190181362 | ISBN 9781459745483 (softcover) | ISBN 9781459745490 (PDF) | ISBN 9781459745506 (EPUB)
Subjects: LCSH: McLeod, Alan Arnett, 1899-1918. | LCSH: McKeever, Andrew Edward, 1894-1919. | LCSH: MacLaren, Donald, 1893-1988. | LCSH: Fighter pilots—Canada—Biography. | LCSH: Great Britain. Royal Flying Corps—Airmen—Biography. | LCSH: World War, 1914-1918—Aerial operations, British. | LCGFT: Biographies.
Classification: LCC D602 .G86 2019 | DDC 940.4/4941092311—dc23

We acknowledge the support of the Canada Council for the Arts and the Ontario Arts Council for our publishing program. We also acknowledge the financial support of the Government of Ontario, through the Ontario Book Publishing Tax Credit and Ontario Creates, and the Government of Canada.

VISIT US AT
 dundurn.com | @dundurnpress | dundurnpress | dundurnpress

Dundurn
3 Church Street, Suite 500
Toronto, Ontario, Canada
M5E 1M2

To my grandchildren. May they never have to fight in a war.

Contents

Introduction

The First World War, fought just over one hundred years ago, saw men fully engaged in a war in the air, shooting each other down at the first opportunity. It had been only a half a dozen years prior that the first known flight in Canada of a heavier-than-air machine, called the Silver Dart, flew across Bras d'Or Lake in Cape Breton, under the watchful eye of Alexander Graham Bell. The famous inventor of the telephone spent his summers in Nova Scotia and took an interest in the creation of a flying machine. Necessity is the mother of invention, and the coming of the First World War advanced the technology of flying a thousandfold.

Much has been written about Billy Bishop, the highest-scoring Canadian pilot in the First World War, and there are some books on William Barker and Raymond Collishaw, two of the other famed Canadian pilots of the war, but none are devoted to three lesser-known Canadian pilots: Alan McLeod, Andrew McKeever, and Donald MacLaren. They were distinctively different from each other. So too were the machines they flew, and their respective roles in the war. McLeod flew reconnaissance and artillery-spotting missions in an Armstrong Whitworth F.K.8, McKeever a two-seat Bristol F.2B Fighter, and MacLaren a Sopwith Camel scout (today we would refer to this as a fighter plane). All three of these pilots are brought to life in this book, which explores their courage, exploits, and near-death experiences in the skies above France. These three men achieved greatness in the air and on the ground in an era of suffering and devotion to duty. They answered the call to go to war. They, like many thousands of others, went overseas to fight for the British Empire. It survived — but was very badly battered. The war would end up destroying monarchies across Europe, and completely alter the way that men and women saw the world.

McLeod, McKeever, and MacLaren were remarkable. These three Canadian pilots of the First World War should be recognized for their accomplishments.

As he lay in his hospital bed, with his head and shoulders propped up by extra pillows, Second Lieutenant Alan Arnett McLeod reflected on the events of March 27, 1918, which had brought him here, to the Prince of Wales Hospital in London. He did not think his actions in the sky over the battlefield of France that day were particularly brave. Yes, he had kept his machine under control while it had been shot about by eight enemy triplanes. But the worst part was the bullet to the petrol tank, causing flames to erupt and practically consume the aircraft. He had somehow managed to land his biplane and, while it was still burning, rescue his observer, Lieutenant Hammond, who was unconscious from the loss of blood from his injuries.

He felt what he had done that day was the same as any pilot would have done to keep himself and his observer (gunner) alive. He contemplated the praise and attention he was receiving now he was back in England, under the care of the medical staff at the London hospital. He felt he really did not deserve it. He was humbled by it all. The visitors, the flowers brought to his bedside by pretty ladies, the mentions in the press. It was all so unnecessary, he felt.

* * *

On March 21, 1918, six days before Second Lieutenant McLeod was shot down, the Germans began their last big offensive: Operation Michael. Seventy-six German divisions engaged twenty-eight British divisions in the Ypres, Armentières, and Béthune areas of the Western Front. General Ludendorff, commander of the German forces, knew that this offensive was his last chance to bring the Allies to their knees, before overwhelming numbers of American soldiers would arrive at the front.

On March 27, the members of No. 11 Squadron moved to the aerodrome at Fienvillers. However, they were without Andrew Edward McKeever and his observer, Leslie Powell, as they had been withdrawn to Home Establishment, in defence of England, on January 15, 1918. By that time, McKeever had destroyed thirty-one enemy aircraft and Powell, with his rear-facing machine gun, had accounted for nineteen more. From Fienvillers the squadron's pilots carried out numerous attacks against the advancing enemy infantry. Flying their Bristol Fighters, No. 11 Squadron pilots carried out low-level strafing and bombing runs, harassing the advancing Germans.

From March 15 to April 7, 1918, squadrons of the Royal Air Force fired no less than two-and-a-half million rounds of ammunition, mostly at ground targets, and dropped 34,154 bombs of all sizes.[1] One pilot carrying out such missions was Donald Roderick MacLaren, of No. 46 Squadron.

On March 27, the same day McLeod was shot down and McKeever was with Home Establishment, Flight Commander MacLaren took off in his Sopwith Camel B9153 with the rest of his flight. It was a clear morning, perfect flying weather. As they were climbing to three thousand feet, MacLaren spotted a German two-seater observation machine flying over British-held territory. MacLaren was first to attack, surprising the German machine. He poured a few rounds into it and saw it dive to the earth. He must have killed the pilot instantly. The poor rear gunner was helpless, and the two-seater toppled downward. It was MacLaren's thirteenth victory. Don MacLaren had joined 46 Squadron in France on November 23, 1917. He went on to be that squadron's highest-scoring ace.

PART 1

Alan Arnett McLeod, VC

ONE

The Early Days and Flight Training

Born on April 20, 1899, in the small town of Stonewall, some twelve miles north of Manitoba's capital, Winnipeg, Alan Arnett McLeod had a reasonably uneventful childhood. His father, Dr. Alexander Neil McLeod, was a prominent member of the community. A general practitioner, he provided all manner of medical services to the community, including delivering babies and tending to the ill, for miles around. He was also the Stony Mountain prison's physician. Alan McLeod's mother was Margaret Lyllian Arnett, who in later life became a noted historian of the Red River and Métis settlements. Alan had two younger sisters, Helen and Marion.

The McLeod family home, constructed in 1900, is at 292 Main Street. A spacious four-bedroom, two-storey building of wood construction, it still stands today and is a historic site. Parts of the original picket fence that surrounded the property still stand, as do some of the trees in the yard. The home is now called McLeod House and functions as a tea house and gift shop.

Growing up in rural Manitoba was simple, and Alan led a straight-forward life, whiling away the hot summer days and barely surviving the bitterly cold and snowy winter storms. Alan's biggest thrill was to accompany his father, in an early model Ford, as Dr. McLeod visited his patients in and around Stonewall and sometimes into Winnipeg.

Although Alan's childhood was in many ways ordinary, even at an early age he displayed an extraordinary willingness to put himself out to aid others. An incident occurred in 1909, when Alan was just nine or ten years old, that typified what kind of man he would turn out to be. The local *Stonewall Argus* newspaper published a story — it is quoted in George Drew's *Canada's Fighting Airmen* — about Alan's efforts to save a dog with a trap on its foot. He apparently chased it for quite some time before he was able to eventually stop the poor animal and remove the trap.[1] This event would foreshadow a larger, more significant saving of a life in which Alan would play a part in the First World War.

McLeod with his mother and sister, Helen.

8

The McLeod House, now operating as a tea house, in Stonewall, Manitoba.

Alan Arnett McLeod, age fourteen, on horseback as a member of the 34th Fort Garry Horse, summer of 1913.

At an early age, Alan developed an interest in the military, which resulted in him enrolling at the age of fourteen in the 34th Fort Garry Horse, the local militia cavalry regiment. Perhaps he, like many, was very pro–British Empire and wanted to serve. Despite the fact that there was a regulation requiring that those enlisting be a minimum of eighteen years of age, McLeod was accepted. His height — he was over six feet tall — and his enthusiasm won over the militia commander. Given menial jobs such as mucking out the stables or feeding the horses, young Alan loved it. He especially loved that he had his own uniform: blue jacket, khaki breeches, and riding boots. He took part in the 1913 summer manoeuvres of the regiment, giving him the opportunity to become an effective horseman.

At the outbreak of the First World War in August of 1914, Alan travelled numerous times to Winnipeg to enlist in the army, but each time he was rejected as he was not yet eighteen. Although over six feet tall, he still had a baby face and looked younger than he was. "War is a man's job," he was repeatedly told.

Alan had read newspaper articles on flying and was fascinated by the notion, so he tried to be accepted into the Royal Flying Corps (RFC). Again, his age prevented him. Finally, on April 12, 1917, Alan McLeod was accepted into the Cadet (Pilot) Wing of the Royal Flying Corps. The letter he received confirming this reads as follows:

Headquarters
Imperial Royal Flying Corps
Toronto, Canada

April 12th, 1917
A.A. McLeod, Esq.,
Stonewall, Man.

Sir:

Reference your application for entry to the Cadet (Pilot) Wing of the Royal Flying Corps, you will report at this Headquarters on the 23rd inst., or as soon thereafter as possible for medical examination, and if passed, attestation and duty.

Transportation Warrant #10341 is enclosed herein to cover transportation. If you will present this to the booking office of your depot, railway ticket will be supplied you. You will please confirm receipt of this by wire.

Yours faithfully,
Lieut. Colonel
Commanding Royal Flying Corps.
Canada[2]

On April 23, just three days after his eighteenth birthday, he was accepted into the RFC, and after receiving a rousing send-off from Principal Burland, his teachers, and classmates at Stonewall High School, Alan boarded the train in Winnipeg with a friend, Allan Fraser, bound for Toronto. On April 26, 1917, he signed his attestation papers, prepared by the recruiting branch of the Royal Flying Corps in Toronto, as Cadet No. 70180. The attestation papers were titled "Short Service (for the Duration of the War)." Alan McLeod's war would last just under a year.

Away from home for the first time, the small-town prairie boy was very lonely. Alan got into the habit of writing home. His letters reveal a young teenager, eager to explore new experiences. Some show his frustration with life as a trainee. McLeod's letters have been transcribed and are now in the Canadian War Museum's library in Ottawa. The letters quoted below are among those found in the George Metcalf Archival Collection, file: 58A1 51.6.

Initially, McLeod and his fellow cadets were housed in the East Residence at the University of Toronto. In one of McLeod's letters home he writes, on April 29, 1917, "For the past few weeks they have been taking on men at a rate of 350 a day and now there are so many they haven't room for them. The plan is that in 3 weeks time, they will pick out the best of them and put the rest in an infantry battalion. I don't want that. Until then we are wearing ordinary private's uniforms with a white band around the hat."

Alan McLeod (centre) boarding a train to Toronto to begin flying school.

McLeod (right) with fellow pilot cadets.

The trainees did infantry drill, also called square bashing, from 7:15 a.m. to 12:15 p.m. They had a rest and then did it all over again from 1:30 p.m. to 5:00 p.m. Alan McLeod was getting used to life in the military. He wrote home on May 3, 1917:

> They are getting very strict now — if our buttons are not polished properly we have to report to the Orderly Room and get extra drill and then we're confined to barracks for 2 weeks — and the same thing if our rooms aren't spic and span. There are so many regulations that you never know when you're treading on forbidden ground — I quake all the time. Often fellows are called out of the ranks for doing something they did not know was wrong — but I'll soon get used to it.

It was not just parade-ground marching that the new recruits learned; there were other subjects, too, like how to fire, dismantle, and put back together again the Lewis machine gun. About that McLeod wrote, "To-day we had a very interesting lecture on the working of Lewis Machine Gun my it is a wonderful instrument of torture. After to-day I think we are going to take 2 hrs a day off drill for lectures that will be nicer because I'm clean played out & my feet are very sore lugging these heavy army boots around. I haven't had time to break mine in yet."

Indeed, the lectures McLeod attended eventually took up most of his day, with drill being limited to an hour and a half. At the School of Military Aeronautics, at the University of Toronto, McLeod and his fellow pilot trainees studied such subjects as the use of wireless and the mechanics of different aeroplane (as they were referred to at the time) engines. He was not impressed in his instructors, as can be seen in this letter home:

> The instructors have no time to explain anything over again, and to-day an officer gave us a lecture on bombing and he talked so fast that we couldn't take it all down, we were supposed to take it word for word and none of us got half of it, and we have all that stuff on exam next week I don't know anything about this dope, I am completely discouraged, that lecture got all our goats, the fellows are all sore & most of them have given up, they are rushing us so fast we haven't time for half the work, they expect too much of us, of course I'll keep on trying but I don't think for a minute that I'll get through and I don't care much for my own sake I don't care if I get through at all, I'm fed up on it and none of the fellows that are out at the camps flying like it, they all wish they were out & advise us not to pass, but I'd like to pass for the sake of you & Dad. I know you'd like it, but I can easily find some other good unit, as good as this if I fail so I'm not worrying … perhaps I will be discharged, a lot of fellows have been put out, but it won't be my fault. You have to have a natural ability for machinery to stay in this and I certainly haven't. I should know more about a car than I do for the time

I've been at it, but I'm sure going to work harder than I ever did before so if I fail it won't be my fault.

Each pilot-in-training had a Royal Flying Corps Transfer Card, which was a record of the training he had received. For example, the Record of Progress, Wireless Training, at the School of Aeronautics included the following subjects:

> Buzzing, with the requirement of, "Six words per minute sending and receiving. Test of 3 minutes duration"; Artillery Code; Artillery Picture Target, the requirement of "Ranging 3 targets correctly, sending their map coordinates and using Artillery Code and Ground Signals without error"; Panneau Signalling, the requirement being, "Reading miniature Panneau accurately from distance of 100 yards, at a rate of 4 words per minute"; Sending on Silenced Key, which required a, "Clearly readable Tape Record produced at rate of 6 words per minute."

Buzzing was the term pilots used for wireless signalling. Panneau signalling involved reading the arrangement of strips of cloth on the ground while flying and communicating the meaning of the arrangement by wireless to ground personnel.

Alan concentrated on his studies, in spite of the fact that many of his instructors had never received training on how to teach adults. One of his courses included map reading. In a letter home he mentioned, "If a fellow gets through this course it will be great training for him, we are taking up map reading now, to qualify for an RFC Officer you have to be able to glance down at the ground and then glance at your map and know where you are at once."

On May 6, 1917, Alan wrote to his parents:

> Well this morning 25 of us were transferred from course No. 1 to course No. 2 that is from the School

of Military Drill & Discipline to the School of Military Aeronautics, in course No. 1 it was all drill & no lectures but now we have only 1 hr. & ½ per day drill and the rest lectures, this morning we had lectures on wireless — we have to be able to send 18 words per minute and receive 12. We also had lectures on the different types of engines in aeroplanes and they are certainly different to car engines. I am going to enjoy this ... I hope I have the natural ability for machinery to stay in this. I know a lot about a car but it is not the same so I am going to work harder than I ever did before.... If all goes well, and I'm fit for air service, I will leave for Deseronto 4 weeks from today. [Deseronto, a town east of Toronto, was another pilot training camp.]

Alan McLeod would write to his parents on May 11, about the importance of the work he was doing and also about his pay.

We hear some very interesting things here about the air work at the front but we are not allowed to tell about it everything we have in our lectures is to be kept secret, because if we told it & the Germans got hold of it, such as secret codes etc, well they would have a better chance at the British planes.... Well, we got paid again today $3 and we were asked to give $2 for a life membership ticket to the Sports Club of the Aviation Corps and of course we couldn't refuse so that meant $1 left. Gee they don't overpay us anyway.

McLeod was supposed to be receiving $7.70; however, from that pay was deducted such things as textbooks, laundry, and the cost of meals at the mess.

McLeod was not impressed by the quality of instruction he received, as can be seen in a letter home dated May 15, 1917: "Today a sloppy looking aviation officer was lecturing us on observing from an aeroplane and he told us about something that we would have to do when we became pilots and then he said 'but I don't expect many of you will ever become pilots though,' he had a poor idea of encouraging a class."

Although initially confident about learning about engines, having worked on car engines, McLeod was becoming discouraged at how different they were. In a letter dated May 16, which appears in C.W. Hunt's *Dancing in the Sky*, McLeod wrote, "I am rather discouraged on this job. I can't understand engines. I have no more mechanical ability than a horse. I pay attention and hear every word of the lecture and I ask questions till the instructor gets mad and all the fellows laugh … those complicated 12 cylinder engines are like a Chinese puzzle to me."[3]

On May 20, 1917, he wrote, "They teach us engines and photography … and they have no engines or camera to demonstrate it on, we just have to imagine we have them … that stuff is hard to understand without actually seeing it, we have been told all about map reading and have been given pages and pages of notes but we haven't seen a map yet and have no practical work at all."

McLeod continued to be frustrated with the level and the kind of instruction he received. His frustration showed in this letter home dated May 22, 1917: "This isn't like school where a teacher is paid to teach you things & has to do it. These fellows rush through things here and are not interested in your welfare like a teacher is. I tell you I find this a lot different than school. You can have everything explained there and the teacher will take turns with you but here they don't care two rats for you but that always is the way with the army."

In spite of the poor teaching methods, there was the requirement to pass the exams with an average of 80 percent. Just days before his exams McLeod wrote home expressing his anxiety about his ability, saying,

> We write our exams next Thursday and then we have from Thursday night until Tuesday night off. About five days and if we pass we'll leave for Deseronto the next day and if not, its good bye to the R.F.C. I don't know what I'll do then, I think I'll join the Cavalry, I fancy it.

I may get through my exams but I'm not counting on it at all, and I don't much care for my own sake, if I do fail, I'm fed up on this business and all the fellows feel the same about it, but for your sake I'd like to get through.

McLeod wrote his exams the end of May and passed, much to his relief. He confirmed this in a letter to his father dated June 2, and also spoke of the death of his friend Allan Fraser:

I suppose you heard Allan Fraser was killed last Thursday at Deseronto, flying with Vernon Castle, the papers said it was an air pocket they struck but the truth of the matter is that Allan lost his nerve and grabbed the control joice [*sic*] and upset them. My I feel awful about it, I can't think of anything else and his poor parents will feel so badly, he only left last Monday for Camp. I think it was his first flight ... I got your letter this morning asking about Allan, is seems awful to think he is dead. I can't realize it.

Vernon Castle was a famous entertainer at the time who gave up his stardom to enlist.

On June 3, 1917, Alan was sent to Long Branch, Ontario, a community just west of Toronto (not to Deseronto, as he had expected). The Long Branch field was part of the Curtiss School of Aviation, established by the famous American aviator Glenn Hammond Curtiss, a pioneer in aviation. In 1907 he had set the land speed record, driving a motorcycle of his own design. Two years later he set the air speed record, winning the Coupe Gordon Bennett at Reims, France, in August.

Glenn Curtiss designed and built the Curtiss JN, a tractor aircraft that would become the main training aircraft for student pilots in North America. The Curtiss School of Aviation at Long Branch used Curtiss JN-4 and JN-4A machines, which became known as "Jennys" to those who flew them. They were two-seater training machines with dual controls, one set for the instructor and one for the trainee. The trainee normally sat in the front seat. Some said that was because, if the aircraft crashed, the trainee was more likely to die than the instructor, who was seated behind him.

Jack R. Lincke, in his book *Jenny Was No Lady: The Story of the JN-4D,* tells the story of this aircraft in a wonderful way, using the analogy of a woman. For example:

> In terms of handling Jenny was a surprising admixture of strengths and weaknesses, of coquettishness and faithfulness, steadfastness and treachery. Although she could on occasion be a lady she seldom touched the stuff. If you flew her badly, for instance, her innate competitive spirit became aroused and she fought back. When this resulted in her spinning-in, the thud was heard in every cadet barracks in America and Canada.[4]

The Jenny was a hybrid of two machines, the Curtiss J model aircraft, designed in England by B. Douglas Thomas, and the N model, designed by Glenn Curtiss himself. The Jenny evolved from the initial JN-1, to the JN-2. Further modifications led to the JN-3 and finally the JN-4 was developed. The JN-4 had a maximum speed of seventy-five miles per hour and climbed at a rate of two hundred feet per minute. Its power plant was an OX5 water-cooled V8, ninety-horsepower (hp) engine.[5]

Over six thousand Jennys were produced for the United States government during the war. In 1917 and 1918, 2,900 Jennys were built in Toronto by Canadian Aeroplanes Ltd. The JN-4 never saw service in battle in Europe, but it was the primary aircraft used to train pilots in Canada and the United States. An agreement between the governments of Canada and the United States created a joint pilot training program in Texas, which began in July 1917.

Alan McLeod's first flight was on the day after he arrived at Long Branch. On June 4 he flew in a Jenny, with pilot Taylor at the controls. It was a short, ten-minute flight, to two thousand feet. Over the next three days, he flew once a day, for only thirty-five minutes on each occasion, flying to between fifteen hundred and two thousand feet. In a letter to his father dated June 6, 1917, Alan described the excitement and exhilaration of flying.

Dear old Dad:

Well I'll just write you a few lines to-day as I haven't much time to spare. Well I was flying for a while this morning again, Gee it was great, I took complete control of the machine, the Lieutenant said that I did really well, so there is some chance that I [might] become an aviator, I feel as much at home in an aeroplane now as I do in a car, Gee its great, travelling 200 miles an hour on a nose dive, its some sensation, when you hit the ground for landing you are travelling about 75 miles per hr. but you never realize it unless you saw the speed indicator.

Well I guess I will close now, I'm in a hurry, I asked for leave to-night so I could go and see mother I don't know whether it will be granted or not. Well good-bye dear old boy.

From your loving son
Alan

Alan was trying to meet his mother who had come to visit him from Manitoba. In a letter to his father the next day, he confirmed that they did end up having a visit.

My Dear old Dad:

Well I just phoned mother up a few minutes ago, she has been down town all day, I was to see her last night also on Monday night and I guess I'll go again to-morrow night, it sure is nice to have her here, but I'll be going away next week so I won't see her for a while.

I had a great flight to-day, I raced with a train, there was an instructor in the back seat though, I sure think it's the greatest thing out to fly, its certainly grand, I just love it, but it makes you awfully tired, so they don't work us hard we lie around most of the day, this sure is a slack place, we just do as we please, there isn't such a thing as a roll here so they never know whether you are present or absent, you could lie in bed all morning if you wanted to and no one would know the difference that is if you weren't on early morning flying, which you are every other morning perhaps oftener, then you have to get up about 4 o'clock, we never clean our buttons or boots or anything, but they started to day giving us 2 hrs. drill a day. I'm sure glad I was sent here the fellows that went to Desoronto [*sic*] have had no flying yet, they have drill nearly all day because they have so many they can't train them so I was lucky in being sent here, I sure like flying. Well I guess I'll close now old boy its only 9 o'clock but I want to go to bed I was up at 4 o'clock this morning, Your own loving son

Alan
Love to all
xxxxxxxxxxxx

Alan soloed for the first time on June 9, 1917, having only spent two hours and fifteen minutes aloft under dual instruction. His first solo flight lasted a mere ten minutes. He was up again flying solo on June 10. Again he was aloft for only ten minutes; reaching an altitude of two thousand feet. The landing McLeod described in his logbook as "bumpy, sprung undercarriage." He went up later on that day solo for fifty-five minutes at one thousand feet and on landing managed to break the propeller. Alan described these events in a letter to his father on June 10, 1917.

My Dear old Dad:

I did not write you yesterday, because as soon as I left work, I went right into town with Mother & Marion, they came down to see me in the morning then I went to town with them, I am afraid I wasn't pleasant company because I had been flying steady pretty nearly from 4 o'clock in the morning and I could hardly stay awake, I did my solo flight yesterday, I made a howling success of it and did really well, but I made up for that this morning, I thought I'd try another solo, so I went down to the Hangars and told the Mechanics to pull out 162, so I went off fine and flew around for a while but it was so bumpy, I couldn't stay out, first the machine would dive and then it would nose up, so I thought I had better land, I was up at 3,000 ft and shut off the engine and began to glide for the aerodrome, but for some unknown reason I misjudged the distance and landed behind the flag instead of in front, I struck hard ground and landed too suddenly, I smashed all the wires on the undercarriage and nearly broke the propeller, but the machine was fixed in about ½ hr. another fellow went up and smashed his machine up pretty well, but got away unhurt, hardly any of the fellows get hurt, after we have our solo, we can take a machine and go up any time we like and we don't have to go up unless we want, they never say anything to you for smashing a machine, I guess I'll try it again this afternoon and make a good landing, this is Sunday but we have to work all the same, but we never work very hard. Well I guess I'll close now old boy.

From your loving Son

Alan had taken to flying like a duck to water, or, rather, a duck to air. He relished going aloft, yet he continued to have mishaps on landing. His letter to his father on June 12 describes what it was like.

I like it here fine, the flying is great, they didn't give some of us enough instruction and as a result we broke a few machines by making bad landings. I had a crash yesterday. I didn't know the wind had changed and I came down with it, instead of against it and smashed the plane all up, but the O.C. [Officer Commanding] just laughed and said, "that was a fine landing" they never care if you have a smash, if you didn't they would think there was something seriously wrong, it is impossible to hurt yourself when making a landing. You may smash the machine but you can't get hurt, the only way you can get hurt is to fall from the air and you can't fall unless you try stunts and I tell you I am mighty careful. I got lost yesterday. I was up for a long time and I couldn't find the aerodrome, I flew right over Toronto but I didn't intent [*sic*] to, at last followed the Lake Shore till I found the Drome [aerodrome].

McLeod was up flying four times on June 15, one flight being seventy-five minutes duration, twice on June 16, and twice on June 17. It is no wonder that he complained to his father that "the flying is not bad but it's tiresome sitting up there and flying all the time, half the time I want to sleep, but it would hardly do."

By the week ending June 17, 1917, McLeod had a total of ten hours and twenty minutes in the air, half of which was flying solo.

On June 18, 1917, Alan McLeod was posted to Camp Borden, home of No. 42 Wing. McLeod was part of No. 79 (Canadian) Reserve Squadron, Royal Flying Corps, commanded by E.W. Smithy. Alan McLeod sent the following letter home to his father on June 19, 1917:

Dear Dad:

I arrived at Camp Borden yesterday. It is an awful hole. I Hate it just now but I guess I'll get used to it. Say but its lonely here, just a mass of sand and tents and the

Flying Corps have a few buildings but they are full up so we are sleeping in tents without floors, there are 10 of us in a tent, we have no dressers or wash stands, we have to walk about ¼ of a mile to the building to get washed, we are put to an awful inconvenience, we have to get up at 3:45 a.m. and there is not time to spare till noon and we just have ½ hour for dinner, then in the afternoon after dinner, we work till 4:30 then have a lunch and fly till 8:15, then we have supper and after supper there are lectures from 9–10:30, then we go to bed, so we haven't very much spare time, we have lots of drill and have to polish our buttons and boots or get Cain. We can have a week-end pass once a month, and I won't be able to get into Toronto for a whole month and I just hate this place.

You ought to be here to see all the Aeroplanes, sometimes there are nearly 100 in the air at once, it is sure a wonderful sight, I am going to phone in to Toronto to mother to-night and see what she is going to do, she can't come near here she won't be allowed in the lines and we can't go out and there is no town within six miles of here, I wish I could see mother, I am getting homesick again I was better but now I'm in a strange place I'm worse again, but I'll soon be better. Well I must close now, dear old boy, I wish I could come home again.

From your loving Son
Alan

The 4:30 p.m. "lunch" McLeod refers to above was the much-loved afternoon tea, adored by the British but not so important to some of the Canadian and American pilots, who did not typically indulge in this custom. The above letter also reveals McLeod's feelings of wanting to be back home, quite normal for a young eighteen-year-old. He was very attached to his parents and dearly wanted to stay in contact with them, if only by mail or a phone call to his mother. Despite the tough living conditions at Camp Borden and his criticism of them, when it came to flying and the reason he was there, he loved being around aeroplanes.

Camp Borden, about sixty miles north of Toronto, in the heart of Simcoe County, was established on July 11, 1916. It was 850 acres, known to the locals as the Sandy Plains, because of its many sand dunes. Named after Sir Frederick Borden, the minister of militia in the Liberal Wilfred Laurier government at the time, it served as an infantry training centre and could accommodate thirty thousand soldiers. It was not until May 2, 1917, that Canada's first military airfield was officially opened at Camp Borden, to house No. 42 Wing. As Alan McLeod mentions, there were no barracks to house the Royal Flying Corps trainees, just bell tents.

McLeod flew on June 19, 20, and 21 at altitudes of between one thousand and three thousand feet. The flights lasted between twenty and eighty minutes, and each flight had to be cut short because of engine failure. Problems with the machines were fairly commonplace. This fact, combined with the lack of experience of the trainees and frequent problems with inclement weather, resulted in there being many incidents. On June 22, 1917, in a letter to his father, Alan McLeod describes one such situation.

> I had a rather exciting time this morning, about 4:30 this morning I went up for a flight with three others, the air looked rather misty but we didn't think anything of it, but as soon as we got about 100 ft. off the ground, we couldn't see a thing it was all mist, you could only tell by feel whether you were going up or down or side slipping or how you were going. As soon as I saw this I thought I would go to the aerodrome and land but I couldn't find it. I flew around for about ½ hour and at last through a spot in the mist I saw land, but not very clearly. I wasn't going to float around so I came and landed, and when I got down I found I was only about ½ mile from the aerodrome so I just ran the machine in. I was sure thankful to get to the ground, one of the other fellows landed in a field about 20 miles away,

another fellow crashed his machine in a swamp and isn't back yet, the other fellow landed in another field about 10 miles away 1 fellow just got back now and it is 12 o'clock the other two aren't back yet, they all phoned in. I was the luckiest of the bunch. Gee I was scared.

In C.W. Hunt's book *Dancing in the Sky*, he describes the attitude of the training instructors and other officers about these sorts of incidents.

The large number of crashes was considered normal by the training hierarchy. They took a laissez-faire attitude to flight training, allowing any cadet who had soloed to take to the air whenever an aircraft was available, regardless of the weather. This policy prevailed despite the fact that the JN4 had none of the sophisticated instruments used by contemporary pilots to deal with poor visibility, turbulent air, or thunderstorms. This permissive policy contributed to the high incidence of crashes and aggravated the shortage of training aircraft.[6]

With so many crashes, the number of airworthy machines decreased markedly. It would take days to repair some of them, others were write-offs. On June 23, Alan would write to his father about this:

Our squadron No. 79 is rather behind the rest. We have the worst machines and the least in proportion to the number of cadets and yesterday four of the machines crashed and there are only 4 machines now for 25 of us so we can't get much flying in. This morning is the first morning since I've been here that I haven't been up before 4 o'clock ... I slept till six, and it was sure great, tomorrow (Sunday) we have to get up at 3:45 just the same, it is hard luck. I wish they would treat us better.

McLeod was in the air practically every day, with his flights getting progressively longer, as he notes in a letter to his father dated June 25, 1917.

> My Dear old Dad:
>
> I am writing this letter in one of the offices in the hangar it is 6:45 A.M. and I have just come down from a nearly two hour flight, when you once get a machine here, you have to hog it, or you wont [*sic*] get your time in I like the air pretty well, but its tiresome sitting in a machine and riding around it gets monotonous, I think no more now of getting in an aeroplane and going for a spin around town in the Maxwell.
>
> I haven't heard from mother for three days perhaps I will hear to-day, I have been writing her in care of Uncle Harry at Anoka if she isn't there, they will probably forward them to her.
>
> Well old boy how are you getting along, I wish I were home with you, my it would fine [*sic*], I like this place all right till I begin to think of home and then I just long for home, but I guess its no use I'll have to make the best of it. Well dear old fellow I must close now, give my love to Helen [his sister] and tell her I enjoy getting her letters I will write her next.
>
> From your loving son
> Alan

Despite trying to fill his days with flying, Alan McLeod could not stop from thinking of home and the parents he so loved.

Toward the end of June and into early July, McLeod and his fellow cadets were practising formation flying and carrying out other tests assigned by their instructors. These included doing figure-eight turns, S-turns, and spins, firing their machine guns at targets, and carrying out cross-country flights.

McLeod was in the air for seven hours on July 5, 1917, flying circuits and practising various manoeuvres. In a letter to his father, he explains some of the required flying tests he took:

My Dear Dad:

I received a letter from you all this morning. My I was surprised to hear about Lou & Bill, congratulate them for me, I haven't time to write them.

Gee I sure have been busy these last few days, I put in about 7 hours flying to-day, I don't know whether I told you that I have been instructing lately, I have all my instructors tests, they were no cinch, I had to make 4 figure eights in the air at a height of 3,000 ft. and come down with the engine off and land in the centre of a circle, you have do [sic] this test 3 times, then the next is harder, you have to go up to 10,000 stay up there a while, come down with the engine off in spiral and S turns and land in the centre of the circle, the next test is a cross country test you have to make a cross country flight of 100 miles and make 3 outside landings, its quite a job. I have a new job it was fun compared with this, but still its not bad firing the machine gun, I put 95 shots out of 100 just near the Bull, I was up to-night in the aeroplane firing with the machine gun at dummy aeroplanes on the ground, I did fairly good shooting the Sergeant said, it was good fun, but hard work, I think it has been definitely decided that we leave on the 2nd and if is so, I will only have four days leave, my I wish I had time to come home, but I guess not.

One of the fellows here Veneberg is his name his people are wealthy Montreal people they were Jews generations back, he asked me to come for a motor trip through the states with him if we got 2 weeks leave, but I certainly would rather go home, although, a trip would be great, Foster wants me to come & visit him & Skall another boy wants me to come to his home Chicago, they are all fine fellows, but I'd rather go home than anywhere, well I must close now old girl.

From you loving son
Alan

N.B. haven't opened the cake yet, thanks very much for it.

As can be seen from this letter, McLeod was becoming a very proficient pilot. The circles he spoke of were forty yards wide and the pilot had to "cut his engine to idle and estimate the glide distance to his target, stalling the wings at just the right height and location over the marked circle."[7]

On July 6, during an altitude test to see how far up he could fly his machine, McLeod broke Camp Borden's record for height, flying up to 12,300 feet, three hundred feet higher than the previous record — quite a feat for Alan McLeod and the fresh-from-the-factory JN-4 he was flying. By that date he had accumulated a total of thirty-three hours in the air, twenty-seven hours and thirty-five minutes of which was flying solo.

On July 10 McLeod was transferred to No. 78 Squadron, a wireless squadron. Throughout the remainder of July, McLeod practised his aerial reconnaissance and aerial gunnery, which, in his logbook, he described as "Panneau and Puffs." Panneau signalling, as previously mentioned, involved flying the airplane while reading Panneau strips on the ground, and then reporting the observations to ground control using wireless transmission. Searching for smoke from artillery was "looking for Puffs." When spotting a puff of smoke, "the pilot was required to determine the smoke's location and send this information to the man in the tent" (on the ground), via wireless. He would communicate to the ground by way of Morse code whether the shot was short, too far, or had hit the target. McLeod describes the task in a letter to his parents: "Tomorrow morning if the weather is good, I have to go up and do a shoot as it is called. Shots are fired in different places and you have to send down by wireless where they hit, so the gunner will know where he is firing. We do just the same as is done in France, it is no cinch I tell you."[8]

Firing the machine gun was also part of the cadet pilots' training. They were taught to operate the gun, dismantle it, and put it together again. At first, they learned to fire the Lewis machine gun on the ground, shooting at bull's-eye targets. Later, while in the air, they used their engine-mounted machine gun, which fired forward, to hit targets on the ground.

The pilots also practised aerial gunnery, firing at drogues, targets pulled by one machine flown by an instructor while another instructor piloted the aeroplane with the cadet in the observer's seat. The cadet fired the Lewis gun on its swivel mounting. The instructor would position the aeroplane so that the cadet could fire on the drogue. The gun could be moved to fire on targets to the left or right of the aeroplane and could be moved up and down in order to hit the moving target.

July saw the arrival of gun cameras. Initially mounted on the upper wing of the aeroplane, the cameras were later mounted to shoot through the propeller. These cameras recorded when the forward-firing machine gun shot against the drogue. Cameras offered an effective instructional tool for teaching the cadets how to carry out deflection shooting — the technique of shooting ahead of a moving target. In battle, the pilot had to aim his gun ahead of the enemy aircraft in order to have the bullets hit the target as it flew into the line of fire.

Mock dogfights were also part of the instruction. Pilots used only their gun cameras when attacking one another and taking defensive action in these exercises. Once they landed and the film was processed, they could determine whether their bullets, had they been used, were on target. These flights were the closest thing to actual combat that the cadets would experience before they were over the trenches of France.

Of this experience, Alan would write home on July 20, 1917, "Gee, I had lots of fun to-night. I had an air fight with another fellow. We both had camera guns, we'd pull the trigger, it would take a picture, it was all kinds of sports. The pictures haven't been developed yet so I don't know how I came out, it seemed all right though."

On July 27, 1917, McLeod had finished his aerial gunnery course and had qualified as a pilot. In early August, he was chosen to be an aerial gunnery pilot, attached to the School of Aerial Gunnery. He wrote home saying, "I am a pilot for aerial gunnery now that is the highest job in the Camp, only officers & experienced Cadets do it. I am all through my course at Camp Borden now, I'm just waiting for my Commission, there's some delay about it, you see it has to come here from England."

In another letter of the same time period he wrote of his disappointment with the role of aerial gunnery pilot, all the while pining to get overseas.

> I'm a pilot for Air Gunnery now, it's a rotten job, the flying is all right but in our spare time we have to clean up the Hangers [sic] and all sorts of stuff. It's rotten. There are 8 of us chosen by Major Tilley as Pilots, we are the Senior Cadets of the Camp and have charge of all the other Cadets & some mechanics.
>
> I guess it was an honour in a way though to be chosen as an Aerial Gunnery pilot ... I take fellows up and they fire the machine gun at dummy aeroplanes and I also pilot for the Camera Gun, two machines go up and have a fight in the air. I drive the machine and the other fellow takes the pictures. Last week I used to take the pictures, but I have graduated from that job now.... The worst part of the work is that half the time your machine isn't working because these Curtiss engines only run when they feel like it ... you have to bum around and see that the mechanics are working on your machine because if you don't watch them they'll quit.... In the mornings and at other times, they put us at sweeping out the hangers [sic] and cutting grass ... in the scorching hot weather.
>
> I don't know when we're going overseas, we couldn't go when we expected on account of ... no boats sailing. Coutts and a bunch of other fellows from here have been sent to different Camps as instructors. I'm sorry they're gone.... I guess we'll go across together but goodness knows when.
>
> We're all going to get leave I think but if we don't, we're all going to take 2 weeks, there would be no use

[you] telling me not to ... all the boys are going to stick together so there will be 30 of us in trouble if any, if they discharge me I won't weep. I'll be mighty glad to get out of the R.F.C., that's the way we all feel ... they won't say much after giving us all the training and commissions.

Eager to get overseas, Alan was getting frustrated by the lack of news. On August 4 he wrote to his sister Helen, "My I wish they would hurry and send us overseas ... we don't know what the delay is, but there is so much red tape in the army, you never know where you're at."

By August 12 Alan McLeod had accumulated a total of forty-three hours and five minutes' solo time in the air. As well, he had acquired six hours of dual. That day, he was told he would be sent overseas in the next draft. He wrote to his mother saying, "I am very sorry I'm going on it because I'll have to leave all my friends behind ... we were told we would probably be a long time in England, might not get to France till next spring because there is no flying in France in the winter time ... of course that is not official so don't take it to heart."

Alan McLeod was sent on leave for a couple of days to say his good-byes to his family. On August 15 he was on a train from Winnipeg to Montreal, arriving on August 17. He hated Montreal, its size, its crowded streets, and, perhaps, the French that was spoken by the majority of the population. He did not have to stay long. He boarded the RMS *Metagama*, which pulled out at 4:20 in the morning of August 20, 1917. McLeod had completed four months of training since his acceptance into the RFC.

TWO

Off to the Old Country

The RMS *Metagama* sailed into Bantry Bay, Ireland, on August 31, 1917, having avoided contact with the prowling German U-boats during the crossing of the Atlantic. On that day McLeod wrote to his mother and father describing his voyage across the Atlantic:

> My but the sea was rough the boat was rolling all over the place, a lot of people were seasick but I wasn't at all thank goodness.
>
> There wasn't much to do in the boat, sometimes we would have sports in the afternoon and concerts in the evening, the first morning I was on the boat I got up for breakfast & that is the only time. I always slept till the one o'clock bugle blows for lunch then

I get up & dressed, I often used to wonder how people could sleep so long but now I know, of course we didn't get to bed till 2 o'clock in the morning, all the R.F.C. boys are on the same deck and about 11 o'clock we all got into our pyjamas and then we used to have fun, some of the boys would stay with the ladies all the time & not associate with us and we'd put them under a shower or torture them some way and all the other fellows who had done wrongs through the day were dealt with, Gee but we had fun, it was the best part of the day, and I never got chastised once, I was lucky, it was usually about 2 o'clock when we got to bed.

After we got into the middle of the danger zone a torpedo boat destroyer met us, and accompanied us here, we did not have an escort with us all the way as we expected a sub took after us and shot a torpedo at us, but it was seen in time and they turned the boat, the destroyer could do nothing, the sub shot the torpedo while it was under water & you couldn't see it, it got away scot free and the next day it torpedoed 4 boats in 5 hours, the *Virginian* was sunk right near us, and some other boats too, we saw them picking up the survivors and we have seen several shop [*sic*] loads of them come in here, it is a naval training station, another time we just missed a mine by about 6 yards and just as were [*sic*] coming in here there was a mine at the mouth of the harbor we nearly hit we saw the mine sweepers at work lifting them out, it is sure a dangerous job.

We stayed here at Bantry for 2 days waiting for the subs to go away, there were 20 or 30 ships of all types in here for refuge from the subs & they couldn't catch them (the subs) while we were there to pass away the time we had boat races, because we couldn't land, I was chosen out of a team for the R.F.C. we were racing the

C.A.M.C. [Canadian Army Medical Corps] in great big life boats there were 8 in a boat I was sitting near the edge of the boat and it lurched as the sea was rough and I fell over, with all my clothes on, that was once I was glad I could swim, Oh but the water was cold and salty and I got a good taste of it too, but I got on again all right, it was sure exciting.

We are on our way to Liverpool now & if all goes well we will be there to-morrow noon, it is 310 miles, we are accompanied by two American torpedo boat destroyers, one on each side of us, but even that doesn't ensure us of safety, the subs have been known to sink escorts & all, in fact it was done right near us, this boat has been going every [*sic*] since the war started and they haven't caught it yet and a submarine Captain told a fellow on this boat who was in another ship when it was sunk, that he was after it, so they may get it yet, but I hope not.

Say those torpedo boat destroyers can trawl there is just a whiz and there [*sic*] gone, we saw some just going past to a boat that has just been sunk near us, I know all this because we get it all by wireless & I know the operator pretty well.

We are supposed to get up every morning at dawn, and stay on deck when in the centre of the danger zone, because that is the time the subs make their attack, but the ladies are the only ones that ever turn out, some are so scared they stay up all night, but we never think of it at all, it seems funny for them to do that. Most of the ladies on board are nurses who have seen service & have been on leave, one of them knew Bill at Salonika, I forget her name but I'll find out & let you know. Well I will close for now as there is no more news, I will write more when we land, if we do and then I can send it right off. Well I want to post my letter now I will write when we get there we are nearly there now only another hour.

Good-bye, From your loving old Son
Alan

P.S. I wired you because I thought you would like to know whether we got torpedoed or not.

At this time, Alan was full of fun, as can be expected of a teenager. He was pulling practical jokes on his fellow RFC companions and staying up late, something new and very daring for him, given his upbringing. One can just picture the lads dressed in pyjamas, racing around the ship getting into all sorts of trouble and making quite a racket. It was all in good fun.

Prior to 1917, merchant ships and troop transport vessels sailed on their own across the Atlantic, taking their chances at being discovered by submarines. In February of 1917, however, Kaiser Wilhelm approved the reintroduction of unrestricted warfare, meaning U-boats were allowed to sink any ship without warning. As a result, Allied shipping losses grew, amounting to about 800,000 tons a month. These losses drove the British Admiralty to establish convoys of ships, in which non-combat ships travelled in groups escorted by warships. Convoys were in place by the time McLeod crossed the Atlantic in the late summer of 1917. However, most destroyers could only meet the convoys once they came near Ireland, an area better known as the war zone, or danger zone, as McLeod referred to it in his letter home. It is understandable the passengers of the *Metagama*, not just the nurses, were afraid of submarines and their deadly torpedoes. The destroyer escorts could do little against the submarine attack but ram them when they had surfaced. It is no wonder, therefore, that McLeod reported four ships sunk in five hours by U-boats. Even in convoys, there was little protection against attack by submerged U-boats. Safety in numbers counted for little at that time. By the end of 1917, the average of forty German U-boats at sea at any one time sank an appalling total of 3,170 ships, a total of 5,938,023 tons.

The United States had entered the war in April 1917 and shortly thereafter were helping the British Navy with escort duties around the British Isles, as McLeod mentions in his letter quoted above.

By September 5, 1917, Alan McLeod was in London on ten days leave. In his letters home Alan bemoaned the cost of everything.

> I got my outfit allowance yesterday it only [*sic*] $120 not $200 as we were told at Borden and this will barely cover the things we need, we have to buy a trench coat $25, Goggles $10 and we have to buy our own blankets bed & pillow, it's really awful, these were the things we were supposed to buy and then were supposed to buy a new uniform for dress reasons they don't wear this kind over here, but I'm doing without most of those things, I don't know whether they'll say anything or not & I don't care, we get $2.50 a day and we'll have to pay $1.50 for mess etc. so I'll have $1.00 a day clear.

London did, however, have its attractions, and was full of soldiers, naval personnel, and airmen on leave, many of whom were as new to the city as were McLeod and his fellow Canadians. There was much to see and do. There were also dangers present, as McLeod writes home in the following letter:

> I was in the theatre last night with another fellow and the Germans started to Bomb London, and some one [*sic*] came in and asked for all Flying Corps Officers and we had to go on the streets and keep the people into the underground passages, I was right near where one bomb dropped, right on Charring [*sic*] Cross near the Savoy Hotel, there was some excitement for a while, but the people here are beginning to take it as a matter of course, there has been a raid every night since we been here [*sic*].

Portrait of Alan McLeod with cane.

The first bombing raid on England occurred on January 19, 1915, when German Zeppelins L-3 and L-4 each dropped six 110-pound bombs and nine incendiaries on the town of Yarmouth. By the summer of 1917, London was the target of massive Gotha bombers. The first Gotha raid on London took place on June 13. These twin-engine, 520 hp machines had a wingspan of seventy-eight feet and carried two machine guns for defence. They had a crew of three and could carry five hundred kilograms of bombs. During the summer and early fall of 1917 giant Staaken R-planes would bomb London. These machines were even larger than the Gothas and had a bigger payload. The Staaken had a wingspan of over 138 feet, a length of 73 feet, and was powered by four Mercedes 260 hp engines. It carried a crew of seven and a payload of about 3,630 pounds of bombs. They were defended by six machine guns.

Alan McLeod was posted to No. 82 Squadron at Waddington, Lincolnshire, on September 14, 1917. From September 15 to 18 he practised his landings in a British B.E.2e aircraft. On September 15 he wrote home, saying,

> Well I am out at camp at last and I'm glad of it, I was tired of London and this place is a nice change, I think I will like it very well, the country around here is very pretty and the machines here are wonderful. I am flying a Bristol Scout (Pup) it is a wee little machine about ¼ the size of the machines mother saw at long branch, the wings are about 8 ft. long whereas the Curtiss were 42 and it is only about 6 ft. long, but it has a 455 H.P. Rolls Royce Engine and it will travel 175 M.P.H. its some bus I tell you, you can do anything in the earth with it and it will be all right, they climb 10,000 ft. in 6 minutes absolutely vertical, that's going some you can imagine the difference for me, when the Engine I had been flying was only 90 H.P. You have to take it up without any instruction because it has only one seat, the Curtiss lands at 50 M.P.H. and the Bristol Bullett (so called because it looks like one) lands at 100 M.P.H.

I wouldn't be afraid of any German in it although they have good machines too.

For the week ending September 25, 1917, McLeod had flown five times in a B.E.2e , and according to his logbook he was doing cross-country flights, practising formation flying, doing bombing runs, and "Panneau" and "ground strips." On September 20, 1917, McLeod wrote,

> If we're on early flying we have to get up at 4:45 and I don't fancy that much. We get through about 7:30 and have to be back at 10 for lectures or flying and we work till 12:15 then come back for dinner. At 2 o'clock we have to be on hand for physical exercise and drill for an hour, you see the main thing for an aviator is to keep fit, they tell us, but they don't feed us that way. After drill there is flying till 6:30 or if you're not flying there are lectures for you to attend and which are very rarely attended … after 6:30 you're through for the day.

From September 26 to 29, McLeod practised air photography and air observation. In a letter to his sister on September 27, he describes what was involved.

> My Dear Helen:
>
> Well there's not much news to tell you, I'm just writing to let you know I'm alive & kicking, I expect to be moved from here next week to another camp to train for a scout pilot, I'll like that job because the Germans have no machines that can catch our scouts, they travel so fast and they are such wee little things my but the're [sic] small there's just room enough for one person to sit in them and they have a great big 450 H.P. engine and have been known to hit up [sic] 300 miles an hour, that hardly seems fast enough, does it.

I was flying very late to-night, I was supposed to be directing a gun fire on the German lines & I would send down in wireless where their shell hit by a code we have when I got down it was pitch dark & they had to put on the lights for me to land by, its all kinds of fun flying at night. Well old girl & must close now, I suppose your working hard at your entrance,

Love to all, from your loving
Bub

Somehow Alan had acquired the nickname of Bub. It is not known how it originated.

By the end of September, McLeod had soloed for fifty-six hours and thirty minutes. He then went on a week's leave to London, where he looked up friends and relatives. By October 6 he was back at Waddington soloing again, now in an Armstrong Whitworth F.K.8.

This machine, designed by Frederick Koolhoven, a Dutch engineer with Armstrong Whitworth, was a two-seater biplane containing either a 120- or a 160-horsepower Beardmore engine. The engine was enclosed in a cowling with two radiators, one on either side of the fuselage, that formed an inverted vee at the upper wing. The F.K.8 had a wingspan of forty-three feet six inches, was thirty-one feet five inches in length and was ten feet eleven inches high. The Armstrong Whitworth had a maximum speed of ninety-eight mph and carried a forward-firing Vickers machine gun for the pilot and a rear-mounted Lewis machine gun for the observer to use. The aircraft's undercarriage could take a tremendous amount of punishment on landing since it had springs built into cylinders within the legs. The A.W. F.K.8 was an ideal machine for reconnaissance and artillery spotting.

Not everyone found this machine easy to fly, however, as Lieutenant Leslie Latham described in *Voices in Flight: Conversations with Air Veterans of the Great War,*

Those machines were like canal barges to fly! They were so sluggish, and very heavy on the controls. If you felt

a bump coming, you'd put some rudder on to counteract it, and the rudder acted about a couple of minutes
later! They were especially difficult to fly in bad weather. Mostly, they were used for artillery observation in
France ... and one of their characteristic features was an
adjustable tail plane.[1]

In a letter to his parents dated October 11, 1917, McLeod describes
his views of the Armstrong Whitworth F.K.8. He also felt they were
heavy and awkward to fly.

> My Dear old Dad & Mother:
>
> Well there's no news to tell you except that I will be
> moving away from here this week, I expected to go be-
> fore but I still have some time to put in on big A.W. the
> flying tank, they weigh about 5,000 lbs, they're some
> bus, I looped one the other day. I was the second per-
> son here to do it, they're perfectly safe but people didn't
> know it, you'd think you were riding in a parlour car
> they ride so smooth, but I'd much rather fly a smaller
> machine, they are easier to stunt with. Well I guess I'll
> ring off.
>
> As ever your loving son
> Alan

In another letter to his father on October 15, 1917, Alan describes
his experience formation flying. The letter reads, in part,

> I had a great experience this afternoon, three of us went
> up to do formation flying, that is flying very close to-
> gether & we had to land at three other aerodromes for
> practice & we had to fly 10,000 ft high, I was leader &
> these aerodromes were a long way off so I had a map & I

had to figure out my course, so the 3 of us started off & we got lost, I took a wrong turn & we flew for 2 hours looking for home & we couldn't find it, so at last I got fed up & came down & landed in an old farmers field, it was so small that I just barely got in without hitting the other side & when I landed all the old farmers in the country came around, they & their families were running from all around to see the wonderful aeroplane, well I fount [*sic*] out I was 120 miles from home, but I wanted to land at their other aerodromes, so they gave me my directions & off I went, after I flew for a while I got to an aerodrome & landed, but it was a naval aerodrome on the coast, I got some gas, I was farther away than ever, you see it was so misty you couldn't see a thing & in the meantime I had lost the other 2 fellows, I went off from the naval aerodrome & flew & flew at last I came to a point where I was fed up, so I landed in another farmers field & again they gathered around, so I got my bearings & away I went, but I gave the crowd some fun first, I got about 500 ft from the ground & took a dive straight at them till & nearly touched their heads & was going about 200 miles an hour & I went at that rate to about 8 ft from the ground, then I pulled her out & went straight in the air when I looked around here they all were lying flat on their stomachs, they were scared I'd hit them my it was funny, I repeated that several times, till I thought they'd be scared & then I beat it, I found the aerodromes I wanted & landed & phoned home I was all right because I had been away 6 hrs, then I beat it for home & it was good & dark when I got there, but I landed safely & one of the fellows had been home for some time, but he didn't land at all, it is now 11 o'clock & the other fellow isn't back yet, they don't know where he is, Gee it was great sport, I enjoyed every minute of my trip.

Part of Alan McLeod's training included attending the Wireless and Observers' Course at Hursley Park, Winchester. He arrived there on October 21, 1917. The course lasted for fourteen days. On October 24 McLeod wrote home about how bored he was at the Hursley Park Camp. "We don't do much at this joint, we attend lectures from about 7.30 or 8 till 12 & then from 1 to 6, sometimes the monotony is broken by doing a bit of flying, but I'm going back to Waddington next week than[k] goodness."

McLeod was tested on artillery observation and the use of wireless. With the aid of ground strips and zone calls, he was able to determine where the artillery targets were and the accuracy of their shots, information that he would communicate via the wireless. Artillery spotting used the "clock code" method, as described in Joseph A. Phelan's book *Aeroplanes and Flyers of the First World War*:

> It was at once graphic and flexible for it depended on unvarying values which were almost impossible to misinterpret — the dial of a clock and true north. The target was considered to be the centre of the dial; twelve o'clock was understood to be true north from the target, and the other hours in their proper position round the dial. These values remained the same regardless of which direction the battery was shooting. Thus, a shot that landed due south of the target was said to land at six o'clock; a shot that landed due west of the target, nine o'clock. Imaginary circles were drawn around the target to represent ranges of 10, 25, 50, 100, 200, 300, 400, and 500 yards. These ranges were identified by code letters: Y, Z, A, B, C, D, E, and F respectively. Thus a shot that landed ENE and 200 yards from the target was signaled "C 1" in Morse code.
>
> Pre-arranged signals were made to the observer in the aeroplane from the batteries, or any ground post, with strips of canvas stretched on the ground.[2]

McLeod passed all his artillery observation and spotting tests. The pass percentages are scratched out in his logbook but they are still discernable. He received one 74 percent and others in the 80 percent to 90 percent range.

On November 18, 1917, No. 82 Squadron left for France, but Alan McLeod and two other pilots were left behind. Alan, in a letter to his parents, explains the situation.

> My Dear old dad & Mother:
>
> I am just going to drop you a few lines before I leave, Kemp & I and another fellow are going to Winchester again, all the rest of our bunch have gone to France, we are going to pilot observers there for a while, I don't know how long we'll be there, I hear it's a good job, we live at a private house so that's all right, but they tell us one thing one minute and in another minute they turn round and tell us something different, but we're really going to Winchester, its much nicer than here, because we are going to another place, not the same one we were at before....
>
> P.S. 82 Squad flew away this morning to France, they were going to land near Folkstone [England] at Limpne first. 24 machines left, 3 machines got there 10 crashed and the remainder haven't been heard of, they had dud machines, of course none are hurt but they have landed all over between here & Limpne.

THREE

In France with No. 2 Squadron

Alan McLeod did not have to wait long to get to France. By November 26 he was in Folkstone waiting to cross the English Channel. He crossed that day and arrived in Boulogne at 3:00 p.m. From there he took a train to Saint-Omer, due east of Boulogne, to join the RFC Pilots' Pool. He had to ride in a cold boxcar during the two-day journey, arriving in Saint-Omer on November 28. He still had not been posted to a squadron. However, the very next day he got word that he was to join No. 2 Squadron of I Brigade, flying out of Hesdigneul located northwest of Arras and south of Béthune. No. 2 Squadron, like most squadrons, was composed of three flights (labelled A, B, and C) of six machines each. McLeod was assigned to B Flight. On November 30 McLeod was back up in the air flying an A.W. F.K.8, number 5773. He was practising landings and broke the aeroplane's undercarriage. As a newly arrived pilot, McLeod had to prove himself to the commanding officer and to the rest of the pilots and observers of No. 2 Squadron. His age and youthful looks detracted from his credibility, but he soon proved to all that he did have the skill required and then some.

That same day he wrote to his parents, giving them his first impressions of France.

My Darling Dad & Mother:

Well here I am at my permanent place at last and it is certainly great, the best I have ever had in the Flying Corps, you see the aerodrome is right in a French town and we are billeted in the houses around the town. I have a peach of a place, I am billeted in a nice little French house the people cannot understand a word of English so you see I have some fun talking French. My room is about the size of my own room at home, it has a large double bed a fireplace 4 or 5 chairs, two great big mirrors, a washstand, dresser & carpet on the floor, electric lights by Jove its great you'd never know there was a war on, I am sitting in front of my fireplace now writing this letter, but I wish I were at home, we eat in our own mess which is rotten, but I am eating that last fruit cake you sent me just now and its scrumptious to say the least.

Gee France is a queer country, so are the people & the cities, I don't like it at all, but I suppose I'll soon get use [*sic*] to it.

We are not very far from the front line trenches & we fly over them every day, we can hear the guns going all the time, they seem to be having a rough time out there.

Just to let you know how safe I am I'll tell you that the Squadron I'm in has only had 1 man killed in the last 6 months and he killed himself by doing a fool trick with his machine, the casualties in the RFC in France are a great deal less than they are in England & Canada, in proportion, why take at Borden 6 were killed one week, so I know you won't worry now you know how safe I am.

I'm having an awful time with my whiskers, I should shave every day now I have such a growth, but usually I put it off for 2 days, so if whiskers make the man I'm a man (my address: No. 2 Squadron R.F.C. B.E.F. France).

What's doing in dear old Stonewall, how I wish I were back there this winter, what a time I would have, is there a rink or do they skate in the quarry or what do they do, the weather is warm here except when it rains, you don't need a coat at all.

Gee I wish I had my old French grammar here it would help me such a lot, there are so many phrases I could use, it would be mighty handy. Well I must close now old dears.

Ever your affectionate son
Alan

Hesdigneul aerodrome consisted of five wooden-and-corrugated-iron hangars, attached to two of which were men's billets. There was a workshop, a smith's shop, an officers' mess, and a sergeants' mess.

No. 2 Squadron RFC had arrived at Hesdigneul on June 30, 1915, and remained until June 1918, an extraordinarily long time to be based in one place, as most units were moved about fairly frequently. The only other squadron that seems to have been stationed here was 21 Squadron, which occupied it for only a week in late October 1918.[1]

No. 2 Squadron was one of the senior squadrons in the RFC and had a brilliant record of achievement before McLeod's arrival. One of the squadron's B.E.s (Blériot Experimental) was the first British plane to land in France after the declaration of war. No. 2 Squadron had suffered the first RFC casualty due to enemy action, in the first British air combat, and

No. 2 Squadron.

also was responsible for winning the first aerial victory for the RFC. This had involved Lieutenant H.D. Harvey-Kelly and his observer, Lieutenant W.H.C. Mansfield. Armed with only a revolver, Harvey-Kelly forced a German monoplane down to the ground. Harvey-Kelly landed nearby and he and Mansfield pursued the two German aviators on foot but lost them when they ran into a forest.

Another of No. 2's pilots, Second Lieutenant W.B. Rhodes-Moorhouse, was awarded the first Victoria Cross for air services on April 26, 1915. That day, Rhodes-Moorhouse, a pilot who had had a distinguished career before the war began, was on a mission to bomb the railway junction at Courtrai, a town behind German lines. Over the target, he encountered heavy anti-aircraft fire. Rhodes-Moorhouse dropped his one-hundred-pound bomb directly on the target but was hit by archie (anti-aircraft) shells. His aircraft was rocked by the explosion. Being only three hundred to four hundred feet above the ground, he was also being fired at from the German troops on the ground. Rhodes-Moorhouse was struck in the stomach by a machine-gun bullet as he attempted to escape. He was hit two more times but managed to fly his machine back to his aerodrome. He was taken to hospital but died the following day. His Victoria Cross was awarded posthumously.

McLeod spent the first week of December on an artillery course. He wrote home about the experience. "I am just at this place taking an artillery course of four days, trying to learn about the huge guns we work with from the air by wireless, you see we direct their shooting it is a rather interesting course and we certainly don't work very hard."

He returned from the course on December 7, 1917. That same day he wrote to his parents.

> My Dear old Dad & Mother:
>
> I received letters from you both by this mornings mail and it was great to hear from home again.
>
> There isn't much doing out here, I'm back from the Artillery School now and I'm glad. You asked what I did all the time, well if I'm not on early flying I get up at 7:45 have breakfast and then if I'm on flying I go off into the air for four hours if I'm not I just bum, if your're [sic] on early flying you get up at 6 am and be in the air by 7 and stay up till 11 or 12 its boring too, if you do that your [sic] usually finished for the rest of the day & you're glad of it because flying is very trying on the nerves, especially when its done in Germany, then lunch is at 12:30 we get some uneatable meat and half cooked potatoes & half cooked rice pudding, then in the afternoon if you don't fly you go out riding when you can get a horse & fire on the machine gun range, its dark at 4 pm. and then we have tea, bread jam & tea, then there's nothing to do until 7:30 then we have dinner, rotten meat half cooked potatoes & rice again it sometimes changes, after dinner we usually sit around & chat & then go to bed if we're not flying, we do a lot

of night flying in our Squadron which is very hard on you, we do not have an awful lot of spare time, we are usually flying day & night. Don't worry over the parcels mother, they always get to me all right and in fine shape.

Gee I wish I were going to be home for Xmas, but I guess I'm not, there's a rumour going around here that we are going to have goose for Xmas dinner. I hardly credit it though. Well I must close now old dears.

Your loving son
Alan

McLeod was in the air twice on December 7, with his observer Second Lieutenant Higgins, flying on artillery patrol in the Lens and Arras area. The more he flew the more he gained credibility with his fellow pilots and their observers, as he showed them he could consistently fly well, and make effortless landings.

On December 8 McLeod wrote to his mother about life in the squadron.

You asked me about the fellows here, well they are a mighty fine bunch, and we get along fine, our Flight Commander Captain Allport is an Australian and is one of the finest fellows I ever met, he's just like one of ourselves & we treat him as such, he's great, you see we mess by flights there are 3 flights in a Squadron, A B & C I'm in B Flight. A major commands a Squadron & a captain a Flight, we never have anything to do with the Major we get all our orders from the Flight Commander, each Flight has 6 pilots & six observers and of course about 50 air mechanics but we never have much to do with them, each Flight has a mess of its own in a little hut so in our mess there are just 13 of us, 6 pilots & observers & the Flight Commander, the pilot runs the machine and does all the work he has a pair of wings, the observer sits in the back & looks out for enemy aircraft & for trains or movement of the troops on the ground he has one wing with an O, the observers don't know how to fly, the 13 of us have a good time in our little mess, we each know each other so well, its [*sic*] very sociable. One of the observers is a fellow by the name of Kelly he's rather an old chap, as soon as he heard I was from the Stonewall he was quite interested, he said he knew Dad & his father knew Dad very well he is evidently an Englishman and he said he came right to Stonewall (this must have been quite a number of years ago) he worked on McFarlanes farm in harvest time for 6 weeks just for his board, he knows the Strattons & all the old timers around there, he said he worked so hard at McFarlanes that he hasn't been able to work since, he's quite an old fellow, he was a Lieut. in some Scottish battalion but transferred to the R.F.C. it was certainly fine to talk about Stonewall to him, he mentioned dozens of people I knew.

Say for goodness sakes don't worry about parcels coming in care of a private address being charged duty, that's rot, don't believe all this stuff you hear mother, you can send what you like, it is never opened or touched & everything comes in first class condition although parcels are often delayed, a parcel coming to an officer is never touched by anyone, do you think for a minute they're going to undo all that & do it up again, they don't care what you send, and no one will keep it as you have suggested you hear an awful lot of rot over there, but let it go in one ear & out the other. Parcels sent to Waddington will get to me all right although it will take time they have my address. Well I must close now dear old girl, heaps of love and kisses to Marion, Helen & dear old Dad.

Your loving son
Alan

McLeod continued to do artillery patrols with his observer Higgins over the front lines. They would fly at heights of one thousand, two thousand, or three thousand feet, getting a fix on enemy gun locations so that the British artillery could fire on them and knock them out. Some days the weather was clear, others, such as December 9, the visibility was very bad, hiding the enemy's guns from observation.

On December 13, 1917, Alan McLeod wrote to his sister Helen about his life at the time.

I am Squadron orderly officer to-day I have to stay in the office and look after all the work of the Squadron I had to sleep here last night, its not a half bad job. I have to go to the cashier in the morning and draw out a whole lot of spon [funds], last night there was a big bomb raid on, the Huns were trying to bomb a large French town right here and our guns were firing at them from the ground and our aeroplanes from the air and with them dropping bombs there was as much row as there is in Stonewall on the 24th of May and that's saying something isn't it. I had to go around and see that all the lights were out because they never know whether they are dropping bombs on anything or not unless they see a light, it's the same with us we go over and bomb Germany at night but its only guess work if we hit anything, night bombings rotten though I don't like it much.

There was a big raid on London this week, they seem to have done a lot of damage. Wasn't that awful about Halifax, we get the papers here the day after they are published, so we can read all about it, that will hold the shipping in Canada back a lot.

I voted the day before yesterday, for Borden too, I met a whole lot of Canadian chaps I knew when I went to vote, everyone voted for Borden but one and I don't know whether he's able to walk now or not. I was [sic] a list of the candidates & J. Adamson is running against conscription, I was surprised, and there was some farmer fellow from St. Andrews as conservative I didn't know him.

I was censoring letters last night there were about 200 to do it's a very tiresome job but there are certainly a variety of letters and some are very funny, you see we officers put our own censor stamp on our letters and we censor the air mechanics letters, some of them write home and tell what awful danger they are in, that there are shells whizzing around their heads etc. but they are as safe as you are in Canada because they never fly, its very funny. One fellow told about how he had been slacking and he was getting promotion for it, which was a lie, you get all kinds of stuff.

Well dear old girl & wish I were home, perhaps I could help you with your work, do you find grade VIII very hard, so you take French do you. You must be quite a scholar now. Well I must close now dear, love and kisses to all.

XXXXX
Your own Bubby

The incident in Halifax that McLeod was referring to was the huge explosion that occurred on December 6, 1917, in the Halifax harbour. The *Mont Blanc*, loaded with high explosives, collided with the *Imo*, a Belgian relief ship. Every building within a mile of the explosion was severely damaged. Smoke from the explosion rose two thousand feet into the air. The blast killed about two thousand people and injured another ten thousand. Whole neighbourhoods were levelled, leaving approximately six thousand people homeless. Relief efforts and the rebuilding process lasted months after the horrible incident.

The biggest issue in the federal election in Canada in December 1917 was conscription. The war was in its fourth year and the supply of willing volunteers had reduced to a trickle. Borden and his fellow Conservatives

Second Lieutenant Alan McLeod (second from right), with fellow officers from No. 2 Squadron, in front of an Armstrong Whitworth F.K.8 aircraft, France.

wanted to force conscription on the male population, making them go to war. Highly unpopular in the province of Quebec, Wilfred Laurier's Liberals fought hard against doing away with voluntary enlistment. The soldiers at the front felt differently, wanting all eligible men in Canada to do their share of the fighting. As can be seen from McLeod's letter, those opposing conscription were dealt with harshly by their fellow soldiers. Borden won the election, but it divided the country for years to come.

On December 14 McLeod got into Armstrong Whitworth number B5773. Pilots were not assigned to only one machine. They took up machines that were available. McLeod had flown five different machines in December alone: B248, B304, B5758, B5773, and B5782. His observer was either Higgins, Second Lieutenant Cundiff, or Second Lieutenant J.O. Comber.

In a letter to his parents on December 17, McLeod discusses his situation at the time, "Things are rather quiet on our section of the line just at present but there is going to be a big drive this spring & we'll have to work day and night."

The quiet section he mentions in the letter above was not without its dangers, however. Enemy aircraft were always on the lookout for the relatively slow-moving two-seater observation aeroplanes that McLeod and others flew. For example, on December 18, 1917, he and his observer Second Lieutenant J.O. Comber, flying Armstrong Whitworth F.K.8 B304, were on an artillery observation patrol over the town of Hulluch, flying at six thousand feet. They had an encounter with an enemy Albatros scout, which dove on them from above. The German machine was driven off by Comber's machine-gun fire. McLeod saw the same enemy aircraft swoop down to low altitude and begin to fire on the Allied trenches. McLeod would have none of that so he went after the Albatros. Diving at top speed, he got behind the enemy aircraft (E.A.) and fired his machine gun. Comber did the same with his gun when the Albatros escaped from McLeod's fire. In their report later that day to Squadron Commander Major Snow, McLeod and Comber categorized the result of the combat as the enemy was "driven off."

On December 19, flying once again with Comber, their Armstrong Whitworth B5782 was attacked from above by eight Albatros scouts between Hulluch and Vermelles, behind the German lines north of Lens. Their report of the combat reads as follows: "When carrying on C.B. [counter-battery] shoot we were attacked by 8 E.A. The observer fired 3 rounds when his gun jammed [sic] badly. One of the E.A. after diving from the front got underneath us, the pilot dived on it firing 30–40 rounds when it started to spin and was still spinning when last seen. The other E.A. dived from behind and each side and followed us down to 3,000 feet."[2]

The two flights of German scouts did not pursue him further. McLeod was credited with an E.A. "driven down."

In a letter to home dated December 20, McLeod admitted to his parents he had started to smoke. Maybe it was due to the stress of combat or maybe he smoked to fit in with the rest of the squadron personnel. McLeod had acquired the nickname "Babe," no doubt due to his baby face and his youth. Still, his peers recognized that as a pilot he showed great maturity and ability.

On artillery patrol or when doing "shoots," observation was often hampered by low cloud or by mist. McLeod and his fellow pilots were

Armstrong Whitworth F.K.8 B5782 flown by Alan McLeod and Arthur Hammond, Hesdigneul Aerodrome, France.

also faced with the threat of anti-aircraft guns firing at them. These guns would throw up shells that were timed to explode at a certain elevation. Often pilots would return to the aerodrome with their machines damaged by this fire. For example, on December 22 McLeod had his elevator controls shot away by "archie."

Flying in the cold and snow of December held its own risks, as McLeod describes to his parents on December 27, 1917.

My Dear old dad & mother:

Well Christmas is over and I had a pretty good time considering where I am, we had a Roast Goose & apple sauce, plum pudding, nuts, raisins, candy, apples & oranges, it was very nice. After dinner we went to a concert that the men gave and after that we had a snowball fight for nearly an hour, it was snowing very heavily and the snow is good and sticky, I enjoyed the snowball fight the best of all, it reminded me of home, I can hardly lift my right arm now as a result. There is an awful lot of snow everyday too, we just get up in the air and get over to the lines when a big snow storm comes up and you have an awful time finding your way home. Yesterday two of us got over to the lines and a regular blizzard came up I came home just jumping over house tops about 30 ft. high. I followed a straight road and I could barely see it from 30 ft and the wind was blowing something awful, when I got to where I thought the aerodrome was I couldn't see the ground I kept circling round and round and at last it cleared a little & I saw I was near the aerodrome so I was going to land I shut off my engine to glide in and the storm came up fierce again and I wouldn't see it, so I put on my engine & kept flying around where I thought the aerodrome was and at last it cleared a little & I caught a glimpse of the aerodrome so I got in position & cut off my engine & glided to where I thought it was & sure enough I landed right in it, by jove it was lucky, I made a peach of a landing too, I never knew I hit the ground, all the squadron had been out watching me, they had been firing up rockets & everything but I could see none, the other fellow landed in a ploughed field quite away off but was all right, Gee it was rotten flying in that blizzard though, I wasn't scared because I knew if anything did go wrong I was so near the ground I couldn't get hurt, but it was mighty unpleasant.

Well there's no more news I'm having a pretty easy time here, there's never an awful lot doing in the winter, I get two weeks leave at the end of February its my turn then, and after 9 months out here we get sent back to England to instruct for a while & Canadians can quite often get to Canada to instruct there, if they have enough pull, so I'm going to try hard. Well I must close now old dears.

Every [*sic*] your loving son
Alan
Love and kisses to the girls & remember me to Mr. & Mrs. B
XXXXXXXXXXXXX

It was the day before he wrote this letter that he got lost in the snowstorm. On December 28 McLeod noted a successful shoot on a section of trench whose coordinates were HW. 15. The next day another successful shoot was mentioned in his logbook as BY. 58.

FOUR

McLeod's Last Three Months at War

By January 9, 1918, Alan McLeod had flown over one hundred hours above the front lines. In a letter home of the same date, he referenced the propaganda campaign against Germany in which he and others were involved: "The only time we know there is a war on is when we get to the lines, we fly over large German cities & drop all kinds of fool messages down asking them when the war is going to be over, we also drop our newspapers sometimes."

Thousands of these propaganda leaflets were dropped into Germany but with little effect. The war ground on with continual casualties.

German anti-aircraft batteries fired on Allied aeroplanes whenever they were above the front lines. On January 12, 1918, McLeod took out his frustration on one such battery by flying low and attacking it with machine-gun fire from his forward-firing Vickers gun. On his way back to the aerodrome after that encounter, McLeod had a forced landing. He described the incident to his parents in a letter the next day.

> Yesterday I had a forced landing in a duck swamp of some kind. My engine quit on me, an inlet valve broke and blew a hole right through the cylinder, I didn't have height enough to glide to the aerodrome so I glided down nice and slowly & settled in the mud, I never broke anything, but I had to stick around till some mechanics came and they went to the wrong place and never got to me till long after dark they hauled the thing out on dry land & fixed it up & I flew it back to-day.

On January 13, at about noon, McLeod and his observer Lieutenant A.W. Hammond were on fighting duty over Wingles at about six thousand feet. They were attacked by eight German aircraft, their Maxim machine guns blazing. McLeod took immediate evasive action, turning and diving away. Two of the enemy machines followed McLeod's Armstrong Whitworth B315 down to one thousand feet near the town of Noeux-les-Mines. All the while observer Hammond fired at the two pursuing German machines, emptying two drums of Lewis gun ammunition in the process. Hammond made several hits, enough to scare the Germans off. McLeod and Hammond returned safely to their aerodrome.

Arthur Hammond had a very interesting background. Before the war he was working as a civil engineer in Argentina. At the outbreak of the war, Hammond first joined the Royal Horse Guards and saw action at the Battle of Loos. He was known to have tracked down a number of German snipers, having scouted in no-man's-land. In 1915 Hammond was commissioned as a second lieutenant in the Royal Engineers and was involved with the 192nd Tunnelling Company, digging mines to blow up the enemy trenches. In 1916 he worked with the 191st Tunnelling Company, who were digging mine shafts under the Messines Ridge. An explosion buried Hammond for thirty-six hours. Luckily, he managed to find one of the mine's breather pipes to get oxygen. In 1917 Hammond joined the Royal Flying Corps and was sent to No. 2 Squadron under the command of Captain Allport. Hammond earned his Military Cross flying with Captain Allport on a photographic mission over the German lines. Despite fierce anti-aircraft fire, Hammond managed to take a number of photos of enemy artillery targets. Then they were attacked by enemy machines. Hopelessly outnumbered, Allport still managed to stunt his aircraft so Hammond in the observer seat could fire his Lewis gun and shoot down three of the enemy planes. They fought a running battle all the way back to their own lines and escaped from what appeared to be certain death. It was Hammond's marksmanship and Allport's flying ability that saved them.

On artillery patrol on January 14, 1918, McLeod and a different observer, Lieutenant Reginald Key, flew over the front lines spotting enemy gun positions. Key was from Northampton and was a few years older than McLeod. The two shared living quarters at the aerodrome and had become the best of friends. They spent many off-hours together, riding or searching out furniture for their accommodation. On January 14, flying their reconnaissance mission, they spotted a German hot-air balloon, or kite balloon as they were called, tethered to the ground by cables that could raise and lower the balloon. The crew of the balloon were housed in a basket that hung below. Normally, it was the role of the Allied single-seat scout machines to attack such balloons. The scouts were faster than the two-seat reconnaissance biplanes and more manoeuvrable, as well. Speed was of the essence when attacking the balloons because they were usually well protected by anti-aircraft guns placed around the balloon site to fire at any intruders. The pilot had to get in and out quickly.

The Armstrong Whitworth F.K.8 (or Big Ack, as it was nicknamed) had a top speed of only about ninety miles per hour, whereas a Sopwith Camel could reach speeds of almost 120 miles per hour. The Big Ack was not designed to strafe anti-aircraft batteries or to go after enemy balloons; it was built for reconnaissance and artillery observation. McLeod did not care; he went after them anyway, and flew his machine as fearlessly as if it were a nimble scout.

On the January 14 flight, McLeod spotted the enemy balloon below while flying near the French town of Bauvin. He dove at the balloon at top speed, and as he got within firing range, he let loose with a burst from his Vickers gun. Veering away from the balloon at the last second, McLeod could see it collapse, falling to the ground. McLeod's combat report describes the encounter as follows: "About 2.45 p.m., I saw a balloon over Bauvin. I flew over above the clouds and dived through firing about 100 rounds from the front gun. The balloon folded up and fell quickly. At the same time the balloon at COURRIERES was slowly drawn down."[1]

Three German Albatros scouts had seen this encounter and raced to the aid of the balloon. They were too far away at the time to save the balloon. The crew managed to jump out of their basket and parachuted safely to the ground. McLeod, though, was met by the attacking enemy Albatros, which dove onto the A.W. McLeod took evasive action, allowing Key to get a clear shot at the nearest oncoming Albatros. His aim was true, hitting the engine of the E.A. Smoke started to appear from the stricken Albatros as it plummeted to earth. Seeing one of their comrades down, the other two German machines did not pursue McLeod as he sped for home. McLeod's ability as a pilot, along with Key's fine shooting, enabled this narrow escape from death. McLeod and Key were both mentioned in dispatches (MID) that day. McLeod's MID read as follows:

No. 2 Squadron. Ref 10.
CONFIDENTIAL
Officer Commanding,
1st. Wing,
Royal Flying Corps.

I would like to bring to your notice the gallantry and devotion to duty displayed by 2/Lieut. A. A. McLeod, General List and R.F.C. of this Squadron.

This officer on the 12th inst. Attacked and dispersed with machine gun fire from 800 feet the crew of a very troublesome anti-aircraft battery in LA BASSEE.

This afternoon while on Artillery Patrol, he attacked a hostile balloon near BAUVIN. This appeared to collapse and was seen to fall rapidly.

2/Lieut. McLeod joined the Squadron on the 29th. November 1917. He has shown keenness in his work, and I regard him as a most capable and reliable Artillery Pilot.

Wilfrid R. Snow
Major,
Commanding No. 2 Squadron,
Royal Flying Corps.
In the Field,
January 14th 1918

It seems clear by his encounters with the anti-aircraft battery, the observation balloon, and the German scouts, McLeod could have and perhaps should have transferred to a single-seat scout squadron. His flying ability was superb. However, he was happy with his No. 2 Squadron and stayed there. His CO let him and Hammond do as they liked once their artillery-spotting patrols were complete.

January 16, 1918, was cold and rainy. The rain and the high winds made flying almost impossible. However, McLeod and his trusty observer, Hammond, were able to take off on an artillery patrol. Near La Bassée, they spotted an anti-aircraft battery and dove to attack it. This particular battery had been especially annoying to other squadrons in the area, so McLeod was eager to destroy it. Facing fierce fire from the anti-aircraft gun, McLeod fired 225 machine-gun rounds at the battery from low altitude. He climbed and circled around for another pass, dropping his two twenty-pound bombs on the battery to finish it off.

McLeod wrote to his parents on January 17 asking them not to worry about him as he was safe and in not much danger. He downplayed his role in the conflict.

Gee whiz mother I wish you'd let up on the "Brave Son" stuff and all the rot about me doing my duty to my country, we fellows out here don't look at it that way, we sort of take it as a matter of course and have a good time, we never think of our country when we do it.

Say please don't take it so seriously about me being in France and don't worry about me, I'm in practically no danger whatever and I'd rather be here than in England anytime. In the R.F.C. after a pilot has done 3 weeks or a month in France and is still alive he's considered safe for the rest of his time in France, 95% of the casualties in the R.F.C. are new pilots out in France that don't know the ropes and in their first two or three trips over the lines they're done in because they are so inexperienced, but after your first bunch of trips over the line you begin to get cunning you know the ropes and then you're safe, do you know that in an official list of casualties in the R.F.C. that came out the other day it showed that there are more pilots killed in training in England that there are in France in the same time we have a regular safety first job out here, this Squadron has had 2 casualties in two years so you know I'm in no danger whatever so don't be foolish and worry over nothing.

You wanted to know about me being in the London air raids, of course I was & I was shot down but that's nothing it didn't worry me in the least, I didn't tell you because you people do worry such an awful lot over nothing I do wish you would stop, it worries me to think you are worrying.

You seem to think I'd mind it an awful lot going among new fellows after leaving 82 Squad. I didn't though, I'm so used to moving around I can go anywhere & meet new fellows and it never worries me the least bit I feel quite at home in no time, that's the way everyone gets in the army and it's a good way to be you seemed to think it queer that I got out to France so soon after being kicked out of 82 for being too young. I did have a hard job to get out here, I had to get down on my knees nearly to an old General guy before I got out here & then he stuck down my age as 19 & told me I could go & said he wished everyone was like me but many were the opposite. I was fed up with England though and I'm glad I got out here now, Mary said I was foolish to insist on going because I'd want to get back as soon as I got here, but I don't, we are worked pretty hard sometimes but as soon as our job is done you can do what you like for the rest of the time you'd never know this was the army, there is no discipline at all, were [*sic*] just like a bunch of fellows gathered together & rule ourselves and it must work all right for this is the crack squadron of France, and anyone who isn't up to the mark gets kicked out.

I'm glad you got those insurance papers all right. I hope they were O.K.

Well old dears there is no more news so I'll go to bed, hugs & kisses for yourselves & the girls.

Ever your affectionate son
Alan

Not much of a reassuring letter, saying he was out of danger but had been in the London raids and admitting he had been shot down once. The insurance papers he refers to are most likely a life insurance policy Alan McLeod took out in case he died in combat: another reason to worry. McLeod was right about the life expectancy of new pilots — about a month. Once a pilot had surpassed that one-month milestone, his chances of survival were considerably greater.

As a reward for McLeod, in part for his successful earlier raid on the anti-aircraft battery, Major Snow sent the young pilot on leave to London for the latter part of January and first part of February. In a letter home on January 28, 1918, he describes in his own words his recent combats.

Now to tell you how I got this leave so soon, it was really nothing but our C.O. thought it was, I brought down a Hun balloon & a bunch of Hun machines and then dived on an anti-aircraft gun the Huns had and shot all the gunners who were crack ones with my machine gun, this gun was very accurate & gave us a lot of trouble so everybody was glad I got its gunners, I then dropped my bombs on the gun & blew it to pieces, it was really nothing, there was no risk in it, the Huns are such cowards & poor fighters in the air that you can always shoot them down if they don't fly away. The C.O. sent my name in and recommended me for a decoration and our General told him he would see I got it and the next day the General was killed he had a bad heart & took heart failure in the air and of course was killed, he was only 26 yrs. old the youngest General in the world, I guess my decoration will fall through, I was mentioned in dispatches from France & in official R.F.C. records so that's just as good, what I did was only fun & not worth a decoration anyway, but the C.O. insisted upon giving me leave, so that's why I am here, there was something in the London papers about me, I didn't see it though some of the fellows told me about it, they wrote for my picture but I wouldn't give it to them.

This letter reflects a different kind of Alan McLeod, a confident pilot and perhaps a bit of a braggart. His dismissal of the German pilots' ability shows a cockiness that would come back to haunt him, as will be pointed out later. If McLeod could not be recognized with the award of a decoration, Major Snow decided to at least reward McLeod with two weeks' leave in London. While on leave McLeod stayed at the Royal Club for Officers. It was from there that he wrote to his grandfather on January 29.

My Dear old Granddad:

I received your most welcome letter yesterday and I was awfully pleased to hear from you, I am awfully sorry I didn't write you before but I have been rather busy out there in France and awfully lazy too, I am just in on two weeks leave I didn't want it, but it was given to me without asking. I like it awfully well out in France, we have a very good time and plenty of excitement I'd rather be there than here although it is nice to be away for a while but I'll be glad to get back.

This morning I met Jack Gunn (Dr) and Billy Gunn and yesterday I saw Ted Skinner, Billy Riley & Ed Stinson, Jack Gunn is going back to France to-morrow & Billy to Canada and Ed Stinson expects to go back at anytime.

This London is a wonderful city, but everything is so expensive and there is such a shortage of food you can hardly get a square meal things are in an awful state.

Last night the Huns bombed London and got a direct hit on a building just by the Savoy Hotel and it smashed all the glass in the Savoy and nearly knocked me off my feet, it seems to me its more dangerous in London than it is in France, they never get that near us there. Well I must close now, remember me to all and please thank Aunt Mamie every so much for the lovely socks she sent me, every your [sic] loving Grandson

Alan

I don't know your address so I'll send this to Dunc.

The bombing raid on London McLeod referred to took place late in the evening of January 28, 1918, when three Gotha bombers dropped their deadly loads on the heart of London. Then, around midnight, a single Staaken giant, serial R39, piloted by Captain Richard von Bentivegni, approached London. He unloaded over two thousand pounds of explosives on the city. Raymond H. Fredette, in *The Sky on Fire: The First Battle of Britain, 1917–1918*, describes the attack.

During the first hour of that homeward journey Bentivegni could see the "red glow" of a large fire burning in the heart of London. He attributed the blaze to a 660-pound bomb which had struck "close to the Admiralty." Actually falling in Long Acre, the bomb wrecked a havoc long remembered for its horror and what then seemed an appalling toll.... Bentivegni's bomb was the deadliest to fall on London during the entire war. The overall casualties of the raid stood at 233, including sixty-seven deaths. Such losses had not been suffered since the daylight raids, a consequence of harsh fate and the huge bombs the Giants were now ferrying to England.[2]

McLeod continued his leave into February, visiting a certain Miss Moll on February 2: "She has offered to take me to dances and all kinds of entertainment but I had to decline as I can't dance and can't do anything one should be able to do in society."

We see here the shy, unassuming, rural boy from Manitoba, somewhat lost in the high society of London. It also should be remembered that he was still only eighteen years of age, a teenager who may have been overwhelmed by British society, as he described in the following portion of a letter home: "I had an invitation to lunch at the Countess of Harrowbys [sic] to-day ... I am too shy to go to see the countess."

McLeod did, however, act the tourist, as all visitors to England do, seeing some of the sights in the area, such as Canterbury Cathedral, on February 6. Alan McLeod's last day of leave was February 9.

By February 11 McLeod was back with No. 2 Squadron, flying reconnaissance missions and supporting the British artillery on spotting missions over the front lines. By this time, he had been in France for nearly three months. He was looking for the opportunity, in a month or two, to be able to get back to Canada for a visit.

On February 15, however, McLeod got the news he was being sent to an artillery battery, in exchange for an artillery officer who would spend time with his squadron. McLeod describes this change in a letter to his parents: "I'm going in liaison with the Artillery to-morrow, that is I go to the Artillery for 3 days and one of the artillery officers comes to us for a while, because we work with them from the air and so if we visit them on the ground we can do the work from the air much better, I'm rather looking forward to it."

McLeod returned to his squadron with a better appreciation of the life of an artillery gunner and the dangers of conducting artillery duels with the Germans. Once he got back he was up in the air almost every day for artillery observation, photo reconnaissance, and bombing raids over the front lines. He wrote to his mother on February 22, 1918, about some of the realities of army life.

My Darling Mother:

I have just received your letters of Jan. 18 and 20th and I also had letters from Attie, Grandma, Cecil, Alice Gray & Edith Mason, it was fine to get so much mail and I guess there will be more to-morrow.

It is nearly ten o'clock now and I have just come back from having dinner with a Major McKenzie from Vancouver, I met him when I was on leave, and found him very nice and I knew a nephew of his so I was the whole cheese with him, he is in another town near here & he sent his car over here for me, we had a peach of a dinner, that reminds me you said you wouldn't let dad talk about the meals he has had and then you sit down to write me and do the very same thing, tell me about roast turkey etc. I think it's a shame.

You were speaking about me getting back to Canada when my time was up in France because you thought I would have done good work out here, that won't help in the least you are not chosen for things like that in the army because you have done good work, they don't look up your record, the man that gets what he wants in the army is the fellow with pull & the best liar, you don't understand the ways at all mother dear, your [sic] out here to do your best and if you do good work they take it as a matter of course, if I get back to Canada it will be because I have a long pathetic yarn to spin, I've begun making it up already but everyone spins that kind of a yarn now and they're wise to it, so I guess I stay in England for the duration, but if I can't get to Canada I'm going to try & stay right here, this is all right.

You were asking me about different kinds of machines we flew. I fly the same kind all the time although I have flown many in my year. I've flown nearly every kind of a machine the British have the scouts just look [*sic*] for scrap with Huns all the time & see how many they can bring down, theirs is a much more dangerous job than ours, we do patrols & reconnaissance & photography etc. in the last 4 days the F.C. brought down 105 german [*sic*] machines in France and they brought down 12 of ours, that is in the whole of France remember, not bad eh!

You have been having quite a time at home lately with snowshoe parties etc. I wish I were home to have some fun with you, never mind I will be next Xmas I hope.

Our aerodrome is ten miles behind the lines, some are more & some less.

McLeod's letter to his parents on March 7, 1918, speaks of his accommodations at the Hesdigneul aerodrome.

My dear old Dad & Mother:

As usual I have no news for you but I'm just going to tell you about my "boudoir" as we call it, I am more comfortable by far in huts here than I ever was in my billet, and that's saying something, it's just grand here, you have the pleasure (also the expense) of fixing up your own hut and its lots of fun, the hut is about 28ft. long and 14ft. wide and its half round, covered with tin that's all the hut is divided into half by a wooden partition & there are six in a hut, 3 in each half, in our half, there are Key who I told you about the other night, Hammond another observer who is now on leave and myself, we each have a small camp bed, two of them are up against the wooden partition and the other against the wall, then we have two sort of cupboards made of old boxes, we fixed them up and draped them with curtains they don't look bad & serve the purpose, then we have a Canadian box heater, that is the drawback of the hut, it's a rotten stove and we can't often get wood for it, we also have a coal oil heater something like ours at home, not so good though, it's a French thing, we have carpet on the floor, (some burlap we pinched) we also have a couple of straw rugs on the floor, in the centre of the room we have a round table 4 ½ ft. in diameter, it has a centre piece on it and a lamp on the centre piece, pretty classy eh, then we have another oblong table which serves as a wash stand, we had to steal & wrangle most of our stuff, but we got it anyway, and in the army that is a recognized way, then we are going to have the tin on the inside painted white, because there are only two small windows & the white paint will help make it light. Well old Dad & Mother I must close now, I have told you all about our hut & there's no more news, heaps of love to the girls

ever your loving son
Alan

The huts McLeod describes in this letter home were Nissen huts, made in the shape of a semicircle. The sides and roof were made out of corrugated metal. Either end of the hut was wooden, containing the two small windows and, between them, the door to the hut. Most huts were raised about two feet off the ground, necessitating a set of four wooden steps to get in and out. Nissen huts were the standard accommodation for airmen in France.

McLeod's B Flight Commander, Captain Allport, left the squadron on March 9, 1918, having spent nine months in France. McLeod describes his emotions about his commander: "Our Flight Commander Capt. Allfort [*sic*] whom we all worship is going home to England to-morrow, he has done his nine months in France we all feel awfully badly about it he's such a nice fellow, we would do anything for him."

McLeod couldn't dwell upon the departure of his Flight Commander, however, as B Flight was in the air the next day over Douvrin on an artillery observation mission, flying at eight thousand feet. McLeod was flying the Big Ack B3377 with Key as his observer. They were pounced upon by four enemy aircraft, two Pfalz and two Albatros. They came from out of the sun, firing all their machine guns. As McLeod made a sharp diving turn, Key fired off a drum of Lewis gun ammunition at the attacking German scouts. Diving west, McLeod and Key shook the E.A., who continued on toward the town of Pont-à-Vendin. McLeod's masterful flying and Key's marksmanship combined to save their skins that day. They lived to fly again.

On March 13, 1918, McLeod's new flight commander, Captain Mitchell, arrived at the aerodrome. McLeod wrote of his first impressions of him, "he seems all right although we haven't had time to know him yet, but he'll never come up to old 'Alfy' as we called him."

There were a number of personnel transfers to and from the squadron, as McLeod writes about on March 14, 1918. "Gee I feel fed up with life, Key the fellow who was in the hut with me has been transferred to another squadron, he was my observer and we were very much devoted to each other, I did hate to see him go & he hated to go too."

Perhaps the stress of daily flight and the ever present danger of combat were beginning to have an effect on Alan McLeod, causing him to be fed up with life. He was also upset with the level of pay he was receiving as a second lieutenant, as can be seen from part of a letter home on

March 16: "A full fledged flying officer got $7 a day eh. I only wish we did, that would be 28s a day and as it is we get 19/6. A captain gets $7 a day, if I got that I'd be a millionaire by now."

March 21, 1918, marked the beginning of the Germans' last attempt to win the war — the Michael offensive. With the fall of the Russian Empire in December 1917 and the signing of the treaty of Brest-Litovsk in March of 1918 between Germany and the new Bolshevik regime, Russia was officially out of the war. The fact that the Eastern Front no longer existed meant that thousands of German troops could be transferred to the Western Front. General Erich Ludendorff, the German quartermaster general and the effective head of the German forces, knew he had to attack the Allies before the Americans could muster enough forces to dominate in France. On the first day of the battle, seventy-six crack German storm trooper divisions fell upon twenty-eight British divisions of the British First and Second armies in the area of Ypres, Armentières, and La Bassée. The artillery bombardment announcing the beginning of the offensive amounted to a massive 3.2 million rounds of high explosives, shrapnel, and chemical shells.

McLeod's squadron was located southwest of the town of Béthune, which was at the southern end of the front being attacked by the Germans as part of the Michael offensive. No. 2 Squadron was, like many other squadrons, called upon to stem the advance of the enemy. Day and night the Ack-Ws flew on bombing raids against supply depots, artillery batteries, roads, and any other military target they could find. They would also strafe, at low altitude, enemy troop concentrations with their forward-firing machine guns. Many air reconnaissance flights recorded the advance of the Germans.

The day after the offensive started, McLeod wrote to his parents.

> My Darling old Dad & Mother:
>
> Well here I am starting off to write to you again with no news at all, except as usual, the weather which has been

beautiful lately, almost like summer, there has been very little work lately so all we do is sun ourselves. I was out for a long ride to-day 3 hrs. we galloped through the woods near here and had a peach of a time, we scared the wits out of old Frenchman [*sic*] by nearly running over them.

Say do you know I'm growing a moustache, it's three weeks old now and believe me it's done some growing in that time, I even had the nerve to have it trimmed the other day, it sure is coming on.

The Huns are shelling this city near where we are and all the people are moving out, it's a shame, it's such a nice place too, now we won't have any place to get things. They sure have long range guns, they shell places 30 miles behind the lines and then their gun is 10 miles behind their lines again, so that is some distance to shoot, we have nothing to shoot that far, so they have it over us there. Well I have come to the end of the little news I had so I guess I'll ring off & go to bed, I wish I could kiss you all good night.

Every [*sic*] your own dear son
Alan

Every day McLeod and Hammond carried out artillery spotting and reconnaissance missions. They also carried out daily bombing raids on enemy positions, dropping twenty-pound Cooper bombs. On March 25, 1918, McLeod and Hammond, in Armstrong Whitworth C3377, were on a special mission around the town of Bapaume. Flying at eighteen hundred feet, they were attacked by a large, twin-engine German machine, which dove on them. Their combat report reads: "Whilst on Special Mission we were attacked by a large two or three seater E.A., which dived on our tail, his observer firing from high up in front of Nacelle. Observer fired 50 rounds and Tracers were seen to enter the front of E. A's Nacelle. He again dived but did not fire. E.A. then turned and flew East."[3]

McLeod (right) and Hammond in front of a Nissen hut.

The attacking German machine was probably a Gotha bomber, which did have a crew of three and had a forward-firing machine gun in the nose (nacelle) of the fuselage.

The following day McLeod wrote to his parents. His letter reflects the increased activity in the air due to the German offensive.

> My darling old Dad & Mother:
>
> I haven't written you for some time, but I've been too busy. I haven't written anyone, we are flying day & night both, they seem to be trying to win the war in the air as well as on the ground and we're having a good try too, we shot down 146 Hun machines in 3 days and only lost about 5 or 6 of our own, that's mighty good eh, and we've bombed every place worth while in all German

territory, they certainly are putting it over us on the ground though, there is the biggest battle going on here now, that the world has ever known, all authorities say so and I well believe it too, to see it from the air where you can watch everything, the Huns are putting it all over us too, they have advanced 20 miles in the last two or three days, my its been a terrible battle, they haven't named it yet, if we don't do something soon it will be all up with us, by the time you get this letter though you will probably know all about it and it will be all over. I don't think anyone could give you a better description of it though than we fellows who saw it from the air, I'll never forget it as long as I live.

I received the two parcels you sent me, the one with the doll, sweater, socks and candy & the one with the cake, the sweater is dandy, I'm wearing it now it was awfully kind of that lady to knit it for me, please thank her for me, also thank Mrs. Gray and Miss Cleland, I'm too busy to write letters now, I probably won't be able to write you very often either. Well my darlings I must close now, hugs & kisses to yourselves & the girls. Every [*sic*] your own dear son

Alan
XXXXXXX
XXXXXXX

FIVE

McLeod's Last Flight

To help counter the German army's final offensive, the RFC threw all it had at the advancing army. Every available machine was used for the strafing of troops and anything else that moved. On March 25 alone, ten squadrons, including five squadrons (No. 2, 4, 5, 16, and 42) from I Brigade operating from the First Army area, and two squadrons from V Brigade, were diverted to low-flying attacks on the advancing German divisions. Reconnaissance machines like McLeod's Armstrong Whitworth were also used for bombing missions. On March 26 McLeod and Hammond flew three bombing raids against enemy targets, operating to late in the day.

The morning of March 27 saw McLeod's aerodrome shrouded in fog and mist. Despite having had little sleep and no breakfast, McLeod and Hammond, along with the crews of six other aeroplanes of No. 2 Squadron, took off to bomb targets behind the German lines. McLeod and Hammond, because of the poor visibility, became separated from the rest of the squadron and lost their way in the fog.

> After twenty-five minutes of flying by compass, McLeod signaled Hammond that he was going down for a look. They came out of the mist so low that they were under heavy fire from machine-guns on the ground. Twice McLeod repeated this effort to locate his position, then turned west in the hope of reaching one of his own airfields. Finally, he managed to land on the field occupied by No. 43 Squadron, but damaged his tail-skid because of his heavy bomb load. While he and Hammond lunched with the commanding officer, a new skid was fitted and one of the squadron's fighters went up to test the weather and visibility. The pilot reported the latter as zero. Nevertheless, McLeod and Hammond decided to try again to find their target, fifteen miles behind the enemy lines, near Bray.[1]

They were on their own, flying to the target area, unaware of the danger that was to befall them.

The day before, Rittmeister Manfred von Richthofen and his fighter wing, *Jagdgeschwader* 1 (JG 1), had taken over a nearby airfield at Léchelle.

> The airfield had been abandoned with such haste six days earlier by No. 15 Squadron, an R.E.8 unit, that fully intact hangars and other buildings offered immediate accommodation to Richthofen. In addition to taking over No. 15 Squadron's installations on March 26, Richthofen shot down and killed one of that unit's aircrews not far from their old 'drome. That R.E.8 marked the 70th aerial victory of Germany's undisputed master fighter pilot and aerial tactician.[2]

JG 1 was made up of a number of *Jastas*, or squadrons, and Richthofen's Flying Circus had a complement of some fifty aeroplanes. (The term *Flying Circus* was derived from the fact JG 1 travelled around the Western Front to whichever location needed its help, just as a circus travels the countryside.)

On March 27, as McLeod and Hammond approached their target near Bray, flying at three thousand feet, the sky cleared enough for them to be able to get into position to bomb a German artillery battery. Just as they were lining up the target, a German Fokker Dr.I triplane came into view and attacked them from above. McLeod turned the Ack-W to enable Hammond to get a good shot at the E.A. He fired three quick bursts of his Vickers and the triplane veered off, spinning toward the ground. This altercation was noticed by aeroplanes from Richthofen's JG 1. Seven Fokker triplanes attacked McLeod and Hammond. As the lead enemy machine got close, Hammond poured machine-gun fire into its fuselage, breaking it in two just aft of the pilot. McLeod, with all his skill, threw his machine around in an attempt to avoid the enemy aircraft. The next triplane to attack, bizarrely painted with black and white diagonal lines, was piloted by Lieutnant Hans Kirschstein, who claimed the paint job made his machine more difficult to aim at and dubbed it the "optical illusion."

> Hans Kirschstein, from Koblenz, was 21 when he began flying the Dr.1. He had already seen war service in Poland and France with the sapper outfit *3.Pionnier-Battaillon 'von Rauch,'* and whilst serving in Galacia [*sic*] in 1915 he contracted malaria. Kirschstein duly returned to his homeland, and upon recovery was sent back to the Western Front, prior to transferring to the air service in May 1917.
>
> After becoming a pilot, he subsequently served with several two-seater *Abteilungen*, and even participated in a bombing raid on Dover on one occasion. Kirschstein eventually volunteered for fighters, and on 13 March 1918 he joined *Jasta 6* – he would eventually become the unit's most successful pilot. During his first week flying fighters he downed a Camel of No. 54 Sqn.[3]

Kirschstein manoeuvred his triplane to a position below McLeod's Armstrong Whitworth B5773 and fired his Maxim machine guns all along the fuselage, wounding both Hammond and McLeod and hitting the engine and fuel tank. The tank caught fire. The fire was starting to spread. The flames licked the fuselage from engine to tail. The bullets from the attacking Fokkers shot out most of the floor underneath Hammond, injuring him again and causing him to have to hold on to the machine-gun ring on the upper part of his cockpit.

McLeod, seeing the danger of the flames engulfing the entire aircraft, had to do something. He eased himself out of his stricken machine, an action akin to getting out of a bathtub with high sides, and managed to extricate himself from the cockpit. He then stepped onto the lower left wing. Although injured with bullet wounds from his attackers and conscious of Hammond being injured too, McLeod focused on trying to control his aeroplane, to minimize the danger of the flames, and to land his Big Ack.

He steered the machine from the wing, holding on to one of the wooden struts that attached the upper plane to the fuselage, while using his other hand to operate the controls. One leg was out of the cockpit, the other inside, on the rudder. He sideslipped the Armstrong Whitworth so that the flames would travel away from the fuselage and not consume the entire machine. All this time they were being attacked by the Fokkers, who were wanting to put an end to McLeod and Hammond.

More shots hit them. The flames were getting worse, and McLeod was trying the best he could to keep the flames under control while attempting to get his machine down and eventually land. Hammond, injured as he was by six gunshot wounds, managed to fire at an approaching triplane. He fired again and the E.A. turned and dove to the ground in flames and out of control.

McLeod was losing altitude. He could feel the heat of the fire as it started to burn through his heavy flying suit, which was stained with sticky blood. McLeod was holding on for dear life and at the same time pushing the control stick forward. He knew that he could not and must not panic. He concentrated on keeping his machine under control and landing it.

Fokkers circled around like a flock of vultures wanting to finish off their prey. The crippled Armstrong Whitworth, now a flaming wreck, was diving toward no-man's-land between the Allied and German trenches. Losing blood from his five wounds, and only semi-conscious, McLeod managed to flatten out his dive just before hitting the ground. He was thrown clear of his machine, falling into a heap on the muddy ground, and lost consciousness. The Fokkers eventually flew away, not wanting to get too near the rifle fire of the British troops.

McLeod and Hammond were Hans Kirchstein's second victory. He would later that day shoot down a Sopwith Camel, his third victory. Kirchstein would go on to down a total of twenty-seven Allied planes, and on June 24, 1918, he would receive Germany's highest decoration, the Prussian order Pour le Mérite, the Blue Max. Hans Kirchstein would die on July 16, 1918, as a result of a flying accident.

Alan McLeod regained consciousness. He saw Hammond a few feet away, who had also been thrown clear of the burning machine when it crashed. McLeod, with his last amount of strength, got up and staggered over to Hammond. He struggled with the dead weight of his injured observer but managed to roll him to a safe distance from the aeroplane. McLeod knew there were still bombs on board the craft, so he had to hurry and get Hammond to safety.

McLeod made slow progress toward the British lines. Both were being fired at by German machine gunners from the enemy trenches. McLeod received another bullet wound. A moment after being hit, he lost consciousness again. Out of the British trenches came a number of soldiers from a South African regiment who, despite being under fire, brought the two men back to safety. Patching up their wounds as well as they could, the troops had to wait until nightfall, around eight o'clock, to evacuate the pair to a reserve trench. From there, stretcher-bearers carried McLeod and Hammond back to the nearest field hospital, behind the lines, where the two flyers received further treatment including shots of morphine.

There is some controversy about whether McLeod had both legs out of the cockpit or just one when he was trying to control the flames consuming his aircraft. Some depictions of McLeod and his machine, like George Tanner's memorial painting, show him totally out of the cockpit, as does the illustration of McLeod in George A. Drew's book *Canada's Fighting Airmen*. If both of his legs were out of the cockpit, he would not have been able to reach the rudder bar, only the control stick. This would have made it virtually impossible to land his machine with any degree of control. Therefore, it is more likely that he had one leg in the cockpit and one leg out of it. In a letter (included at the end of this chapter) that Hammond wrote to McLeod's mother after the war, he confirms that McLeod had only one leg out of the cockpit and not two. Given that, it is clear that he would not have been able to totally escape the flames, and McLeod's lower body must have received some burns. However, McLeod makes no mention of his burns in his letters home. Perhaps he did not want to alarm the family by mentioning the burns; or perhaps, in fact, he was totally out of the cockpit and miraculously landed his machine that way.

When McLeod and Hammond did not return to their aerodrome the squadron members, as well as Commander Snow, were very worried. The next day, March 28, 1918, Squadron Major Wilfrid Snow wrote to Alan's father.

> Dear Mr. McLeod,
>
> It is with the deepest regret that I have to advise you that your son, Lieut. A.A. McLeod has been missing since yesterday morning. He left the aerodrome about 9.40 in formation with five other machines to take part in the battle which is now raging. After landing at another aerodrome nothing further has been heard of him. He was with others engaged in low flying, bombing and machine gun attacks on massed hostile troops moving up to attack, a job which your Son with his unbounded courage and complete ignorance of the meaning of the word "fear," would delight in.
>
> It is my finest conviction that your son is a prisoner is [*sic*] quite all right. Where he was operating is sixty miles from this aerodrome and with the immense battle which is now raging particulars come through very slowly. There

is a faint possibility of his being wounded and in one of our hospitals though I don't think is very likely. My opinion is that he and his observer are unwounded and prisoners of war. All the machines of this work suffered from ground machine gun fire and with the large target the engine presents the chances are that it was hit and put out of action so that they were forced to land.

It is possible that news may come through by means of a message dropped from an enemy machine stating what has happened.

The whole Squadron is plunged into gloom at the loss of your son. Without exaggerating he was the most gallant and fearless officer I have ever met in the Flying Corps and his invariable cheeriness and good humor had endered [*sic*] him to everyone.

His kit will be packed and sent on to you in due course. As soon as there is any news I will let you know immediately.

With very many sympathies
Yours sincerely,
(Sqd.) Wilfrid R. Snow,
Major O.C. N0. 2 Squad,
R.F.C.[4]

By March 29, 1918, McLeod and Hammond had been moved from the hospital in the field (known as a Casualty Clearing Station) to the St. John Ambulance Brigade Hospital in Étaples, France, on the English Channel south of Calais. From there he started a letter to his parents. He sent it once he arrived in hospital in London.

My Dear old Dad & Mother:

Well I got into a scrap with some unfriendly Huns day before yesterday and they sort of shot me up a bit. My wounds are absolutely nothing though they don't hurt a bit. They are good clean ones too, so there is no need for you to worry, in fact there may be room for you to rejoice because I may be able to get back to Canada. Dr. Gunn is just about 100 yds. from here and I have sent for him to ask his advice about it. Well I have nothing else to say only, don't worry.

Heaps of love and kisses for yourselves and the girls.

Ever your loving son
Alan

I am now in Prince of Wales Hospital London, very comfortable.

In the meantime, the British Secretary of War Office had telegrammed the McLeods to inform them of their son being admitted to St. John's Hospital in Étaples with gunshot wounds to the leg and buttock. In the telegram, these wounds were described as "severe."

McLeod had arrived in England on April 1, 1918, and was in the Prince of Wales Hospital the next day being treated for his injuries. The day McLeod was admitted to hospital his commanding officer, Major Wilfrid R. Snow, sent a confidential communiqué to headquarters 1st Wing RAF.

Further to my No. 10 of 14/1/18. I would like to again bring to your notice with a recommendation for immediate reward the gallantry and devotion to duty displayed by 2/Lieut. ALAN ARNETT McLEOD. General List & R.F.C., and of Lieut. ARTHUR WILLIAM HAMMOND, M.C., Royal Engineers & R.F.C. of this Squadron.

2/Lt. A.A. McLeod joined the R.F.C. 23/6/17, was first commissioned 17/8/17, and joined this Squadron as a pilot 29/11/17.

As an artillery pilot, he has always been exceptionally keen in his work and has shewn [sic] great ability and perseverance. As mentioned before, on January

10th. While on artillery patrol he successfully attacked the BAUVIN balloon. He also on two accaissions [*sic*] attacked with machine gun fire from a height of 50 and 800 feet a particularly active anti-aircraft battery at LA BASSEE. Each time that battery was silenced, and some of the personnel were seen to fall to the ground.

On March 27th. 1918 while on special mission (bombing) over ALBERT he and Lieut. HAMMOND were attacked by eight enemy triplanes. During the ensuing fight, three of these were seen to go down out of control after a burst from the observer's gun. Their machine then took fire and 2/Lieut. McLEOD by standing on the side of the fuselage, brought it down under control though in flames. The machine crashed on landing in "No Man's Land" and 2/Lt. McLEOD, though himself wounded in five places and under machine gun fire from the enemy trenches, dragged the observer, who was more seriously hit than himself, away from the crash in order that he might not be hit by the explosion of the bombs on the machine. 2/Lt. McLEOD was again wounded while doing this.

Lieut. A.W. HAMMOND, M.C. though seriously wounded in six places, continued to engage the enemy aircraft, who were following them down while their machine was in flames, thereby shewing [*sic*] a gallantry and determination which I consider to merit some recognition.

Both pilots and observer were eventually rescued by our Infantry.

In the Field
Wilfrid R. Snow
2/4/18
Major
Commanding No. 2 Squadron
Royal Air Force [5]

Lieutenant Hammond would later receive a bar to his Military Cross for his bravery that day. The official announcement of Hammond's award reads as follows:

On March 27, 1918, while flying with his pilot, Second Lieutenant A. A. McLeod, east of Albert, attacking hostile troops and transport with machine gun fire and bombs from 5,000 feet, he was attacked by eight enemy triplanes which dived from all directions firing their front guns. Lieutenant Hammond fired bursts at each machine in turn, shooting three of them down out of control.

During this engagement he was wounded six times. He was continuing fire on the hostile machines, when a bullet penetrated the petrol tank, setting the machine on fire. The pilot, Second Lieutenant McLeod, although wounded five times, with great skill and coolness managed to climb on to the left-hand bottom plane, and controlled the machine from the side of the fuselage, sideslipping to the ground. Lieutenant Hammond, despite his wounds and surrounded by flames, continued to fire upon the enemy machines while descending. The machine crashed in "No Man's Land." Second Lieutenant McLeod managed to extricate Lieutenant Hammond from the flames and heated bombs and dragged him to a shell hole, from which they were both subsequently rescued by our infantry under heavy fire from the enemy lines.[6]

On April 2, 1918, Major Snow again wrote to Alan McLeod's father, giving him the good news, Alan was not a prisoner of war, and extolled the bravery of his son.

Dear Mr. McLeod,

I am delighted to be able to write you what no doubt have heard from your son himself., Viz. that he is on our side of the lines and not as was before supposed a prisoner of war. Wounded and in a hospital at the Base was the first news we had of him some days ago and you can't imagine the relief and delight of all the officers of the Squadron and myself as well to know he was safe.

Of his wonderful gallantry in bringing his machine down under control though in flames and then after crashing on the ground dragging from the [*sic*] his observer who was more seriously wounded than himself, I will say no more than it is just what I would have expected him to do. His fearlessness and courage while in the Squadron I had several times brought to the notice of the Colonel and now this crowning act of all which I hope will be rewarded as it deserves.

With very many congratulations
Yours sincerely,
Wilfrid R. Snow
Major [7]

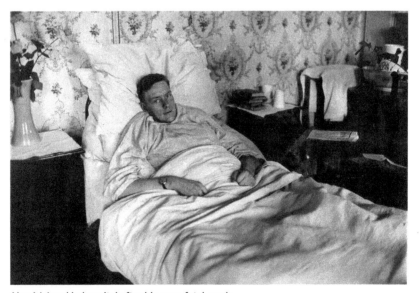

Alan McLeod in hospital after his near-fatal crash.

On the same day his CO was recommending McLeod for a decoration for bravery, he penned a letter, the day he arrived in hospital, to his parents giving his own rendition of the events of March 27.

Prince of Wales Hospital
Marylebone Road
London, W. W. 1.
April 2nd, 1918.

My Dear Old Dad and Mother,

Well this is a great old war. Here I am in a London Hospital, feeling as fit as ever I did, but mighty sorry to have left France now the fun has begun. If I could, I'd go back today, for we were having loads of fun; beaucoup Huns to scrap with and everything, it was grand.

The work we were doing when I left was lots of fun, working on the front where the great Push was around Albert, Bray, Perronne [*sic*] and Baupaume [*sic*], not very far from Amiens. Our aerodrome was about sixty miles away, but we used to fly down and work there. The Huns took all that ground there because they wasted their men, just jammed them in. We would go over in our machines, drop bombs on them and rake them with our machine gun fire. It was just slaughter, but they always had more men to take the places of the fallen. They out-numbered us about ten to one. Our fellows made a mighty good fight for it tho [*sic*]. A lot of it was open warfare and hand to hand fighting like the old days. We flew very low and got a great view of what was going on. I'll never forget it as long as I live.

When I got it, it was a cloudy day and the clouds were low. Six of us started out in the morning for Albert in formation. It was so cloudy that we all lost each other. We didn't know where we were. I wandered around the country and as I did not know that part of the line, I did not know which were our fellows and which were Huns. So I went back to an aerodrome near there, had some lunch and then found my way over from there.

When we got to the lines we were the only one of our machines around, and there were lost [*sic*] of Boches. We went quite a piece over the lines and were just going to drop our bombs on a Hun battery that was in action, when suddenly a bunch of Boches came out of the clouds on us. There must have been eight of them. I foolishly stayed to scrap with them. We jumped up to about five or six thousand feet and fought for a while and got three of them down in flames. Then they got us. By this time I had a few bullets in me and they were beginning to hurt, when our machine burst into flames. As soon as I saw this I put the machine into a dive to try to get to the ground. We stood out on the side of the machine as soon as we got near enough and jumped for the ground. Our flying suits were burned off us and our clothes partly burned, but we were hardly burned at all ourselves. My observer, Hammond, was certainly a hero. When we were coming down in flames it looked like certain death and he was badly wounded, he still fired at the Huns and brought one down too. That takes some nerve, believe me.

The machine came down near us. It had 8 bombs and 1000 rounds of ammunition on it and was in flames, so that was not a very safe place to stay. My observer was nearly all in. He couldn't move, so I managed to drag him far enough away from the machine so that when the bombs went off he wouldn't get hurt. The machine gun bullets were going off all around us from the heat of the machine, so it wasn't very pleasant. Soon the bombs went off and blew the whole machine over us, but nothing hurt us.

We didn't know where we were — on the Boches side or ours — but we were being shelled. The Boches from above were still using their machine guns on us, the snipers were at work on us too, so we decided we were on the Hun side. Suddenly we saw some of our Tommies [British soldiers] rush out of the trenches to our rescue. It turned out we were in No Man's Land. The Huns rushed out of their trenches too, and had a scrap with our fellows, but they got us into our trenches O.K. I had been hit again while we were on the ground so had Hammond. Then after we were in the trenches the Hums were shelling us, so we couldn't leave there until night. It was about noon when they dragged us in, and there was no doctor there. About eight that night, under cover of darkness, they carried us on stretchers to a reserve trench about a mile away. We got our wounds dressed there and I had some bullets taken out that weren't very far in. The doctor gave us some morphine and we were carried again by stretcher bearers for another three miles to another dressing station. There we had a lot of dope injected to keep us from getting lockjaw poison, etc. Then we were put in an ambulance and taken to a casualty clearing station at Amiens. It was a Canadian one and some of the doctors and nurses knew Dad. They were from the W.G.H., but I forgot their names.

We had our wounds dressed again and about four in the morning we started on a very dirty slow train for the base at Etaples. We arrived there at six p.m. the next day. In Etaples Hammond and I got separated. I don't know where he was sent and can't find trace of him. I was taken to St. John's Hospital and the first person I met was a pal of mine from our squadron. He had a bullet in his leg, had been shot down too. I was awfully glad to see him. He is a Canadian from Hamilton. My hospital was just a hundred yards or so from Col. Gunn's. I sent for him and he came to see me. I left Etaples at one a.m. went to Calais and form [*sic*] there got a boat to Dover. Believe me the channel was rough. I got here at 8 the next night.

This is a pretty good place. It used to be one of London's good hotel [*sic*]. They put about five of us into one big room, and in my room we are having a peach of a time. None of us are seriously wounded, and we have pillow fights, scraps and all kind of sport. The meals are not much, worse than France, but they can't get food in England.

I have only one wound of consequence, on the right heel. The bullet went into the bone and is there yet. I am going to have an operation soon to extract it. I got two or three flesh wounds on the right leg — they were just flesh wounds never touched the bone and some more of the same kind in the hip. The doctor at the first dressing station took some bullets out, but they were nothing, didn't even hurt. The one in my heel hurt though, I nearly fainted with pain. Hammond had a lot of bullets in him too, he was much worse that I was.

The doctor says it will take some time for the wound in my heel to get better, tho [*sic*] it isn't of much consequence. When I get my Medical Board I am going to apply for leave to go back to Canada till I get better, but I couldn't stay long. Not likely I get it tho. Leave is hard to get. I won't know what to do all the time here. I wish I could get either to France or Canada right away. I hated to leave the old squadron. I did like it. Now all my kit is there and will be lost I suppose. I had a good suit on be burnt [*sic*] as well as my flying suit. Address my mail in care of Mrs. Thom and send me some sugar please, its not to be had here now.

Heaps of love and kisses to the girls and yourselves.
Ever you own dear son,
Alan

P.S. Please don't worry. It would just be like you both, and I'm as fit as a fiddle. I believe our escape was one of the most remarkable I ever heard of. Here I am six days after, feeling like a prize fighter, and have just shown one of the fellows in this room that I am one.

It was just like Alan McLeod to put on a brave face for his family. That was the nature of the man. He did not want his family to worry about him. In fact, the bullet wounds to his hip were quite serious. So too were those to his heel. McLeod would use a cane as a result. On April 12, 1918, McLeod wrote to his family of his recovery, of the visitors he had in hospital, and of the fate of his observer, Hammond.

My Dear old Dad & Mother:

I guess it's time to write again but there's no news as usual, I'm so afraid some of you are on you're [sic] way over here because I haven't had a wire or anything from you acknowledging my wire and Bill's too.

I'm afraid it's all up about me going to Canada because a new rule has just been passed saying that no one can go to Canada on leave unless they are ill enough to stay six months so that puts the hat on me, it doesn't matter much though.

I have had Miss Moll in this afternoon, also a couple of Hammond's (my observers) sisters, I was delighted to see them & find out all about old Hammond, I'm sorry to say the news was bad, he has had his leg taken off and his right arm is so bad they are going to take it off soon, I do feel so sorry for him, he was such a stout chap too, his father is an admiral in the Navy they are awfully well off, so he will probably have good care taken of him, he is still at Rouen in France, his father & mother went over to see him but they couldn't stay long as there are about 5 or 600 cases of smallpox in Rouen, well I guess

I'll ring off now. I do hope none of you come over because I'm going out to France very soon if I can.

Ever your own dear son
Alan
Hugs and kisses to the girls

Alan ended the letter writing twenty-four *x*'s. He truly loved his family but he was itching to get back to France and continue his air war against the Huns. That was his commitment to his Squadron. Many airmen expressed the same thing: whether injured or on leave, they were eager to get back to their fellow flyers. The squadron was the environment they knew best, and they were comfortable there. They had a routine: to fly, to be with their mates in the air, and on the ground relaxing at the aerodrome.

On April 17, 1918, McLeod wrote again to his parents.

My Dad & Mother:

I received two letters from you dated Mar. 8th & 11th, I was very glad to get them. Marion's letter was enclosed in one of them.

Well I'm still coming on fine and anxiously looking forward to see whoever is coming over, I guess it will be Dad, but I don't know.

Mrs. Moore is coming to see me this afternoon also Kathleen.

I no longer belong to the R.F.C. but the Royal Air Force. I've also been promoted I've got my other pip so I'm a full Lieut. Now, it's not much of a promotion but better than nothing I suppose, if I'd only been a bit older I could have been a Capt. By this time just my luck isn't it. I have to buy a new uniform now, and I don't get any allowance for it either, & now this new R.A.F. business has bone in [*sic*] we are being paid a month in arrears instead of a month in advance, so means no pay this month. I have enough money to keep me going but that is because I had some saved to send home and now I can't spare it, every time I go to send money home something always turns up to stop me.

I send [*sic*] Dad a pipe some time ago but forgot to mention it, I hope he'll like it, they are considered good pipes on this side, the best that can be bought.

I am going to see the Surgical specialist about my heel tomorrow and I expect I'll have the operation the day after, I wish they'd hurry & get it over, I hop around on one foot now but I have no clothes as my spare uniform is in France & my other is burnt. Well I'll close now old dears, love & kisses to the girls & yourselves. Your own dear son.

XXXXXXXXXXXXXXXX Alan

The Royal Flying Corps was merged with the Royal Naval Air Service on April 1, 1918, and became the Royal Air Force. This was done to create a unified, separate air arm, not part of either the army or the navy. The RAF had new, blue uniforms, different from the existing khaki of the RFC and the dark blue of the RNAS. Some pilots, however, kept wearing their old kit and did not convert to the new one.

On Wednesday, May 1, 1918, shortly after McLeod's nineteenth birthday on April 20, the Air Ministry announced in the *London Gazette* the award of two Victoria Crosses, one to Lieutenant Alan Jerrard, Royal Air Force, and the other to Alan McLeod. The announcement reads as follows:

His Majesty the KING has been graciously pleased to award the Victoria Cross to the undermentioned Officers of the Royal Air Force, for services displaying outstanding bravery:

2nd Lt. Alan Arnett McLeod, Royal Air Force.

Whilst flying with his observer (Lt. A. W. Hammond, M.C.), attacking hostile formations by bombs and machine-gun fire, he was assailed at a height of 5,000 feet by eight enemy triplanes, which dived at him from all directions, firing from their front guns. By skilful manœuvring he enabled his observer to fire bursts at each machine in turn, shooting three of them down out of control. By this time Lt. McLeod had received five wounds, and whilst continuing the engagement a bullet penetrated his petrol tank and set the machine on fire.

He then climbed out on to the left bottom plane, controlling his machine from the side of the fuselage, and by side-slipping steeply kept the flames to one side, thus enabling the observer to continue firing until the ground was reached.

The observer had been wounded six times when the machine crashed in "No Man's Land," and 2nd Lt. McLeod, notwithstanding his own wounds, dragged him away from the burning wreckage at great personal risk from heavy machine-gun fire from the enemy's lines. This very gallant pilot was again wounded by a bomb whilst engaged in this act of rescue, but he persevered until he had placed Lt. Hammond in comparative safety, before falling himself from exhaustion and loss of blood.[8]

The Victoria Cross is the British Empire's highest decoration for gallantry. It was established in 1856 when Queen Victoria wanted to reward valour by soldiers fighting in the Crimean War of 1853–56. The Victoria Cross can be bestowed upon officers and men of any rank. The first Victoria Crosses were fashioned out of a captured Russian bronze cannon. A good description of a Victoria Cross is found in John D. Clarke's *Gallantry Medals & Awards of the World*. "Victoria Cross is a bronze straight-armed cross pattée, obverse centre a lion standing upon the Royal crown, below a draped semi-circular scroll with the words FOR VALOUR. *Reverse* the recipient's name and details appear along the suspender clasp, the date of the act of valour appear engraved within the centre circle of the cross. *Ribbon*: Plain crimson for all services."[9]

Replica Victoria Cross.

With the award of the Victoria Cross announced in the London papers, McLeod was becoming somewhat of a celebrity. Congratulations were pouring in, including this one from his commander of 1 Wing:

Dear McLeod,

I write to congratulate you most heartily on having obtained the most coveted honour which it is possible to obtain in the British Army, and if ever the many brave deeds which have gained it have truly earned it, yours most certainly has.

I am more proud than words can tell that I should have had the honour to command the Wing while you were in it and obtained the Victoria Cross.

Not only does it reflect the greatest credit on yourself, but also upon the excellent squadron in which you served. Your earlier achievements in the squadron would in the earlier days of the war have earned you rewards, but I felt sure from what I had seen and heard of you that given the chance, you would put up a most magnificent show and I was not wrong!

Once more I congratulate you and your observer on the most remarkable and plucky show it has ever been my privilege to record.

With all best wishes.
Ever yours sincerely,
E. D. Gossage,
Lieut.-/Col.,
Commanding 1st Wing, R.A.F.[10]

Members of the press swarmed the hospital wanting an interview with McLeod, which did not go over very well with him. He hated the attention the press was giving him, as can be seen in a letter home dated May 18, 1918.

My Dear old Dad & Mother:

Here I am making another attempt at letter writing, I am feeling fine, but my fingers are numb and I can hardly hold the pen, I don't know what it is, my legs are the same, the Dr's say they will soon come round.

I guess you'll be glad to hear I'm coming home as soon as I'm fit to travel, I never even asked to go, the Air Board just sent a notice her [sic] that I was to go to Canada to convalesce and when I was better I was to stay there to instruct, so I can stay a year if I want, but I won't want to stay that long. The sister has just told me that I can't fly for a year, that's mighty hard luck, I hardly believe it though.

Some Major in the C.A.M.C. [Canadian Army Medical Corps] was up here and said Dad was trying to get a passport and at least he succeeded and got one dated May 10th, I didn't know whether it was true or not but I guess you'd wire me if he is coming.

Gee they've had some write ups in all the London papers about me, every day in every paper there is something about me, it makes me sick, there were a whole line up of reporters with their cameras out in the hall several days, but I would only see one and that was the Canadian war records, they took my picture and are going to send some to you, they are awful though and it was in all the London papers. I got your wire of congrats, also one from the school the town and Dr. Montgomery. Well my darlings I'll close now, heaps of love & kisses to all, ever your own dear son.

Alan

Having now spent almost two months in hospital, McLeod was struggling with the pain of his injuries. He had trouble sleeping and was suffering from pneumonia. He describes what he was going through in a letter to his parents dated May 22, 1918.

My Darling old Dad & Mother:

Well I have no news for you, I'm getting on fine, nearly a complete cure now, my heel is all healed up now and my pneumonia is nearly over my worst trouble is I can't sleep at nights, not through pain I just don't know why, gee it's rotten lying awake all night, when I was very ill & in great pain I used to get an injection of morphia about 3 times in 24 hrs. first they used ⅙ and then ¼ & then a little over ¼ but I got so used to it that it didn't help me at all, so I haven't had it for a couple of weeks now, they tried other kinds of sleeping drafts but only one kind will send me off and it makes me sick to take it, however I suppose my natural sleep will soon come back now I am getting well.

Gee I got an awful swab of letters from you the other day, about 25, you wrote me every day nearly, I hardly like it that often so go easier you'd better cut out writing altogether soon because I'll be leaving for home in a month I am coming on a hospital ship.

I got those pictures of all of you out at Madell's this last mail & I'm very proud of them, I was showing them to the head sister here, sister Grazebrook, she looked at it & said, which is Helen and which is Marion, I said "what, how did you know their names," she said "Oh you told us all them one night when you were delirious" gee I was surprised.

I fully realize how impossible it is for Dad to come over here, because you always have to have your picture on your passport and I believe dear old dad would rather face death than a real photographers camera, am I right. Well me darlings I guess I'll ring off now, heaps of hugs & kisses to yourselves & the girls.

Ever your own dear son

Alan
DAD
XXXXXXXXXXX
MOTHER
XXXXXXXXXXX
MARION
XXXXXXXXXXX
HELEN
XXXXXXXXXXX

Alan knew his father wanted to be with him by his bedside. Initially not wanting his family to take the long voyage to England, he had a premonition his father would make the trip to be there in person. In fact, McLeod's father, as soon as he received word Alan had developed pneumonia and was dangerously ill, made the arrangements to get to London as quickly as possible. He was, as mentioned at the start of this book, a medical doctor. Civilians were not encouraged by the authorities to cross the Atlantic in wartime, so obtaining the necessary documents took time. Once on board ship, there was the threat of a U-boat attack. McLeod's father did not forewarn Alan of his visit but showed up unannounced and spent the summer with him helping the convalescence process, until Alan was well enough to return to Canada in September 1918.

McLeod was still in hospital at the end of August although he was allowed to go out on occasion, such as to the theatre, as is described in this letter dated August 29, 1918, to his mother:

My Darling old Mother:

Here I am laid up in bed again, nothing serious thank goodness, only grippe, I guess I'll be up again to-morrow.

I got your cablegram to-day and I was awfully glad to hear from you, and to hear about Helen's birthday. I'll certainly do my best to persuade old dad to go to Scotland and I know he'll go if he knows it won't prevent me getting home earlier.

I was sitting in a box in the theatre the other night with some other boys from the Squadron I was sitting away forward on the edge of it, in quite plain view of everybody, quite unintentionally of course and the leading lady ?? was singing a song and here were two lines of it.

Maybe you'll get a flying boy to take you out to tea
or maybe you'll get a flight with McLeod V.C.

& she pointed me out & she swung the light on me.

The other fellows got it doped up and I never knew, gee I nearly fell through the floor, the whole theatre simply roared and all looked at me, and for the rest of the show I was stared at from all sides. It's rather nice in a way to be a V.C. everyone thinks your [*sic*] great. Well dear I must close now I hope we'll be home soon.

Love to the kiddies.
Ever your own dear son
Alan

The grippe that Alan McLeod mentioned was a cold that could develop into full-fledged influenza. Because of his illness, McLeod and his father had to turn down a personal invitation from the king and queen to visit them at Windsor Castle and to have McLeod's VC conferred on him privately.

Alan McLeod and his father were able to go to Buckingham Palace on September 4, 1918, for a public investiture ceremony where King George V pinned the Victoria Cross on McLeod's new blue RAF tunic. In the picture taken of McLeod that day, he is leaning on a cane for support, his heel injury still giving him trouble. Alan looks gaunt and thin of cheeks. His bouts with pneumonia must have taken pounds off his frame. No longer looking the baby-faced teenager, there he stood, a man who had aged due to combat, his injuries, and his illnesses. His father must have been bursting with pride as he looked on and saw his son receive from the king of England and the Empire its highest decoration for bravery and gallantry. He overheard King George V say to his son, "I am proud to know you." The king was amazed that such a young man could have accomplished such a brave deed.

That evening, Billy Bishop, Canada's first air VC, hosted a dinner for McLeod at the Savoy Hotel, where the champagne flowed freely. McLeod was one of only three Canadian flyers to receive the Victoria Cross in the First World War, the other two being Bishop and William George Barker. McLeod was the youngest of the three, only nineteen. He was, in fact, the youngest man to receive the VC in all of the First World War.

Alan McLeod was sent home to Canada to convalesce. He and his father departed England on a White Star Line ship on September 25, 1918, bound for the United States and then on to Winnipeg. They arrived at Winnipeg on September 30, 1918, on the CPR's Imperial Limited train, pulling up to the station at 10:20 p.m. For hours, a crowd had been forming to greet the returning war hero. By the time the train

McLeod at Buckingham
Palace investiture.

Portrait of Alan A. McLeod.

had arrived, the crowd had grown to the thousands, most from Winnipeg but also many families from McLeod's hometown of Stonewall. Mayor Davidson adjourned a council meeting in time to allow him and members of council time to get to the train depot. The *Winnipeg Free Press Bulletin* the next day recorded the homecoming.

> As the young V.C., with his mother fondly holding his arm, came down the steps leading from the platform the crowd closed in on them, while adults who had watched the young hero grow from a boy warmly wrung the lad's hand, and the boys wearing returned soldiers' buttons and who had his school chums perhaps, yelled "What's the matter with 'Buster'? He's all right."
>
> Upon reaching the rotunda the mass of citizens parted to allow the hero and his parents to mount the steps from which a number of brief words of welcome were delivered by prominent citizens, while the crowd punctuated the proceedings with "Three more cheers."
>
> R. D. Waugh, calling the crowd to order, said: "We are met to do honor to this gallant young man who has brought great honor to our country. You all know the act that won for him the highest honor the empire can confer on a soldier. We all know how severely he was wounded in winning the Victoria Cross while saving the life of his comrade. We the citizens of Winnipeg and Stonewall, want to congratulate him and his father and mother for his great attainment in this war. Our hearts have gone out for many months to his father and mother in their days of anguish. Tonight we rejoice with that mother and father in having the boy back again."
>
> Brig.-Gen. Ketchen extended a welcome to the young hero on behalf of the officers and men of M.D. 10. "I offer to him, on behalf of those who have been in France and those who are yet to go, the most hearty welcome and congratulations…. His name in the Air Force

today is one that will always be remembered. It has been said among military men that if a man could win two V.C.'s then Lieut. McLeod should have had them."

Mayor Davidson … extended a welcome on behalf of the city. "The citizens of Winnipeg extend to you the very heartiest welcome … and wish that you may speedily recover from your wounds. Your name will live in history long after you are dead."

It was only at this juncture when Mr. Waugh called upon the young V.C. to speak a few words that he showed any indication of embarrassment.

His remarks, however, by their brevity and modesty, were entirely characteristic of the real hero and British soldier.

Falteringly he said: "I am no speechmaker, you know. I want to thank you very, very much for your welcome. I only hope I deserve it."

While the crowd cheered itself hoarse the hero accompanied by his parents and Stonewall friends, passed through the mass of citizens to a decorated street car which was to convey the party home to Stonewall.[11]

The same newspaper article went on to describe the reception McLeod and his parents received in his hometown.

The pretty town of Stonewall wore a gala dress in honor of the occasion, every house in town being especially decorated. The streets were well lighted, while flags and bunting floated everywhere. Colored lanterns brightened up the whole town, and every house and building made a splendid showing of flags and colors.…

After leaving the car, the airman and his closest relatives stepped into a gayly decorated automobile, and then began a great parade all around town. Pipe Major Collie and his pipers and drummers of the 79th headed the procession, and then came the hero's car, followed by an enthusiastic crowd, including many happy boys and girls. Old school chums greeted McLeod with cries of "Hello Bus!" and sang "For He's a Jolly Good Fellow!"

Finally the parade came to an end outside the McLeod residence, and the hero was welcomed by a shower of sky rockets and other brilliant fireworks. W. Inkster, president of the Returned Soldiers' association, read a letter of welcome which had been signed by the mayor of the town and other leading citizens. The letter simply but eloquently expressed the feelings of the people of Stonewall and Rockwood towards Lieut. McLeod. It conveyed the great admiration and esteem the people had for the hero, and the deep appreciation they felt for the deed he had done for the empire....

The address was strongly backed up by most hearty and prolonged cheers for the hero, which were later followed by cheers for his parents. In a few words Lieut. McLeod conveyed his heartfelt appreciation of the welcome that had been extended to him. Although his words were few and simple, they carried deep feeling, and expressed more than any brilliant speech would have done....

The crowd stood bareheaded under the stars of the early morning and heartily joined in the National Anthem to the strains of a coronet. The celebration was concluded, but the event for which it was arranged, and the man for whom it was a welcome will live forever in the hearts of the people of the empire.[12]

One can only imagine how Alan McLeod and his parents felt about the welcome they received and the appreciation they felt for all the work that went into planning the Stonewall parade. Finally, Alan was home. In the wee hours of the morning, he climbed into his own bed and reflected on the events of the day. He was truly loved by the people of Manitoba. He could now get back to living a normal life.

Bust of
McLeod.

In a month and a week, however, Alan McLeod was dead. He was recovering well from his injuries but bouts of pneumonia returned. He got weaker and weaker. Finally, he succumbed to the flu.

The Spanish flu, as it was called, struck millions of people around the world from 1918 to 1919. Estimates of the number of deaths caused by this flu range from twenty to forty million. Even at the low end of the estimates, twenty million is a huge number, and of those succumbing to the influenza, about fifty thousand were Canadian. More people were killed by the Spanish flu than died in the First World War. It was a worldwide pandemic, greater than the cholera and smallpox epidemics of the early nineteenth century.

In 1918 and 1919, there were no inoculations for the flu. The medical community did not know how to treat those suffering from this pandemic, nor did they know how to prevent it from attacking those most at risk. The flu spread to Canada by returning servicemen and decimated communities, rural and urban. It struck the rich and the poor. It was most deadly to those between the ages of twenty and forty, but the young were particularly vulnerable. Those brave men returning from combat were also afflicted. It began with a high fever, and the victim would be dead in a matter of days.

The final 1918 edition of the *Journal of the American Medical Association* reflected upon this epidemic.

> The year 1918 had gone: a year momentous as the termination of the most cruel war in the annals of the human race; a year which marked, the end at least for a time, of man's destruction of man; unfortunately a year in which developed a most fatal infectious disease causing the death of hundreds of thousands of human beings. Medical science for four and one-half years devoted itself to putting men on the firing line and keeping them there. Now it must turn with its whole might to combating the greatest enemy of all — infectious disease.[13]

Alan McLeod was not the only one struck by the flu in Stonewall. McLeod's father was the local health officer, and in a special edition of the *Stonewall Argus* newspaper in October 1918 he set out a warning to the public on the Spanish flu, what it was, and how it was spread. A number of the local Stonewall residents had contracted the flu, resulting in Dr. McLeod's closing indefinitely the local schools and the theatre. A number of volunteer nurses, helping to stem the epidemic, were staying at the McLeod home. As accommodation for them was limited, a call went out to other homes to take in the growing number of volunteer nurses. It is difficult to say how the Spanish flu travelled to Stonewall. The town was certainly caught in its grip. Many died from it — including Alan McLeod.

Alan McLeod died in his sleep at the Winnipeg General Hospital on November 6, 1918, five days before the end of the First World War. He was given an elaborate military funeral in Winnipeg. A newspaper article describing the event read as follows:

> Never has a military funeral in Winnipeg been so elaborate as that of Lieut, Alan McLeod, V.C. who was buried this afternoon in Kildonan cemetery. He died Thursday from Spanish influenza after having won out in a lengthy fight against death in English hospitals.
>
> The pall bearers were six members of the Royal Air Force to which Lieut. McLeod belonged. They carried the casket on their shoulders from Thomson's undertaking establishment to the gun carriage waiting a block to the north. They marched through lines formed by the escort of 100 officers and men from Depot Battalion and 50 from the Engineering and Railroad Construction unit.
>
> The gun carriage, draped with the Union Jack, was in charge of officers and men of No. 10 Artillery Depot, in command of Major E. Nixon. The firing party was composed of troopers of the Fort Gary Horse, and that regiment also supplied the buglers to sound the "Last Post."
>
> Major S. Graham, senior garrison chaplain, said a short service at the undertaking rooms. The internment was private, the military leaving the cortege on the outskirts of the city.[14]

On January 9, 1919, McLeod's father received a letter from the Privy Purse Office of Buckingham Palace that read: "I am commanded by the King and Queen to express their sincere sympathy to you at the loss you have sustained by the death of your gallant son, Lieutenant A. A. McLeod, VC, who, Their Majesties regret to hear, has succumbed to the illness while in the service of his country."[15]

Mrs. McLeod sent letters out to Alan's friends in the RAF, telling them of his passing. One of them, Reg Key, one of McLeod's observers

McLeod's gravesite, Kildonan Presbyterian Cemetery, Winnipeg, Manitoba.

and a hut mate in No. 2 Squadron, wrote her back on March 15, 1919, from Northampton. Here is his letter, quoted in part:

Dear Mrs. McLeod:

It was very kind of you to write to me, Alan's death came as a great shock to me, we were more than pal's and I simply thought the world of him, I was his observer for a time and we used to live together, did Alan never mention our little hut, and the excursions we used to make to buy furniture, how we scoured half France to get a round table, and how eventually when we had the happiest and most luxurious little nest in the camp, I was sent away to reinforce a Squadron which had had a lot of casualties, I shall never forget that morning, for I could have howled like a kid, Alan begged the C.O. to let him come too, it seemed so hard to part us just as we were so happy and comfortable, we were willing volunteers for any sticky job that came along providing we were in it together, Alan would take on anything and I was willing to go anywhere with him, I had absolute confidence in him, he was the finest pilot I have ever flown with, devoid of fear and always merry and bright, we were in many scraps together, and often after getting out of a very tight corner, by sheer [will], with six or seven Lui's at our tail he would turn around to me and laugh out loud, Alan had so many lovable qualities, that is [sic] was impossible to live, fly and sleep with him, without getting very fond of him, and I just loved him, being a little older I used to try and restrain him from taking too many risks, I knew he was your only son and I could just imagine how you must have worshipped him, he would listen and agree to everything I said, but once we got into the air it was all forgotten, and if there was anything doing, we had to be in it. I believe he told you in one of his letters that I was trying to nurse him, he referred to me as a "comic little Englishman" I remember I had a few words, remonstrating about it in the same letter, and when I met Mr. McLeod in London he didn't quite see where the littleness came in. I visited Alan several times at the Prince of Wales Hospital and it was there that I met his father, perhaps he will recall Lieut. Key (little Quay) as Alan used to say. He was mentioned in dispatches for a particularly daring piece of work in strafing a Hun observation balloon, it was a long way over the lines and we were all on our own, any one that has done any flying at all will tell you that it needs a pretty stout heart to go 10 to 12 miles over the German lines in the machine we were flying (A. W.) without an escort, but he had set his mind on getting it, so he made for it, archied the whole way, and he got it with his front gun, it went down in flames, on the way back we ran into three Albatross, and thanks to Alan's splendid maneuvering I bagged my first Hun, on another occasion, whilst doing a shoot with the artillery he was very much troubled by an Archie Battery in La Bassee, which was some distance behind the line, flying over he dived to within 50 ft. of them, shot up the crew, then after emptying two or three magazines on the Boches, went back and carried on the shoot. I doubt very much if it is possible to get copies of these acts, as they [sic] only intimation given was just the names on the Gazette along with hundreds of others as being mentioned in Dispatches, no record of the deeds being given, just mentioned as having "done good work" I guess, Mac earned the D.F.C. times over. I wish so, that I could see you, I could tell you so much better than I can write there is so much that it seems hopeless to try and put in a letter we had some wonderful times together apart from the flying, we had three horses at the Squadron for the use of officers, and Alan and I certainly had our share of the use of them, we had great sport together riding around the country. There was an Artillery Major that we used to go and see, I can't recall his name, but he came from Winnipeg and he was awfully fond of Alan, one day on our way over we put the horses at a brook, mine got over alright, but Alan's sort of changed it's mind half way over, with the result that they both flopped in the middle, seeing Mac was alright I grabbed the horse, with the result that the ungrateful animal immediately pulled me in, Alan of course roared with laughter, and when we both arrived at the Battery the Gunner's did likewise, anyway they fixed us up with clothes and we finished up with a very merry evening. I could write much more but am afraid I might weary you I am such a clumsy hand at writing letters, perhaps some day I may have the great pleasure of meeting you, at present I am very unsettled, not knowing whether the Army is keeping me or not, if they pitch me out it is more than likely that I shall come to Canada, as I have no prospects whatever in this country, in which case if I may I would like to call and see you …

I will say good-bye now thanking you once more for your very kind letter, accept the photograph of myself with best wishes.

Trusting you are all well at home with kind regards to Dr. McLeod

I remain
Yours very sincerely
Reg Key
Alan's pal.[16]

Arthur Hammond also returned a letter from Mrs. McLeod on February 28, 1920. Writing from his home in Essex, he gave this account of that fateful day in March 1918 when he and McLeod were shot down:

My Dear Mrs. McLeod:

What must you really be thinking of me? for not answering your very kind letter, which I only received three days ago although I see it is dated three months ago, but as it has come via the Air Ministry, I can understand the cause of its speedy delivery.

I have also made two attempts to write to you, once to Winnipeg and again through the Air Ministry but from your letter I gather that you received neither of them, however very happy I am to find that I am at last in direct communication with poor Alan's family.

I fully understand your feelings in waiting [sic] to know all about your brave boy when we were in France together I only just wish I could go to you in person and express to you my thoughts of him and tell you of the various flying escapades we had together, as during his time in France we shared the same quarters and nearly always flew together and consequently we were always just the very best of "pals" and I always regret that we were separated when we were wounded on that eventful 27th of March which ended the career of war for both of us. Fortunately I can remember every detail of that day we were brought down so I will give you herewith a record of what actually happened.

On the early morning of the 27th we returned to the aerodrome at about 2 a.m. after a night of bombing raid in Hunland and found that we were under orders to stand by at 9 a.m. on the same day for a bomb raid on a place called Bruay sur Somme near Albert, where the Germans were pressing so hard. However for the moment we turned in to get some sleep expecting that the weather to be too bad for flying, but notwithstanding that we and five other machines started off and very soon lost sight of each other in the clouds and it was even impossible to see the ground, consequently we very soon got lost and decided to go down close and try to pick up our whereabouts when we were heavily bombarded with German aircraft guns, so we again returned to the clouds, going west for our own lines, again we descended and got a similar reception so we realized that we must have been a good way in hunland, however we tried again and found that we had gained our own side at last & we hunted round & at last found an English aerodrome where we landed & found that it was 43 Sqd. We had lunch and got our bearings for our destination and tried to get an escort to go with us, but the C.O. thought the weather too bad for his scout machines to go up, so off we started and arrived over Albert keeping a good look out for the massed German reinforcements that we were ordered to attack, we kept well under the clouds, so we were safe more or less from being attacked from above, however we were, by this, some miles in hunland, when to my surprise I saw a German "Fokker" triplane below us about 200 yds. away and its pilot had not seen us, I signaled to Alan and we closed up to the hun and I got my chance and he went down without hardly firing a shot, we were both so pleased and trying to congratulate each other when the clouds suddenly broke up and another triplane suddenly dived on us from above firing away but not hitting us very seriously and thanks to poor Alan's clever manipulation of our machine, I got my chance and the hun suddenly started to clear off when he nosed dived, spinning very fast to the ground, but the air suddenly seemed to be filled with German machines and I think we both realized that it was all up with us, as we were getting hit badly, my legs seemed to come in for a lot of it, and Alan must have been hit as well, but I had no time to find out how serious and we were then on fire and my right arm was hit and got so numb that I could not use the gun and the German machines closed up close to us, I then made an effort & started again and put another enemy out of action, but all the rest except one cleared away and he under cover of our smoke followed us down to the ground just giving us short bursts which were wonderfully accurate. During this time we were side slipping and Alan was standing up with one foot on the rudder bar and the other outside on the wing and I was standing on the bracing wires at the side of the fuselage as the bottom of my cockpit has fallen out and as we neared the ground I climbed on the top ring so that when we hit the ground I was thrown forward on the ground, I had all my senses but my body was quite numb consequently I could not move. I saw Alan jump out of the machine and look for me but evidently thought that I had fallen out, but he came to me and tried to pull me towards our lines but it was too much for him so I found I could roll and with his help I rolled to where some of our own infantry took us in to a trench, I afterwards found out from Alan that he was again hit while rolling me along the ground and I can remember hearing a machine gun firing quite close to us. We laid all that afternoon in the trench and that was I think, the worst experience of all, especially as the infantry seemed to expect that the Germans would advance and take us all, but as soon as it was dark enough we were taken away and I don't remember anymore after that and I came to in hospital and I never saw Alan again until we were both in England, and this to my surprise he was very bad, I was confident that he would pull through it all, and when I saw in a Canadian Magazine that he had been taken from us, I just did not know what to do or think.

I have quite recovered from my wounds, but life in England is not very happy as my disability prevents me from going back to my old work in South America where I was before the war, so I am at the moment attending classes for a business training, but things do not look very hopeful, however I must be thankful for so many things and take them as they come. I would have liked to have had a talk with Dr. McLeod when he was in England but I was sent up to the North of England to a convalescent home which was very nice but I would have rather remained in London with Alan.

Well I think I will end this narrative and hope that if at any time I could be of any service to Mr. McLeod or yourself I would always be anxious to do it and for the moment I send my regards and very best wishes from

Yours very sincerely
Arthur W. Hammond[17]

Reunion of the three Canadian First World War pilots who won the Victoria Cross: (left to right) William George Barker; Mrs. McLeod, representing her late son; William A. Bishop, 1928.

These letters from his two closest pals describe how fond they were of Alan McLeod and how much they were shocked by his passing. He was well liked by all.

Both Reginald Key and Arthur Hammond immigrated to Canada, Key in 1920, and Hammond in 1921. Hammond came to Canada at the invitation of the McLeod family, and lived in Winnipeg; Key in Toronto. Hammond worked for the Great-West Life Assurance Company and served with the RCAF in Canada during the Second World War. He died in 1959 in Victoria, British Columbia.

The spirit and enthusiasm of Alan McLeod is typified in the following quote found in Mike O'Connor's book in the Battleground Europe series, *Airfields & Airmen: Arras*:

> P. E. Butcher, an NCO with 2 Squadron, who had served with it in France since the outbreak of war, wrote in his autobiography, *Skill and Devotion*:

Alan McLeod, head and shoulders portrait.

Towards the end of 1917, a very young Canadian officer, in fact only seventeen [*sic*] years of age, named Alan McLeod joined the Squadron. He reminded me very much of McCudden and would walk around and get into conversation with the mechanics, wanting to know all about the peculiarities of the F.K.8 which he was going to fly. We all liked him as he was an officer full of life and, for a lad of his age, knew no fear. At first he was not keen about the Ack W, as the machines were termed by us, but he soon got the hang of this heavy reconnaissance bomber. It seemed he had heard such glowing reports about the famous No. 2 Squadron, that he had asked to be posted to us, where, he told me he put all his confidence in his N.C.O. and mechanics. He was always wanting to know all about the Squadron's history and past doings, I remember.

The general consensus of opinion amongst us all was that he was going to get somewhere by his keenness, and almost before we knew it, he and his observer, Lieut. Camber, had brought down a Fokker, the first to an F.K.8. Later this was confirmed by the Balloon Observers, but he seemed cut out for something bigger, and the New Year was to prove us right.[18]

McLeod was the youngest Canadian to win the Victoria Cross. In 1967 McLeod's medals and personal letters were donated to the Canadian War Museum by his sister Mrs. Helen Annetts. Alan McLeod was named a Member of Canada's Aviation Hall of Fame in 1973.

PART 2

Andrew Edward McKeever

SIX

The Listowel Boy Joins the RFC

The town of Listowel, Ontario, is to the west of Toronto, about halfway between Lake Huron and Lake Ontario in southern Ontario. Originally known as Mapleton, it changed its name to Listowel in 1856. A tiny village, nestled in the heart of a farming community, Listowel is bordered by Elma Township. The township increased its population by one when Andrew Edward McKeever was born on August 21, 1894. His mother was Anna Belle Henderson and his father, William, was a farmer. The family farm was located on the second concession of Elma Township.

Some documents show Andrew McKeever's birth as August 21, 1895. The plaque placed in his honour at the cenotaph in Listowel gives his birth year as 1895; however, his tombstone shows 1894. Many official documents, such as the Royal Flying Corps Military Wing Form of Application and the Officers' Declaration Paper, Overseas Military Forces of Canada, both signed by McKeever himself, give his birthdate as August 21, 1894. So, using the best-evidence rule, one can conclude he was born in 1894. Ontario's vital statistics records for 1894 and 1895 do not mention any Andrew Edward McKeevers being born in August of either year. Having ten children, Mr. and Mrs. William McKeever may have forgotten to register their son Andrew.

Andrew (Andy, as he was called by his friends) attended Listowel's public school and high school. When not in school, Andrew would help his father on the family farm. After high school, Andrew enrolled at the Central Business College in Toronto. He graduated as an accountant and worked as a bank teller in Listowel.

Little is documented about McKeever's upbringing and early life. He was five feet ten inches tall, had grey-hazel eyes and dark brown hair. In October 1915, McKeever, at the age of twenty-one, joined a militia unit in Toronto, the Queen's Own Rifles of Canada. He served as a private until November 1916. There is no evidence McKeever served in any capacity with the Canadian Expeditionary Force overseas. In a postwar document titled Officers' Declaration Paper, Overseas Military Forces of Canada, McKeever recorded his militia unit as the Queen's Own Rifles of Canada and stated, regarding former military service, that he had transferred from the Queen's Own Rifles of Canada to the RAF. There is no mention of other service overseas.

The Queen's Own Rifles of Canada is one of the oldest militia units in Canadian history. It dates back to 1860 when it was called the Second Battalion Volunteer Militia Rifles. In March 1863 Queen Victoria approved a change in the unit's name to the Queen's Own Rifles of Toronto. Then, in January 1882, the name was changed again, to the Second Battalion Queen's Own Rifles of Canada. The battalion had a rich history. The QOR was involved at Ridgeway against the Fenian raiders from the United States into Ontario in 1866. The Second Battalion fought in the Northwest Rebellion of 1885 and sent soldiers to South Africa in 1899 and 1900 to fight in the Boer War.

The Queen's Own contributed volunteers to seven major battalions of the Canadian Expeditionary Force (CEF) in the First World War: the 19th, the 35th, the 58th, the 74th, the 81st, the 123rd, and the 216th. "In addition ... 938 members of the regiment volunteered for other units in the

Canadian Expeditionary Force. These units included the 20th, 75th, 92nd, 116th, 124th, 134th, 169th, 170th, 180th, and 216th battalions, *The Royal Air Force* [emphasis mine], Canadian Field Artillery, Eaton Machine Gun Battery, Cyclist Battalions, Pioneer Battalions, Canadian Railway Troops, Army Service Corps and Army Medical Corps."[1]

McKeever was one of those who applied from the QOR for transfer to the air service. He made his application on November 4, 1916, to join the Royal Flying Corps (which became the Royal Air Force on April 1, 1918), and was accepted as a candidate. He left Listowel on November 20, 1916, arriving in Toronto on the twenty-second. From there, he travelled by train to Montreal, arriving the next day. He sailed on the *Grampian* on November 25, bound for Liverpool, England. McKeever claimed reimbursement of his expenses for travel to England from Listowel, but got reimbursement only for the portion from Listowel to Montreal, amounting to one pound thirteen shillings. (His penchant for numbers and his bank experience was showing through in this instance.)

McKeever was selected for appointment as a second lieutenant, on probation, in the RFC, Special Reserve, effective December 5, 1916. He took a train from Liverpool to London that day. He requested reimbursement for this stage of the trip as well, but was not successful. (The accountant in McKeever never left him.)

A letter to the Commandant, School of Military Aeronautics, Oxford, dated December 6, 1916, announced the arrival of a number of gentlemen, one of whom was Andrew McKeever. The letter read as follows:

> I am directed to inform you that orders have been issued for the undermentioned gentlemen to report at Oxford to-day, for preliminary instruction in aviation. These gentlemen have been selected in Canada for Commissions in the Royal Flying Corps Special Reserve, under the conditions laid down in War Office letter dated the 4th October, 1916, number as above
>
> Coghill, Frank Street
> Moloney, Peter Joseph

Clerk, Ronze Douglas
Crossland, Ernest Ford
Shibley, George Rustin
McKeever, Andrew Edward
Rushworth, Charles Evard

Sqd: E.F. Hausburg
Major,
For Director of Air Organization[2]

That same day, McKeever was told by a certain Captain Innes-Ker to report to Adastral House, London, where he would receive written instructions. These took the form of a letter telling him to report to the Commandant, School of Military Aeronautics, RFC, by 4:00 p.m. for preliminary instruction in aviation. It went on to state, "Your appointment as a Second Lieutenant, on probation, in the Royal Flying Corps Special Reserve, with effect from the date of your arrival in England (5th instant) will appear in the *London Gazette* in due course."[3]

As a student, McKeever flew old, out-of-date Maurice Farman Shorthorn and Longhorn machines. These antiquated aircraft, dating back to 1912, were two-seaters, with the student sitting in the front, in the nacelle, whose shape resembled a bathtub. The pilot instructor sat behind the student and behind him were the engine and propeller. They were "pusher" aircraft — the machine's propeller, which was pointed to the rear, pushed the aircraft forward. The Farmans had two wings, or planes, and the fuselage was a series of wooden longerons strung together with wire. About thirty-and-a-half feet long, the Shorthorn had a wingspan of about fifty-two feet and a top speed of seventy-two mph. Students initially were just observers, assigned to see what it was like to take off, fly circuits, and land, with the pilot doing all the work.

The students also attended classes on a variety of topics. In the ground school, they studied such subjects as the theory of flight, engine maintenance, rigging, map reading, aerial navigation, meteorology, and cross-country flying. For the latter, students were instructed to look for significant geographical landmarks to assist them in locating where they

Portrait of Andrew E. McKeever in flying gear.

were and how to get home. Rigging training related to the cross-wires of the aircraft, which reinforced the struts and the two wings and kept everything strong and taut.

McKeever had an opportunity to fly a number of different aircraft types, including B.E.2cs and B.E.2ds, as well as R.E.8s. These more modern and faster machines were two-seater, tractor types with an inline engine and the propeller in the front, an arrangement that meant the aircraft was pulled along. It would have been in these types of aeroplanes that McKeever mastered manoeuvres such as takeoffs, looping, rolling, turning, diving, climbing, and landing.

He also trained on the new Bristol F.2A Fighter, designed by Frank Barnwell. This two-seater entered squadron service in April 1917.* It was a sturdily built machine that could withstand a lot of punishment. The pilot and observer sat back to back, allowing them to communicate to one another with relative ease — important in the middle of an encounter with enemy aircraft.

McKeever learned the versatility of the Bristol Fighter and put it through its paces. He could manoeuvre this machine as if it were a single-seat scout. The agility of the "Brisfit," as it became known to those who flew it, was amazing.

Andrew McKeever would spend over four months training on the Bristol Fighter and various other aircraft. In March 1917, he was transferred to Northolt for further instruction.

The Bristol F.2A first entered combat on April 5, 1917, when Captain Leefe Robinson, VC, of No. 48 Squadron, led a flight of six of the new two-seaters into action over Douai, France, against Manfred

---

* Built with a Rolls-Royce V12 Falcon 190 hp engine, it had a total all-in weight of 2,754 pounds. The wingspan was thirty-nine feet three inches, it had a height of over nine feet, and was twenty-five feet nine inches in length. The Bristol F.2A could climb to ten thousand feet in 14.5 minutes and had a maximum speed of 110 mph. The armament included a fixed, forward-firing Vickers machine gun and a rear-mounted Lewis gun for the observer to fire. The pilot's ammunition load was up to 1,200 rounds for the forward-firing Vickers and almost seven hundred rounds (seven drums of ninety-seven rounds each) for the rear gunner's Lewis machine gun.

A distinctive feature of the F.2A and F.2B was the fuselage was tapered toward the tail. The rear fin and rudder had a sleek design, meaning it did not impede the rear gunner's field of fire. In addition, the Bristol's upper wing was placed close to the fuselage enabling the rear gunner to fire forward, above the pilot's head.

Bristol F.2B fighter A7135.

von Richthofen's Flying Circus. Von Richthofen and his pilots in their Albatros D.IIIs shot down four of the six Bristols. Robinson himself was taken prisoner. This led to a comment on the worth of the Bristol by Richthofen: "It was a new type of aircraft, which we had not seen before, and it appears to be quick and handy, with a powerful motor 'V' shaped and twelve cylinders. Its name could not be recognized. The D.III Albatros was, both in speed and ability to climb, undoubtedly superior."[4]

The maiden combat flight of the Bristol Fighter was a disaster. This was due in part to the way the machines were flown. The pilots treated them like any other two-seater, flying in formation and at the same height, which made them easy prey for the German fighters. The RFC eventually learned their lesson and utilized the Bristol like a single-seater scout. McKeever was one of the pilots who showed the RFC the true capability of the Bristol as a forward-firing aircraft, able to withstand harsh turns and other manoeuvres.

As John H. Morrow points out in his book *The Great War in the Air: Military Aviation from 1909 to 1921*, "The Bristol crews, unfamiliar with a plane that they feared was structurally weak, flew it like a two-seat reconnaissance plane. In time they would learn that this two-seater was superior to most single-seat fighters if flown aggressively, with the gunner merely to protect the tail and not as the main armament."[5]

On April 19, 1917, McKeever was appointed flying officer and later that month it was recommended that his rank of second lieutenant be confirmed. He was eager to be posted to a squadron in France. His wish would come true in May.

SEVEN

No. 11 Squadron, RFC

Andrew McKeever joined No. 11 Squadron on May 28, 1917.[1] This squadron was formed at the beginning of 1915 and on July 25 of that year became one of the first British squadrons to arrive in France. Its work consisted primarily of photography and reconnaissance missions using F.E.8s, a small scout with a one-hundred-horsepower monosoupape rotary engine.

> These shows usually resulted in a good deal of fighting, as the Hun was much in evidence in the air all the winter and spring of 1917. Many E.A. were brought down and the Squadron also suffered rather heavy casualties.
>
> At the end of March 1917 Major Maclean took over from Major Atkinson and the Squadron continued

its good work, many photos being taken for the Arras offensive on April 9th.

Towards the end of May the F.E.'s were replaced by Bristol Fighters. The pilots were given instruction on B.F's to accustom them to tractor machines. The first Bristol pilot posted to the Squadron was Lieut. A.E. McKeever who became one of the most brilliant pilots the Squadron has ever had.

While the change of machines was being effected the Bristols used to escort the F.E.'s on reconnaissance etc.

At the beginning of June the Squadron moved to Belle Vue aerodrome with 48 Squadron where reconnaissance, photography and offensive patrols were carried out. Large numbers of E.A. were still being met with and the Bristols did great execution.[2]

During the battle of Arras in April 1917, the British aeroplanes faced much superior German models. The pusher F.E.s were outclassed by the German Albatros scouts. Consequently, the British lost 319 aircrew that month, a month that became known as Bloody April. No. 11 Squadron received its share of casualties.

By 22 April they had lost three crews, with another three members wounded, plus one killed, but on this day suffered terrible losses with seven men wounded, one died of wounds and one crew missing in action. They made three attempts to reconnoiter the Drocourt–Queant line and one must question the wisdom of repeatedly sending machines to the same target. The missing FE2b was flown by Sergeant John Kenneth Hollis and his observer Lieutenant Bernard Joseph Tolhurst. The squadron had the misfortune to encounter the highly experienced and proficient *Jasta* 11, based at Roucourt … led by Manfred von Richthofen. Von Richthofen sent one FE down to crash just on the British side of the lines with a wounded crew and Kurt Wolff brought down Hollis and Tolhurst. It was his nineteenth victory and on 4 May he received the *Pour le Mérite*.[3]

McKeever was a welcome addition to the squadron after the losses received in April. He got on well with his fellow airmen. According to Eric R. Dodds of Newport Beach, New South Wales, Australia,

> Andy McKeever was a bright, wide-eyed young man of medium height and good physique. He had a friendly nature but tended to keep to himself a good deal. He was never involved in men's gags or binges. To my knowledge he neither drank nor smoked. He was modest and unassuming, and I liked him.[4]

McKeever was fastidious in his dress, never going on patrol unless dressed in full uniform. He kept a spare shaving kit in his pocket in case he was shot down and taken prisoner.

By the end of May 1917, the powerful Bristol Fighters replaced the squadron's F.E.s. No. 11 Squadron had received the latest version, the F.2B. This was more powerful than the F.2A. Some models of the F.2B were equipped with a Rolls-Royce Falcon II 220 hp, others by a Hispano-Suiza 200 hp engine. In the Hispano-Suiza the top speed was only about 105 mph.

Jon Guttman, in *Bristol F2 Fighter Aces of World War I*, describes the features of this machine:

> The F 2B had a wingspan of 39 ft. 3 in., was 25 ft. 10 in. long and had a height of 9 ft. 9 in. Its empty weight was 2145 lb. and maximum take-off weight was 3243 lb. The aeroplane boasted a maximum speed of 123 mph at 5,000 ft. and it climbed at an average rate of 889 ft. per minute to a ceiling of 18,000 ft. and a maximum ceiling

of 21,500 ft. Armament originally consisted of a single synchronized forward-firing Vickers machine gun and a Scarff-ring-mounted Lewis for the observer, as well as up to 240 lb. of either 20-lb. Cooper or 112 lb. Hale bombs. In the field, Bristol crews often augmented their firepower with a second Lewis on the Scarff ring or on a forward-firing mounting above the upper wing.[5]

A second description of the Bristol Fighter can be found in Leonard Bridgman and Oliver Stewart's *The Clouds Remember: The Aeroplanes of World War I*:

In this relatively small aeroplane, with pilot and observer crammed close together in the fabric-covered distinctively rectangular fuselage, some of the greatest combats of the War were fought…. The high speed — for the time — the powers of manoeuvre and the immense strength of the Bristol Fighter ministered to this form of tactics.

The pilot could enter a dog-fight and turn almost as quickly and on almost as small a radius as the best single-seater. He could fling his machine about, go into vertical dives, pull it out quickly, turn it on its back, spin it, roll it and generally do every sort of manoeuvre if the need arose. And all the time there was the comfortable feeling that the observer was there with his pair of Lewis guns, watching and protecting.[6]

A more conservative view of the F.2B's capabilities is found in Aaron Norman's *The Great Air War: The Men, The Planes, The Saga of Military Aviation: 1914–1918*:

Its maximum speed at ten thousand feet was 105 miles per hour, which equaled or surpassed that of coeval

German fighter craft, but its maneuverability, while remarkable for its size and weight, was less sprightly than that of opposing single-seaters. Though its speed enabled it to outdistance most enemy interceptors, and its rear guns provided a sting in the tail, the Bristol was at a distinct disadvantage in close-range dogfights where aerobatic agility often meant the difference between success and failure. It needed more room for a turn, for example, and was clumsier to loop or roll. These handicaps could be diminished by an adroit pilot and sharp-shooting observer, as Captain McKeever and Sergeant Powell* certainly demonstrated, but the Bristol was not the complete answer for renewed Allied air supremacy that spring.[7]

By the end of the war over 3,500 Bristol Fighters had been produced.

At first, it was expected that the pilots and observers in the Bristols would fly the machine in the conventional way most photography and reconnaissance aeroplanes flew. That is to say, in a straight line. The pilot would manoeuvre his machine to allow the rear-facing observer to defend against enemy attack. The forward-facing machine gun was to be used only in emergency situations. Pilots like McKeever, however, treated their Brisfits (a nickname attached to the machine after the war) as if it were a scout, attacking the enemy head-on and maximizing the speed and agility of the aircraft. These pursuit tactics revolutionized two-seater combat methods. The machine was a true fighter with the added protection of a rear gunner. The two-seater fighter team of pilot and gunner was a potent force to be reckoned with. The Bristol Fighter thus played a significant role in British aviation in the last year and a half of the war.

---

* Leslie Archibald Powell, born on June 27, 1896, was a former journalist with the *Western Press*, and hailed from Redland, Bristol, England. He joined No. 11 Squadron in early July and would be McKeever's main observer for most of the next five months, figuring greatly in Andrew McKeever's success.

* * *

The move to La Bellevue aerodrome on June 1, 1917, brought the squadron closer to the front lines and closer to the German aerodromes at the same time. La Bellevue was situated about halfway between the town of Doullens and the major city of Arras, just miles from the front lines. The aerodrome had three sets of four or five hangars to the north and east of a farm and orchard. The pilots, observers, and ground crew were housed in five sets of huts behind the hangars. La Bellevue was home to a number of squadrons during the war. By the end of June, No. 11 Squadron had been entirely re-equipped with eighteen Bristol Fighters.

On June 20, 1917, Lieutenant McKeever was able to prove the ability of the F.2B. By this time, he had been promoted from second lieutenant to lieutenant. McKeever and his observer, Second Lieutenant Duncan, were returning from an uneventful reconnaissance patrol when they spotted a German Albatros, which spotted them at the same time. The German pilot, seeing a two-seater, was confident of victory. The E.A. attacked head-on. He no doubt thought that McKeever's slow-moving machine would be an easy target and that he could just fire a broadside on the British aeroplane as it turned to allow the observer to get a shot in. McKeever had other thoughts, though.

He did not turn but continued to fly straight at the Albatros, firing a stream of bullets from his Vickers machine right at the approaching enemy. The Albatros took immediate evasive action, going into an almost vertical dive. McKeever swung his Brisfit around and followed the enemy aircraft down, getting into a position on the German's tail. McKeever shot again, firing a burst that scored a number of hits. The Albatros spiralled toward the ground and escaped, the pilot wondering what had just happened.

This encounter with the enemy proved McKeever's theory, that the Bristol Fighter could be flown like a single-seat scout. The front gun was the main weapon of attack. The observer's role was to be a lookout from behind. In time, most of the other pilots of No. 11 Squadron adopted the same aggressive tactics with the Bristol Fighters they flew.

The next day, June 21, 1917, McKeever and Duncan were on a morning observation patrol, along with other Brisfits, flying at eight thousand feet over the town of Villers. A German Albatros dove onto the formation of F.2Bs. He did not know what he was getting himself into.

McKeever vigorously attacked the Albatros, firing about fifty rounds from a distance of 150 yards. Then his gun jammed. He turned off to the right to allow observer Duncan to fire at the E.A., a blast of thirty rounds at one hundred yards. The Albatros beat a hasty retreat, diving to safety. Since the German machine did not appear to be shot down, neither McKeever nor Duncan were given credit for it.

On an observation patrol in the afternoon of June 23, McKeever and Duncan were on patrol again, flying in formation east of Arras with other planes from the squadron. They spotted an Albatros scout flying west high above them. The formation left this E.A. alone, wanting to gain height. There they awaited the Albatros's return to the front lines. Once they spotted the returning Albatros, McKeever's observer fired three drums of ammunition at him. The tracers went right at the German machine, but as it was a thousand feet above them their fire was not very accurate, so did not do much damage. The Albatros was seen flying off toward its own front lines.

June 26 was to have a a different, and decisive, result for McKeever. Flying F.2B number A7144 at 12,500 feet, near the towns of Étaing and Dury, with observer Lieutenant D. Oake, McKeever was attacked by six Albatros scouts. Andy McKeever noticed they were painted in what he referred to as "comic colours." Some were red and blue; others green, white, and yellow; and still others were a mottled green, brown, and grey.

Two of the Albatros machines attacked McKeever from the rear. Observer Oake aimed his Lewis gun at the nearest one, getting off a burst of about twenty-five rounds at one hundred yards and a similar burst at the other oncoming enemy at about 150 yards. One of the Albatros scouts veered away but the other went down, completely out of control. McKeever then dove at the remaining Albatros aircraft. After diving a thousand feet, he got into position to be able to open fire on one of the machines, which was hit and dove seven thousand feet toward the ground. McKeever could not watch it fall to earth, however, as he was picking out his next target.

Now at nine thousand feet, McKeever flew at another E.A. He got to within fifty yards and let loose a vicious stream of tracer bullets. The

German machine fell to the ground out of control. It was seen to crash straight into the ground. McKeever then fired at the nearest enemy aircraft, from a distance of about three hundred yards. It flew off, seemingly unharmed, with the rest of the group. Andrew Edward McKeever was credited by his squadron commander, Major C.T. Maclean with one machine destroyed and one out of control, his first and second victories.

In the fall of 1916 and throughout 1917, the Albatros scout was the mainstay of the German air arm. The Albatros D.III saw action in 1916, but by the summer of 1917 it had been replaced with the faster and more manoeuvrable Albatros D.V. Jack Herris and Bob Pearson, in *Aircraft of World War I: 1914–1918*, provide the aircraft's specifications: "This aircraft was powered by a 160 hp Mercedes in-line piston engine, giving it a top speed of 105.6 mph. It could fly for two hours to a ceiling of 18,700 feet. It had a wing span of 29 feet 7 inches, a length of 24 feet and a height of 8 feet 10 inches. Its armament was two Maxim (Spandau) machine guns."[8]

McKeever wrote a combat report on July 2, 1917, describing a photography mission he and observer Lieutenant W.B. McKay had that morning, during which they encountered seven Albatros scouts. It reads as follows:

> Pilot dived and opened fire at about 200 yards distance, fired about 15 rounds, the E.A. dived and went in an eastward direction.
>
> The observer opened fire at an E.A. which was attacking our rear machine. Fire was opened at about 150 yards range and about ninety shots were fired. The E.A. then dived, appearing to be out of control, but recovered about 2,000 feet below, and did not take further part in the combat.[9]

On July 7, 1917, again flying F.2B number A7144, but this time with observer Second Lieutenant L.A. Powell, McKeever patrolled at nine thousand feet over Vitry and the Sensée Canal. It was a beautiful

Lieutenant Leslie Powell and Major Andrew Edward McKeever (right) in their Bristol F.2B aircraft.

summer evening, with clear skies and terrific visibility. Below them, they noticed seven Albatros scouts and what appeared to be a British Nieuport scout with German black-and-white crosses painted on its wings and fuselage. The enemy aircraft had not noticed the Bristol Fighters. Down went the British machines, each picking out an enemy aircraft to attack. McKeever dove at one and fired fifty rounds from about twenty-five yards. The Albatros had no warning of the attack and took no evasive action. It plummeted to the earth completely out of control. McKeever followed it down to about five thousand feet and saw it crash just south of Vitry. After they had climbed back to the fight, Powell got in seventy-five rounds from his Lewis gun at an enemy aircraft about one hundred yards away. It fell away completely out of control and was seen still falling to the ground at a low altitude.

Major Andrew Edward McKeever (left) and Lieutenant Leslie Powell standing in front of a Bristol F.2B aircraft.

McKeever continued to climb in order to make another dive on the remaining enemy aircraft. He reached 7,500 feet, turned, and dove on another Albatros. He fired a twenty-five round burst at it, but the E.A. took evasive measures, turning over and diving east to get out of danger. McKeever lined up another Albatros and was able to get within 150 yards of it and let loose with a stream of seventy-five rounds, hitting the German machine from tail to engine. It fell out of control with smoke streaming from it all the way down to the ground.

Powell was hard at work as well, firing fifty rounds from 250 yards at the Nieuport, which was above them. It took off to the east to avoid further contact with the British aeroplanes, apparently not damaged. McKeever fired at a retreating Albatros from two hundred yards but did no damage to it. The remaining Albatros flew home safely. McKeever was credited with one enemy machine destroyed and two driven down out of control. Second Lieutenant Powell was credited with a destroyed machine.

McKeever was flying again on July 10, this time with observer Second Lieutenant E.V. de G. Dodd. McKeever spotted an Albatros D.V below him and dove to intercept the E.A. The D.V could not escape and received a number of bullets in the engine. It dropped from the sky out of control.

On July 13, with observer de G. Dodd, McKeever flew an observation patrol over the town of Haynecourt. Flying at fourteen thousand feet, they encountered seven Albatros D.Vs and three captured Nieuports. McKeever's combat report, completed after landing safely back at La Bellevue aerodrome, read as follows:

> I dived on an E.A. opened fire at 200 yards, fired 50 rounds, the E.A. went East losing height apparently undamaged.
>
> The observer opened fire on another E.A. at 150 yards, fired 70 rounds, the E.A. went down in a nose dive for a long distance but appeared to be in control.
>
> I dived on an E.A. and opened fire at 150 yards, the E.A. fell out of control, was seen at a very low altitude still absolutely out of control, the observer opened fire on another E.A. at 100 yards, fired 75 rounds. The E.A. went East and did not pursue.
>
> I opened fire on another E.A. 100 yards, fired 75 rounds. The E.A. was seen to fire a red light and fell out of control.
>
> The observer opened fire on another E.A. 200 yards range [sic], fired 50 rounds. The E.A. went East apparently under control.
>
> I opened fire at 250 yards on an E.A. fired 50 rounds the E.A. went East apparently not damaged.[10]

McKeever's commanding officer, Major C.T. Maclean, credited him with two enemy aircraft shot down.

This combat report just states the facts; it does not give any indication of what this battle in the air must have been like. It does not refer to the various manoeuvres McKeever must have made to avoid being shot down, such as rolling, sharp turns to the left or the right, looping and split-S turns. One can only imagine the skill he employed.

His first initial dive would have scattered the group of German aircraft, who would then attempt to get the upper hand. Some would attempt to get behind McKeever's F.2B, only to be shot at by observer de G. Dodd. Other German machines would be circling above the melee, just waiting for their turn to pounce. After each dive McKeever would have climbed to gain altitude, putting him in a vulnerable position. However, as mentioned above, the Bristol Fighter's rate of climb was as good as, or better than, that of the Albatros D.V.

With McKeever battling against so many enemy aircraft, the Germans faced the possibility of crashing into one another, so they had to be on the lookout for each other, as well as getting into position to attack McKeever and Dodd. The two held their own against great odds and managed to fire on seven of the ten German machines, who were not up for much of a fight after that and escaped back to their aerodrome.

In his book *Open Cockpit*, Arthur Gould Lee, a pilot in No. 46 Squadron, describes how airmen of the war were described in the press and perceived by the public and how different that was from reality. He lists McKeever as one of the aces who was absolutely fearless.

> We were often cynically amused at the falseness of the image of the R.F.C. which was held by the public in England ... but we were far from being the impossible creatures created by the newspapers. That we were all intrepid, daredevil, hell-bent birdmen.... It would have been nice had things been even remotely like that ... Yet although we may have often flinched from our jobs, we did them to the best of our will-power and our nerves.
>
> These qualities naturally varied from man to man, and to even the dullest of us it became clear that in the matter of fear and courage we were all made differently. Some pilots and observers, not a very large proportion, really did not know the meaning of fear.... And such

Military Cross.

aces as Bishop, McCudden, Collishaw, MacLaren, Nungesser, McKeever, and the American, Luke, ruthless killers all, apparently never knew a twinge of fear in even their most desperate exploits.[11]

In just three weeks, June 26 to July 13, 1917, McKeever had destroyed or driven down out of control a total of eight enemy aircraft. For this feat he received the Military Cross. The citation for this decoration read,

> For conspicuous gallantry and devotion to duty, particularly when on offensive patrol. He attacked eight enemy aircraft single-handed at close range, and by his splendid dash and determination destroyed one and

drove five down completely out of control. He had previously shown exceptional fearlessness in attacking the enemy when in superior numbers, and in the space of three weeks he destroyed eight hostile machines, setting a very fine example to his squadron.[12]

This citation was published in the *London Gazette* on September 17, 1917. McKeever now was nicknamed "Hawkeye" by the rest of No. 11 Squadron for his marksmanship. Around this time, Second Lieutenant Powell also received the Military Cross for his victories as an observer.

EIGHT

August and September 1917

In the summer of 1917, the Allies did not have mastery of the air — far from it. The famous German ace Werner Voss, the commander of Jasta 10, had forty victories by the end of July. By mid-August, Manfred von Richthofen had shot down his fifty-eighth victim and helped celebrate his Jasta 11's one hundredth victory. On the ground the British were in the midst of an offensive in Flanders, but in the air there was a war of attrition.

In this stern battle, the monthly toll of British casualties rose by over one hundred during August, from 209 in the four weeks ending July 27, to 328 in the four weeks ending August 31.

In August, No. 11 Squadron conducted two standard reconnaissance patrol routes, one from Douai to Denain and on to Cambrai, and the other from Bray to Doignies to Artois. The squadron also carried out escort missions for bombing squadrons. Offensive patrols were very popular with the Bristol Fighter pilots as they now realized the power and agility of the "Biff," a nickname that the Bristol F.2 had acquired.

August 5, 1917, found McKeever and observer Powell on one of these offensive patrols. At 7:50 p.m., the flight of four Bristols from No. 11 Squadron took off and flew in the direction of Quéant. All eyes were peeled, looking for hostile aircraft. They soon spotted a flight of six single-seater Albatros scouts a thousand feet below them and slightly to the right. McKeever, in a diving turn, pounced upon his unsuspecting quarry, firing his Vickers machine gun at them, spraying twenty-five rounds from two hundred yards at the one E.A. he had picked out for his first attack. The Albatros dove away, seeking refuge in the clouds. In the meantime, Powell had fired seventy-five rounds at another D.V from two hundred yards. His fire was accurate and deadly. The German machine turned on its back and fell toward the ground, completely out of control. Its final fate was obliterated by clouds.

McKeever now focused on an E.A. coming out of the clouds. He flew to within twenty-five yards of the Albatros, which was attempting to escape just like a jackrabbit would when being chased by a coyote. McKeever pulled the trigger on his machine gun, letting loose fifty rounds at close range. The Albatros burst into flames and plummeted to earth.

Seeing another of the Albatros escaping into the clouds, McKeever quickly turned his machine and dove to attack. He fired fifty rounds of tracer bullets from seventy-five yards but the German machine managed to take evasive action and left the combat as quickly as he could.

Powell fired his Lewis at two E.A., sending a stream of two hundred bullets from a distance of 150 yards. Of course, the greater the distance between friend and foe, the less accurate the shooting, and at a range of 150 yards plus, it is difficult to gauge where the aircraft will be once the bullets arrive on target. Powell's targets managed to avoid his fire and headed east to safety.

McKeever noticed a straggler, some distance from the other Albatros. He dove onto that E.A., sending seventy-five rounds into it from fifty yards away. The German aircraft turned and fell out of control but McKeever lost it in the clouds and thick mist. The four Bristols then returned to their aerodrome to file their combat reports. McKeever was credited with one E.A. in flames, which was observed and verified by the other three Bristols on the flight, and two E.A. out of control.

Lieutenant T.W. Morse was McKeever's observer on an evening offensive patrol on August 9, 1917, over Vis-en-Artois. They flew at an altitude of between five thousand and seven thousand feet through the clouds. Below them, a German two-seater Aviatik was taking photos of the front lines, escorted by an Albatros scout. (The Aviatik first appeared in 1916. Its maximum speed was seventy-five mph. The interesting thing about this aircraft was the observer was in the front seat, near the engine, and the pilot sat in the rear seat facing forward. The observer had to fire his single machine gun [some machines had two machine guns] without hitting the engine, the propeller, the pilot, the bracing wires, or the struts. Future German two-seaters had the observer in the rear seat.)

McKeever dove on the slow-moving Aviatik and sent a burst of fifty rounds from seventy-five yards. The Aviatik went into a near-vertical dive to one thousand feet and was lost in the mist and clouds. Turning to the Albatros, which by now was also into a dive, McKeever tried to catch up to it and fired seventy-five rounds from one hundred yards. The German machine had too much of a lead, however, and escaped to the east.

August 21 saw a change in command of No. 11 Squadron. Major Maclean was replaced as commanding officer by Major R.S. Norton. The evening before his departure, the squadron gave Maclean a real send-off party. Many bottles of champagne were consumed and many songs sung around the piano in the officers' mess. Whisky followed the champagne and the singing got remarkably loud and boisterous. McKeever sang a few songs with his mates but did not drink. He stood off to one side of the revellers, just taking it all in.

Lieutenant Morse was with McKeever again on a patrol in the morning of August 22. They flew at six thousand feet over the town of Biache.

They saw another Aviatik below them. Morse filed this report of the combat: "The pilot dived down after an E.A., which was just over the German lines the E.A., went East and the observer fired about 50 rounds at a range of 250 yards, the E.A. spiraled down and was seen to land on the ground between some trenches."[1]

Major Norton categorized this as an indecisive combat.

On an evening flight that same day, McKeever and observer Second Lieutenant L.F. Ebbutt, in F.2B number A7159, were flying at twelve thousand feet over Auby and Douai. They encountered eight Albatros scouts. McKeever, known for his bravery and initiative in combat, did not think twice about going after enemy aircraft, whether it was one or eight. With his marksmanship and flying skill, he could put his Bristol through its paces, outmanoeuvring the German machines.

He picked out one of the Albatros D.Vs and dove straight at it, firing off a stream of fifty bullets from a distance of 150 yards. The enemy aircraft rolled over onto its back and spun down for about one hundred feet and then was seen to regain control. McKeever focused on his next target, firing fifty rounds again but at a range of one hundred yards. The E.A. escaped to the east, apparently in control and not damaged. Aiming at a third Albatros, McKeever flew to within thirty yards of it and sent seventy-five rounds into its fuselage and engine. That Albatros tumbled earthward completely out of control, and, at about five thousand feet below him, McKeever saw it break up in mid-air, pieces of wing and tail floating away like leaves in a summer breeze. The heavy fuselage and engine, with the pilot trapped inside and probably dead, plummeted to the ground.

A British Nieuport joined the dogfight but quickly found itself being attacked from behind by a German aircraft. McKeever was quick to position his Bristol for a shot at the enemy to drive him off. Firing warning shots from three hundred yards, McKeever was able to distract the Albatros, which flew east to home. He then turned his attention to one of the two remaining Albatros, diving on it from a distance of 150 yards and firing twenty-five rounds. This Albatros also flew off east, not wanting any more contact with the Bristol Fighter. Observer Ebbutt fired twenty-five rounds at an escaping Albatros from two hundred yards but with no effect. McKeever was credited with one enemy machine, the one that broke up in the air and crashed.

To finish out the month, on August 26 McKeever and observer Morse were on an offensive patrol at five thousand feet over Le Catelet, looking for enemy reconnaissance machines. They saw two German machines flying together and pounced on them from above. McKeever sent fifty rounds into one, from 250 yards. The German two-seater quickly dove to low altitude and escaped east. Turning and climbing into position to attack the other German aircraft, McKeever had to fire from a long distance as the two-seater dove for home. He let loose fifty rounds from three hundred yards but did no perceptible damage to the fleeing German.

By the end of August, the Flanders offensive had cost the British army over sixty-eight thousand casualties and had gained little ground. All of the air squadrons were pressed to provide more aid to the troops on the ground in their struggle.

No. 11 Squadron tried its hand at night flying. The whole squadron successfully passed their night flying tests in a week. Their role was to patrol over the Albert district, but they never saw any German machines. Gotha bombers often flew raids over the lines at night, but No. 11 Squadron had no contact with them.

No. 11 Squadron was not without its losses. "On September 19, 1917, Bristol F.2B number A7130 was shot down by Friedrich Gille of *Jasta* 12, southwest of Sailly. It was his sixth victory. Second Lieutenant H.T. Taylor and Lieutenant G.W. Mumford crashed behind enemy lines. Wounded, they were taken prisoner."[2]

McKeever's next notable full engagement with the enemy occurred on September 23, 1917. Flying F.2B A7159 over Vitry, with his faithful observer Powell, they came upon a sole multicoloured Albatros D.V flying directly toward them. McKeever, without any sign of trepidation, attacked head-on, firing right into the oncoming Albatros. The Albatros was doing the same to them. It seemed neither would give way. At the last moment, the E.A. flew below the Bristol. McKeever looped his craft and at the top of the loop rolled his machine so that he ended up behind the German machine. McKeever fired as he completed the manoeuvre, and the Albatros, mortally wounded, fell out of control toward the ground. Later that day, both McKeever and Powell, again in the area of Vitry, attacked a flight of Albatros, sending one down out of control.

On September 25, McKeever and Dodd were flying in flight formation with Lieutenant Niall-Smith and Second Lieutenant S.S. Stanley over Le Catelet at nine thousand feet. The Bristols encountered two German two-seaters, one green and the other mostly white. Niall-Smith dove down on one of the E.A. but overshot it, allowing the enemy machine to get a good shot at him. McKeever saw Niall-Smith's F.2B break up in the air. Following closely behind, McKeever attacked the German aircraft at twenty-five yards distance, firing twenty-five rounds at one of the two-seaters. It fell, completely out of control. Second Lieutenant Stanley dove and fired on the other German machine, about twenty-five rounds at one hundred yards, but it managed to escape through the nearby cloud formations. Members of No. 41 Squadron were able to verify the machine McKeever sent down out of control had in fact crashed.

There were a few air battles on September 28, and in these the German airmen suffered. The Bristol Fighter and the S.E.5 dominated the enemy's fighters. In one encounter, south of the main battle area, a formation of nine Albatros scouts, four Bristol Fighters of No. 11 Squadron, and eight DH.5s of No. 41 Squadron tangled. The German pilots, although they fought with courage, were routed. Only one survived. Three were destroyed in the air and five were sent down out of control.

A.M. Hewitt was McKeever's observer on September 28, 1917. Taking off in the early morning, they climbed to about nine thousand feet. Searching for enemy aircraft over Bugnicourt, they spotted a formation of Albatros scouts nearby. Outnumbered five to one, McKeever dove on the nearest E.A. Getting in behind it, McKeever sent a stream of tracer bullets into the cockpit and engine area of the German machine. It fell to earth, completely out of control. He then veered off to the right, avoiding being attacked from behind. At that very moment, another

Royal Aircraft Factory S.E.5 fitted with cockpit screens.

Albatros was flying across his sights. McKeever quickly fired a burst from his Vickers. The Albatros faltered for a moment then fell to the ground, spinning uncontrollably. The remaining Albatros scouts fled the scene, retreating east to more friendly skies.

That evening, McKeever and Hewitt went looking for more prey over Bugnicourt. Another flight of Albatros scouts had the misfortune to get in the way of McKeever's Bristol. Although each E.A. tried to get into firing position, McKeever was able to take evasive action. He then got behind one of the German machines and sent a burst of bullets into it at twenty-five yards. It started to smoke as it fell, out of control. Suddenly, the sky was clear of all enemy aircraft. McKeever had bagged three Albatros in one day!

At this point McKeever had accumulated eighteen victories.

McKeever would assist his fellow pilots from other squadrons when he came upon them in dogfights with German aircraft, as explained by John Norman Harris in *Knights of the Air*:

Albatros D.IIIs of Jagdstaffel 11 and Jagdstaffel 4 parked in a line at La Brayelle near Douai, France. Manfred von Richthofen's aircraft is second in line.

One Canadian fighter ace tells a story of McKeever in action. This particular ace, with a flight of SE-5s, was engaged in a furious dogfight with a flight of Albatros fighters. All were skilled pilots, and nobody could get an advantageous shot, but time was distinctly against the

Manfred von Richthofen in the cockpit of his Albatros with officers of Jagdstaffel 11.

SE-5s, for they were over enemy territory; if they could not disengage, they ran the risk of running short of fuel.

"Suddenly," he said, "a single Bristol fighter appeared, diving into the midst of the melee. Instantly, the battle broke up, and the Germans headed for home. We were extremely grateful for the rescue, but at the same time it was a little humiliating for the SE-5s to be rescued by a two-seater."[3]

NINE

October and November 1917

The first day of October saw McKeever and observer Lieutenant H.G. Kent flying F.2B number A7121. They, along with the rest of the flight of Bristols, were on an offensive patrol over Douai. McKeever noticed one of the F.2Bs leave the formation with engine trouble and head back to the aerodrome. When it was several thousand feet below the formation, McKeever saw the Bristol being attacked by a German two-seater. Quickly turning and diving to the rescue of his fellow squadron pilot, McKeever dove to 4,500 feet and got onto the two-seater's tail, pouring twenty-five rounds into it at point-blank range. The German keeled over and was seen by both McKeever and observer Kent crashing into the ground.

The next day, two flights of Bristols, eight machines in all, took off at 6:00 p.m. to patrol an area from Douai to Cambrai. On this flight,

McKeever had L.A. Powell with him as observer. The two flights were in formation at fourteen thousand feet when they spotted a formation of seven Albatros scouts, two thousand feet below them. McKeever dove onto one of the German machines. While he was doing that, Powell fixed his Lewis on an E.A. that was firing on a Bristol. Powell got off a burst of a hundred rounds at seventy-five yards. The German machine fell to the ground in flames. This was observed by three other Bristol crew members.

In the meantime, a Bristol was attacked by three hostile aircraft, two from behind and one from the front. The pilot fired sixty rounds at his attacker, while the observer, Second Lieutenant Fosse, fired off three drums of ammunition into the other two E.A. One of them was seen by both the pilot and observer falling down completely out of control, turning over and over, tail over engine, toward the ground.

Lieutenant McKenna and his observer Second Lieutenant Sutcliffe engaged a German machine that was attacking one of the Bristols. McKenna and another pilot, Second Lieutenant Wookey, fired about eight hundred rounds into the Albatros, which, after taking such a terrible beating, rolled over and over, and then plummeted toward the ground, completely out of control.

Another one of the Bristols took on an Albatros, firing 150 rounds of tracer ammunition from a distance of about one hundred yards. Some of the bullets were seen to go into the E.A.'s engine, forcing it to dive straight down and then recover into a glide. This combat was labelled "indecisive" by Commander Norton.

Having destroyed or brought down out of control twenty enemy aircraft, McKeever was awarded a bar to his Military Cross, signifying he had won the decoration twice. The announcement of this award appeared in the *London Gazette* on October 27, 1917. It read as follows:

> For conspicuous gallantry and devotion to duty in aerial combats. He has recently destroyed five enemy aeroplanes and driven down six out of control. On one occasion he encountered five enemy scouts, and drove down two out of control. Later, while leading a patrol,

he engaged nine enemy scouts. He destroyed two, drove down one out of control, and dispersed the remainder. His dash and determination have been a fine example to his squadron.[1]

On October 16, 1917, McKeever and Powell were on a reconnaissance and photography mission around Brebières. Flying at sixteen thousand feet, they noticed below them two German two-seaters being escorted by six Albatros scouts. McKeever attacked from out of the clouds. He fired about fifty rounds at the E.A. from a distance of seventy-five yards. It tumbled earthward, obviously damaged, and did not rejoin the scrap. Powell then fired on a German machine that was diving toward them, pouring fifty rounds at fifty yards with deadly accuracy. The E.A. was seen by both Powell and McKeever to float in midair then fall to the ground completely out of control. They saw it crash east of Erre.

McKeever then attacked another German machine, firing twenty-five rounds from fifty yards and sending it crashing to the ground near Douai. Both McKeever and Powell witnessed its demise. The dogfight was not over yet. Both McKeever and Powell fired their machine guns at the remaining enemy aircraft. The German machines broke off the engagement and flew home. McKeever was credited with two E.A. destroyed and Powell with an E.A. out of control.

Powell submitted the following report of their reconnaissance that day to Commander Norton, who passed it on to army headquarters:

> Troops with transport, covering about 1 mile of road, moving N.W. from Dechy to Douai.
> Several trains with steam up, apparently goods trains, going north westerly direction.
> Three trains with steam up stationary, facing west.
> Three barges observed on Scarpe River.
> Visibility good; clouds 16,000 feet.[2]

No. 11 Squadron certainly had multiple functions to perform. They did not just engage in offensive patrols, as can be seen from the above report, they also carried out observation, reconnaissance, and photography shoots.

The day after McKeever submitted his report, a formation of Bristol Fighters was on a similar photography and reconnaissance mission from the Sensée Canal to Cambrai. One of the F.2Bs was piloted by Lieutenant R.F.S. Mauduit, with observer Second Lieutenant L.H. McRobert. The formation was attacked by ten Albatros scouts. In this engagement, one E.A. was seen to go down in an uncontrollable spin, falling five thousand feet. This enemy aircraft was probably the victim of Second Lieutenant Stanley.

After the Bristols had scared off the first group of German machines, another ten Albatros scouts arrived and continued the attack on the Biffs. Two of the E.A. dove onto the British machines from the flank. McRobert fired fifty rounds at each of the two enemy aircraft from one hundred yards, inflicting severe damage to both machines. He saw one of them flutter momentarily before turning over and falling uncontrollably to earth. The other one was seen to spin down, free-falling several thousand feet toward the ground.

On October 20, a flight of four Bristol Fighters was flying northwest of Cambrai, behind enemy lines. McKeever was flight commander. His observer was H.G. Kent. The others included Sergeant Stephenson and observer A.M. Flatel, Second Lieutenant Perney and observer Corporal MacMenigall, and Second Lieutenant Handall with observer Second Lieutenant Jones. The flight spotted two formations of Albatros, one of four aircraft, the other of five. McKeever was the first to dive, getting off fifty rounds at between fifty and seventy-five yards. The German machine was caught totally unaware. It dove away almost vertically and then burst into flames two thousand feet below McKeever's aeroplane. In the ensuing melee, McKeever shot seventy-five rounds at another German Albatros but with no apparent result. A German machine had in the meantime manoeuvred in behind McKeever's Bristol, only to be met with eighty accurate rounds of fire from observer Kent. That burst scared off the Albatros, which headed east for home.

Sergeant Stephenson, meanwhile, dove onto an Albatros, firing a stream of fifty bullets into it at a range of seventy-five yards. The fire was very accurate, and the German machine rolled onto its back then went into a flat spin to the ground. Stephenson did not see it crash, as it went into clouds below. Perney's Bristol had an Albatros on its tail, so the observer, Corporal MacMenigall, fired a burst of fifty rounds at it from one hundred yards and saw the German aircraft bank to the right to avoid the fire and dive. MacMenigall thought it was out of control but could not verify this, as the E.A. dove down through clouds as well. Pilot Handall and observer Jones were also involved in this scrap but did not have any decisive results against the attacking German machines. In the space of a few minutes of combat, over nine hundred rounds had been fired at the enemy. One E.A. had gone down in flames and another two were shot down out of control. The Bristols suffered no losses.

Flight Commander Lieutenant McKeever (promoted to this rank on October 26, 1917), with observer Powell, led three other Bristols — piloted by Second Lieutenant E.D. Perney (Corporal Lee, observer), Second Lieutenant M.S. West (Lieutenant L.V. Pogson, observer), and Second Lieutenant R.W. Perkins (Sub-lieutenant D.S. Allison, observer) — on an afternoon mission on October 31, 1917, over Fresse at fourteen thousand feet. "Hawkeye" McKeever spotted eleven Albatros scouts below them. Outnumbered almost three to one, McKeever led his squadron into a dive. He picked out a target and fired fifty rounds at fifty yards. He saw the E.A. flutter for an instant then fall completely out of control toward the earth. McKeever watched it until it was swallowed up by clouds near the ground.

Powell, in the meantime, had fired on an Albatros that was getting into position to shoot at McKeever's Bristol. Powell got his machine gun firing first and poured a hundred rounds at the Albatros from seventy-five yards. The E.A. stalled for a moment, went into a dive, then burst into flames. Powell quickly changed the drum of ammunition for his Lewis machine gun in time to fire at another Albatros that had got into range. He fired eighty-five rounds at the German machine from only fifty yards away. It spun down to the ground like a top, completely out of control. McKeever was credited with one machine out of control, and Powell was credited with one machine down in flames and two machines downed out of control.

The rest of the flight of Bristols had their fair share of action during this dogfight, firing off between seventy-five and eighty rounds from the pilots and a total of about 330 rounds from their observers. These Bristols did not send any German aircraft to the ground, however.

As the third battle of Ypres was ending (it had continued from July to November 1917), British General Headquarters had given its approval, on October 20, for an offensive of the British Third Army against the enemy at Cambrai. This battle marked the introduction of the tank as an offensive weapon on a large scale. While the army was making its preparations, so too was the RFC. S.F. Wise, in his comprehensive *Canadian Airmen and the First World War: The Official History of the Royal Canadian Air Force*, volume 1, notes the magnitude of the battle.

> Nonetheless, the air planning was carried out with a care and thoroughness not previously seen in the RFC, at least as far as ground attack was concerned. The designated 3 Brigade was quietly reinforcing until it mustered 125 corps machines, 134 single-seater fighters, eighteen Bristol Fighters, and twelve DH4 bombers, and arrangements were made for it to draw additional fighting and bombing squadrons from 1 Brigade and 9 (HQ) Wing on demand. Against this force, the enemy could, at the opening of battle, count on only seventy-eight machines, of which twelve were fighters. III Brigade alone outnumbered the opposing units of the German air force by about four to one, with a superiority of ten to one in fighters.[3]

No. 11 Squadron played an active part in the battle of Cambrai. As a lead-up to the infantry offensive, much of No. 11 Squadron's work was photography reconnaissance. McKeever and observer Pogson flew one such mission on November 11, 1917. Flying at thirteen thousand

Portrait of Manfred von Richthofen with the order Pour le Mérite.

feet over the area of Brebières, while Pogson took his photos, McKeever kept an eye out for hostile aircraft. He could not see any. After finishing the shoot and while on their return to base, McKeever noticed two German DFW two-seaters ten thousand feet below. He must have had quite incredible eyesight to spot them from such a distance; perhaps, he used a telescope to scan the area. McKeever dove onto one of the German machines. From one hundred yards he fired fifty rounds into the somewhat slow-moving German reconnaissance aircraft. The E.A. turned over and spun to the ground, first to the left then to the right, out of control. McKeever lost sight of the first DFW as he engaged the second one. Right when he was about to fire, his guns jammed. The German machine escaped unharmed and McKeever and Pogson returned to their aerodrome. McKeever was credited with another victory.

During most of November, the weather was appalling and the machines were compelled to work with mist and cloud at about three hundred feet. Luckily the casualties were light and the results achieved, excellent. British pilots were flying low-level support for their troops. Light casualties were not to last. The Germans transferred a number of squadrons south from Ypres to Cambrai, including Manfred von Richthofen's *Geschwader*. By November 23, the pilots noticed a distinct increase in the number of combats and German machines in the air. The number of British aircraft shot down was on the increase, due both to ground fire and the increase in German aircraft in the area.

By the third day of fighting (November 23), III Brigade had lost, from one cause or another, 30 percent of the aircraft initially available. Despite the losses, the RFC continued its tactics of close support for the British infantry, flying low-level missions against the front-line German troops. Meanwhile, German reserves poured south from Douai to Cambrai. Reconnaissance aircraft reported much activity and troop movement south to the battle lines.

Up to the time of the arrival of the reinforcing Jagdstaffeln, the orders for No.11 Squadron allowed for a maximum of four Bristol Fighters for one reconnaissance formation, but, on November 23, the reconnaissance formation was increased to eight, and, on November 28, to twelve. According to S.F. Wise:

> Air reconnaissance was still greatly hampered by bad weather, but both GHQ and Third Army felt that any counter-attack which did develop would be launched against the northern flank, around Bourlon. However, on 30 November the Germans focused the weight of a major assault against the southern flank, between Masnières and Vendhuille, catching the British badly off balance.... III Brigade could muster only 230 serviceable aircraft now, ninety-nine of them corps

machines, but around Burlon Wood the sky was "black with German and British machines." Fighter patrols of both sides were busy as sixty-one combats were reported, twenty-three of them being claimed as "decisive."[4]

McKeever was among them in the air battle that raged that day. Although most pilots of No. 11 Squadron thought the weather conditions were too overcast and rainy for flying, McKeever and Powell volunteered for a line patrol and reconnaissance mission south of Cambrai, some sixty miles from their aerodrome. They climbed into their Sidcot flying suits, donned their leather helmets, and placed their goggles over their eyes. With the help of their ground crew, they fired up the Bristol.

McKeever, now an acting captain, and Powell took off, unaccompanied, in F.2B number A7288. Climbing to get to the target, they flew through low clouds. At that altitude, there was only fair visibility. Once they were over the front lines, McKeever and Powell descended to only about 1,500 feet, back into the patchy cloud formations. Flying in a northerly direction, they were observing enemy troop movements. Harris, in *Knights of the Air*, described what happened next.

"He completed the reconnaissance job, collecting valuable information, and was about to turn for home when he saw a large explosion some miles ahead, and decided to investigate. He found that a British shell had scored a direct hit on a huge German ammunition dump. Fires were raging everywhere, and exploding shells were hampering the efforts of hundreds of firefighters. McKeever at 1,000 feet, had just decided to dive down and hamper their efforts further by means of his guns...."[5]

Suddenly, through the clouds to their right came two red German two-seaters along with seven black Albatros scouts. McKeever sprung to the attack, making a sharp turn to the east and getting his machine underneath the enemy aircraft. Coming to within only fifteen yards of one German machine, he fired ten rounds at point-blank range, aiming for the engine and fuel tanks. He scored a perfect hit and his opponent fell to earth and burst into flames.

Thinking this victory would scare off the other E.A., McKeever turned in the direction of his own lines. However, five of the Albatros dove at McKeever and got onto his tail, all of them firing their machine guns. Lieutenant Powell shot a stream of bullets at one of them from a distance of twenty yards, making many direct hits. This E.A. fell to the ground and crashed. Quickly picking out another German aircraft, he fired again, sending it to its death. Powell kept firing at two other Albatros but with no apparent effect.

The fifth attacking Albatros was going so fast it overshot McKeever's Bristol, allowing him to get in about twenty-five shots as it passed over him. He saw it flutter in mid-air then fall, spinning down until it crashed to the ground. McKeever then turned to other German machines and fired bursts at them but with little results. By now, McKeever was within twenty feet of the ground. Powell's gun jammed, so it was up to McKeever to defend against two Albatros that dove at him from a height of one hundred feet. One of the enemy bullets tore into one of McKeever's flying boots, grazing his leg. Dozens of German rounds hit the Bristol.

McKeever had to think quickly about how to get out of this extremely dangerous situation. He pulled a trick on the Germans, shutting off his engine and doing a sideslip toward the ground. The enemy flew off, thinking they had shot McKeever down. They could not see him through the mist and cloud. McKeever then gunned his engine back to life and quickly escaped.

Flying at only twenty feet through the spotty clouds, he followed a row of trees along a roadway for about five miles. He turned his aircraft toward the front lines. As they crossed the lines, they were met with a barrage of rifle and machine-gun fire from German troops. McKeever, at full throttle, put as much distance between him and the hostile fire as quickly as he could, relying on the low clouds to help hide his machine as it sped past the infantry. Now safely away from the enemy aircraft and the enemy ground fire, he turned for home.

Upon landing, pilots and members of the ground crew of the squadron ran toward McKeever's Bristol. As McKeever and Powell alighted from the aircraft, the others gathered around them. They were astounded by the damage inflicted on the Biff by German E.A. and by ground fire. One line of bullet holes went from the tail fin right up the fuselage to where Powell had been sitting. More bullet holes were spotted in and around the cockpit. Several others had ripped large holes in the upper and lower wings of the Bristol. It was a tough machine that could withstand lots of punishment.

McKeever was credited with one E.A. having crashed in flames and another E.A. having crashed. Powell was credited with two E.A. having crashed. Four enemy machines out of nine shot down in one aerial encounter was a tremendous feat of courage, good shooting, and excellent flying. Many pilots would have attempted merely to escape the nine enemy aircraft, but not McKeever. This action, on November 30, 1917, did not go unnoticed. King George V announced the granting of the Distinguished Service Order to McKeever. On July 5, the *London Gazette* described the reasons he received this decoration:

> For conspicuous gallantry and devotion to duty. While on patrol by himself over the enemy's lines in very bad weather he encountered two enemy two-seater machines and seven scouts. By skillful maneuvering he engaged one and destroyed it. As he turned to get back to the lines five of the enemy dived on his tail and his observer engaged and destroyed two of them. After an indecisive combat with two others he attacked and destroyed one of enemy which had overshot him. He continued the fight with the remainder until he was within twenty feet of the ground, when the enemy machines climbed and left him. He has recently destroyed ten enemy machines and has shown great courage and initiative.[6]

For his work that day, Lieutenant Powell was awarded the Distinguished Conduct Medal. At some point while with No. 11 Squadron, McKeever was awarded the French Croix de Guerre, with palm.

These were the last victories McKeever was to see. He went up once more with Powell on December 5, 1917. On a line reconnaissance mission over Gouy, flying at 2,500 feet, McKeever spotted a formation of three enemy aircraft that had crossed the lines into British-held territory. He dove on them, firing about twenty-five rounds at one of the E.A. It spun down five hundred feet and then levelled off. McKeever lost sight of it. The other two E.A. disengaged and flew home. It was an indecisive combat for McKeever.

By some accounts, McKeever's number of victories was thirty-one. In their book *Above the Trenches: A Complete Record of the Fighter Aces and Units of the British Empire Air Forces, 1915–1920,* authors Shores, Franks, and Guest give McKeever credit for thirty-one victories but they have included Powell's two victories on November 30, 1917, and other victories by his observers, in McKeever's score.[7]

Royal Flying Corps communiques put McKeever's score at twenty-seven. They credit him with the following victories:

June 26, 1917	one out of control, one destroyed
July 7, 1917	one destroyed, two out of control
July 10, 1917	one out of control
July 13, 1917	one out of control
August 5, 1917	two out of control, one destroyed
August 22, 1917	one destroyed
August 23, 1917	one destroyed
September 23, 1917	two out of control
September 25, 1917	one destroyed
September 28, 1917	one out of control, two destroyed
October 1, 1917	one destroyed
October 2, 1917	one destroyed
October 16, 1917	two destroyed
October 20, 1917	one destroyed
October 31, 1917	one out of control
November 11, 1917	one out of control
November 30, 1917	two destroyed [8]

Brigade summaries have his score at twenty-three, with four possible victories, which adds up to twenty-seven. In any event, McKeever was "the king of the two-seaters." In the space of five and a half months, McKeever and his observers managed to shoot down thirty-one enemy aircraft, or about one-and-a-half machines a week — an incredible feat! McKeever bagged more enemy planes in a Bristol Fighter than any other pilot in the war.

Norm Shannon, in *From Baddeck to the Yalu: Stories of Canada's Airmen at War*, mentions other Canadian pilots who scored victories in Bristol Fighters over a short space of time. "Ken Conn of Almonte, Ont., figured in 20 victories in a Bristol Fighter between June and November of 1918. Montreal's Wilfred Beaver accounted for 15 of his 20 victories during the spring and summer of 1918 as well. Alfred Atkey, a former reporter for the *Toronto Evening Telegram,* remains an enigma. The RFC credits him with being instrumental in 38 victories but many of these were acquired by his different gunners."[9]

Lieutenant Leslie Archibald Powell would end the war with a score of nineteen enemy aircraft destroyed or downed out of control. McKeever and Powell could be described as "aces back to back."

Arthur Gould Lee, in his book *Open Cockpit*, was reminded of McKeever and Powell as he flew over the Bellevue aerodrome, home of No. 11 Squadron.

> Still another was Andrew McKeever of 11 Squadron at Bellevue and at this moment, looking down, I saw Bellevue aerodrome over to our left. I'd been there often and talked to him, a normal friendly Canadian, yet here was a man, flying Bristol Fighters at a time when they weren't supposed to cross the Lines except in formation of at least six, who on three occasions, while alone except for his rear-gunner, Sergeant Powell, as brave as himself — had attacked Albatros formations of seven,

eight and nine, and each time had shot down three or four, and got away almost unscathed.

But neither McKeever nor any of the other risk-takers could have won through without great luck, for even the bravest, most skilful fighter could be caught by a chance bullet. They were blessed with luck, and nobody in air fighting could get far without it.[10]

Luck was responsible for part of his success but extraordinary skill should be credited for most of it. McKeever never cracked up any of the Bristols he flew and received only one minor wound, to his lower leg when an enemy bullet ripped into his flying boot. McKeever looked after his observers as well, never losing one of them in combat. His flying prowess was second to none and his marksmanship with a forward-firing machine gun incredible.

TEN

Home Establishment and the Canadian Air Force

For most of December 1917 and January 1918, little flying occurred as the weather was so bad. On January 25, 1918, both McKeever and Powell, who by now had a bar to his Military Cross, were transferred back to England, to what was called the Home Establishment. There, they parted. McKeever took command of a training school, with the rank of acting captain. His valuable skills were too precious to lose, so he spent the balance of the war in England.

On February 23, 1918, McKeever was one of a number of soldiers, sailors, and airmen waiting in line to be invested by King George V at Buckingham Palace. At five feet ten inches in height, McKeever had to bow from the waist somewhat to enable the diminutive King George V to pin the Distinguished Service Order (DSO), the MC, and bar on to the left breast of McKeever's tunic. The King congratulated him on his many victories and his courageous deeds. Andrew McKeever was very much impressed with the pomp and ceremony of the investiture.

On April 1, 1918, McKeever was confirmed in the rank of captain.

McKeever would continue his instructional duties until the end of April 1918, when he was granted home leave. When he arrived in Listowel on May 9, 1918, the whole town, almost every man, woman, and child, was at the CPR station to greet this returning hero. It was a time to reconnect with friends and family. After a couple of months leave, he was back on his way to England and an entirely new challenge.

As early as 1917, the Canadian public had been talking of the feasibility of creating a Canadian Air Force. The Aero Club of Canada supported the idea and pressed the Canadian government to pursue it. Canadian newspapers were onside as well. Respected Canadian pilots like Billy Bishop and Wing Commander R.H. Mulock of the Royal Naval Air Service advocated for the establishment of a distinctive Canadian air force. Canadian governmental officials, including Canadian embassy officials, began discussions with the British Air Ministry. They knew the part being played by Canadians in the Royal Air Force, and the Royal Naval Air Service, was very significant. Prime Minister Sir Robert Borden, a long-time opponent of the idea, now embraced it. Canada had a distinct Canadian Army Corps, under the leadership of General Arthur Currie, so why should it not have a distinct air service? General Currie was in favour of the idea as well. So too was Brigadier General A.C. Critchley, the highest-ranking Canadian in the RAF.

Another factor, which may well have influenced the Air Ministry not to block the formation of the Canadian Air Force (CAF), was the awareness of its senior officials that yet another Canadian air force, the Royal Canadian Naval Air Service, was in the process of being created.

The British Air Ministry came around, and in August 1918 agreed that two squadrons, first designated 93 and 123 Squadrons by the RAF, were to be manned entirely by Canadian personnel and would become the foundation of the CAF. S.F. Wise's *Canadian Airmen and the First World War: The Official History of the Royal Canadian Air Force*, volume 1, describes the Air Ministry's decision:

The Air Council had decided that 93 was to be a fighter squadron, equipped with Sopwith Dolphins, while the 123 would be a day-bomber squadron, equipped with DH9s. In order to allow time for the assembling of personnel and necessary training of groundcrew, the mobilization date for the two squadrons was tentatively set as 10 October....

Prime responsibility for assembling the officers and other ranks belonged to Bishop, who was promoted to temporary lieutenant-colonel and attached to HQ OMFC [Overseas Military Forces of Canada] at the head of the CAF Section. He was given general liaison responsibilities with the RAF, and was to act as the minister's adviser for all questions respecting the organization and training of the CAF and for the selection of personnel.[1]

The two squadrons were renamed 1 Squadron (fighters) and 2 Squadron (day-bombing). They would be stationed at an RAF training base, Upper Heyford in Oxfordshire. Wise's official history goes on to explain McKeever's involvement:

To command 1 Squadron, Bishop's first choice was Major Raymond Collishaw, but when he proved unavailable, Bishop secured the services of Captain A.E. McKeever. For 2 Squadron, Bishop recommended Captain Walter B. Lawson. When, in early October, Bishop decided to relinquish his position and return to Canada, he had put together a list of officers for the fighter squadron which McKeever accepted, but Lawson was left the job of finding suitable bomber pilots. Complete lists were not in the hands of the Air Ministry until 19 November. None of those named were to be offered permanent appointments, partly because McKeever and Lawson wished to leave room for airmen with outstanding operational records. The whole selection process had been slowed by Bishop's departure, by delays in securing the services of McKeever and Lawson from the RAF, and by the uncertainty of whether or not the CAF would survive the end of hostilities.[2]

The end of the war came and went, and still those in charge of the operations of the CAF were looking for staff. The most pressing need was for ground crew. Most of the recruits were sent to RAF Halton Park to train as mechanics and riggers. Others were sent to Uxbridge for armament training. One Squadron and 2 Squadron were officially mobilized between November 20 and 25 at their airfield at Upper Heyford. However, no one had planned for or was working on the necessary administrative structure and policies to make an independent air force a reality. The highly skilled veteran pilots selected for the two squadrons did not have the administrative or organizational experience or ability to prove to the Canadian government that the CAF could be a viable force into the future. Wise describes the state of affairs as follows:

> At Halton Camp, early in January 1919, the Canadians still there refused in a body to obey orders to drill. An investigation officer dispatched by HQ OMFC found that a British RAF officer had "fallen in the parade on a ground which was in a deplorable condition and began to drill the men before a crowd of young soldiers who obviously took much pleasure in seeing the detail drilling in the mud." No sooner was this trouble quelled than McKeever reported a "crisis" with the men at Upper Heyford. This station was under RAF command, and Canadian other ranks had been detailed for fatigue duties by British officers. On 7 January the men refused to move off from morning parade to duty at their flights. As it turned out, they had a number of legitimate complaints. They had had no Christmas

leave; because the CAF had no real administrative organization, they had been given no trades pay since mobilization; their messing was atrocious; they were anxious to know when the squadrons would be returning to Canada; and some expressed the fear that they would not be permitted to demobilize....

There was much dissatisfaction among the flying officers as well. The chief cause was the aircraft furnished by the RAF. Neither the Dolphin nor the DH9a was held in any respect by men who knew their operational performance. McKeever wanted Snipes for his squadron, and Lawson Bristol Fighters for his, but junior staff officers at HQ OMFC found no willingness on the part of the Air Ministry to change the original allocations.[3]

The safety of the Dolphins was being questioned. There had already been one fatality. In February 1919 the Air Ministry ordered all service flying of Dolphins to cease until modifications could be made.

In spite of being promoted to the rank of major in the CAF on January 22, 1919, within a week McKeever's frustration with the whole situation reached the boiling point. Wise elaborates:

He called upon the Overseas Ministry to appoint a senior officer to command the CAF, in order that some stability could be given the fledgling organization and also to make some impression upon the Air Ministry. Beyond that, he was as perturbed by the hazy status of the CAF as were the other ranks. "A definite policy should be arrived at as soon as possible by the Canadian Authorities as to the purpose of the two Canadian Squadrons," he wrote. "Is it the intention to use these two Squadrons as the nucleus of the Canadian Royal Air Force?" If it was, then arrangements must be made in Canada for their reception in the form of accommodation, hangars, and other installations, and it was vital to determine what aircraft were most appropriate for a Canada-based force. McKeever's views were received sympathetically at HQ OMFC. "I cannot help feeling," wrote Lieutenant Colonel C.M. Edwards, "although I hesitate to make the statement, that the Air Ministry take very little interest in our organization and equipment." In fact, Canadian Headquarters had already been exploring the question of a commander for the CAF.[4]

Colonel R.H. Mulock was offered the position but turned it down. Mulock did agree, however, to spend some considerable time and attention, beginning on February 20, 1919, to gathering material on the current state of affairs of the CAF and to formulate a policy proposal for the Canadian Cabinet. His proposal was received by Cabinet, but ignored.

In the meantime, Lieutenant Colonel G.C. St. P. de Dombasle, one of the senior Canadians in the RAF, was appointed to command the CAF. De Dombasle proposed a move to a better airfield and the replacement of the Dolphins with the more operationally sound S.E.5a fighter aircraft. The Air Ministry agreed with both recommendations.

On March 31, 1919, the two squadrons of the CAF moved to Shoreham-by-Sea. The two squadrons were formed into 1 Canadian Wing, commanded by the distinguished former RNAS pilot Major Robert Leckie, who was also Shoreham's station commander. By April–May 1919, there were forty-nine officers on strength at 1 Wing. S.F. Wise names many Canadians involved in the CAF at the time.

> Of the forty-two officers on flying duties, twenty-two had been decorated for gallantry and ten had at least two such decorations. The fighter squadron's flight commanders were Captains C.F. Falkenberg, DFC and Bar, G.O. Johnson, MC, and D.R. MacLaren, DSO, MC and Bar, DFC; while those of the bomber squadron were Major A.D. Carter, DSO and Bar, Captain

Major A.E. McKeever, Commanding Officer, No. 1 Squadron, Canadian Air Force, in front of a captured German Fokker D.VII, Upper Heyford, Oxfordshire, 1919.

A.E. McKeever, in flying gear, climbs into the cockpit of Fokker D.VII 5924/18 at Hounslow, Middlesex, 1919.

Major A.E. McKeever.

McKeever in flying gear in front of a Sopwith.

J.O. Leach, MC, AFC, and Captain T.F. Hazell, DSO, MC, DFC. The CAF, in other words, had become an organization weighted towards those with operational experience, outstanding records, and a background of army service on the Western Front.[5]

Despite the impressive talent pool in the CAF, its days were numbered. So too was the Royal Canadian Naval Air Service, recently formed at the end of the war. The RCNAS ceased to exist shortly after the armistice and all of their cadets were released in early January 1919. With the future of the CAF in doubt, the British government proposed a gift of sixty-two Avro 504s, twelve DH.9s, twelve S.E.5s, ten DH.4s, two Curtiss H-16 flying boats, two Bristol Fighters, and a Snipe. Ottawa agreed. But how would the maintenance and transportation of these machines to Canada be financed? No one in the Canadian government seemed willing to commit funds to this matter. On May 30, the Cabinet decided it would no longer fund the CAF. All that was left to do was disband it and send home all its pilots, ground crew, and other staff.

Andrew McKeever was demobilized on August 1, 1919. He sailed from Liverpool on the SS *Belgic* on August 16, 1919, for North America. He took his personal Bristol Fighter, number F4336, with him (this aircraft was later entered on the Canadian Civil Aircraft Register as G-CYBC). He and his machine were on their way home.

ELEVEN

A Tragic Ending

McKeever returned to Listowel in late August 1919. He had accepted the position offered to him by the United States government to be the manager of the Mineola airport near New York. The salary was to be ten thousand dollars per year, an enormous sum in those days, and reflected the high esteem in which McKeever was held by all. This post would have insured McKeever a place in postwar aviation in North America. At the young age of twenty-five it seemed his future was assured.

Fate intervened, however. On September 2, 1919, just days after McKeever arrived home, he and five other young friends decided to borrow the big Hudson Six owned by J.W. Scott of Listowel, and take it for an evening ride to Stratford. Morton Scott, the driver, was accompanied by Major McKeever, Aerial Schinbein, and three ladies, Fredda Smith, Francis McDonald, and Elva Sanderson. Just two miles north of the town of Mitchell, the car either hit a stone and swerved into the ditch or perhaps slid into the ditch after hitting some water on the road. McKeever was the only one to be injured, having broken his leg.

He was taken to the Stratford Hospital to have his leg set. It was not properly set, healing in a manner that resulted in the injured leg being three inches shorter than the other one. On December 15, 1919, McKeever entered the Toronto General Hospital to have an operation to have the leg rebroken, reset, and fixed in place with a silver plate. The operation took place on Monday, December 22. The *Listowel Standard* reported the outcome:

> At first it was thought that he was getting along fine. Tuesday morning he was conscious and was able to converse with his doctor. In the afternoon he had a good sleep and was much improved on Wednesday. Early Thursday he took a turn for the worse and quickly grew weaker. At nine o'clock no hopes were held for his recovery and at 10:40 p.m. the great soldier had gone to his reward.[1]

Major McKeever died on Christmas Day 1919, from either uremic poisoning or a blood clot in the brain. It is ironic that McKeever, who had escaped the many air combat missions against German aircraft during the war and avoided the constant dangers of death in the air, ended up succumbing to an injury sustained in an auto accident. His father, William, took possession of Andrew's medals and decorations. His mother, Bella, received the Memorial Cross, as did all mothers of deceased soldiers.

The town of Listowel was in shock. Their favourite son and war hero was dead at the age of twenty-five years, four months, and four days. The funeral, held on December 31, 1919, was attended by over five thousand people. A private service at the McKeever residence on Queen Street was held at 1:00 p.m., with a procession at 1:30 p.m. to Christ Church for a public service at two o'clock, followed by the interment at the Fairview Cemetery. The *Listowel Standard* reported on the public service:

With full military honors Major McKeever was laid to rest on Wednesday afternoon in Fairview cemetery. Thousands of citizens from Listowel, the community and other parts of the province were present to pay their respects in tribute to the gallant soldier. A private service was held at the family residence after which the remains were taken to Christ church where a public service was held. The church edifice was not nearly large enough to accommodate all who wished to attend the service and many hundreds had to remain outside.

The rector, Rev. W.H. Dunbar, conducted the service, assisted by C.H. Buckland, of Guelph. The rector's sermon was eloquent and very appropriate. His text was from 2 Samuel 1: 22, 23; "From the blood of the slain, from the fat of the mighty, the bow of Jonathan turned not back, and the sword of Saul returned not empty. Saul and Jonathan were lovely in their lives, and in their death they were not divided; they were swifter than eagles, they were stronger than lions." Speaking of the most beautiful lamentation of King David over Saul and Johnathan, Rev. Mr. Dunbar felt he could choose no more appropriate words for the present occasion. "But it is not so much the tribute which he pays to Saul that I am concerned about today," said the speaker, "but the glowing and deserving tribute paid to a gallant soldier of Israel, to a friend and brother. He feels that no common man have fallen, but the beauty of Israel, her ornament and her glory, men of indomitable courage who had overcome seemingly insurmountable difficulties again and again on "the field of battle." The speaker felt that these words were most appropriate in the present occasion.

Referring to Major McKeever, he said: "There lies the hero of a hundred flights, a man who risked his own life many times that we might breathe the air of freedom, yea, that we might live, and because he was swifter than eagles and stronger than lions, he did his part nobly and well to crown our arms with victory and to make the name of Canada ring throughout the world and to cast a halo of glory around this town and parish; a young man 25 years of age whom King George had decorated and Canada idolized. His life as a soldier is well known to all but his life as a civilian is not so well known. Having known him for years," continued the speaker, "I could say nothing more suitable than 'He was lovely and pleasant in life.' He had a way of winning himself into the hearts of all and all who knew him loved him. It is with heavy hearts we bow in humble submission to the will of God and say 'Thy Will Be Done.'"

As the choir sang the Nunc Dimmittis the remains were reverently taken to the rear of the church, where for over an hour throngs of sympathizing friends marched past the casket to view for the last time the great soldier.

Led by a firing party of 60 returned men under the command of Lieut. G.E. Harron, to the strains of the "Dead March" played by the G.W.V.A. band of Stratford, the solemn funeral procession marched from the church to the cemetery. Following the firing party and band was the gun carriage carrying the fallen hero, then the mourners and ... 75 returned veterans and the Mayor and members of the town Council. The funeral services at Fairview cemetery were conducted by Capt. C.H. Buckland, of Guelph, a retired chaplain and a former rector here. Three volleys were fired in honor of the dead and as the solemn notes of the "Last Post" were sounded the brave and gallant soldier was laid to rest. The pallbearers were Capts. Morse, Johnson, Salter, Brookbell, and Lieuts. Kerruish, (Harry G.) Kent, McIntosh and (Lyle) Kidd.

In honor of Major McKeever, the flags were flying at half mast since the news of his death reached town,

Fairview Cemetery, Listowel, Ontario.

McKeever's gravesite,
Fairview Cemetery.

and at the request of Mayor Watson, all business in Listowel ceased from one to four p.m. Wednesday. The W.P.L., the I.O.D.E., the town council and the Board of Education attended the funeral in a body. In addition to all the local soldiers, many officers from other points were present. Col Bishop, V.C., and Col Barker, V.C., could not be present and Capt Salter represented them.

Besides his bereaved parents Major McKeever is survived by his two sisters, Miss Marjorie McKeever, General Hospital, Hamilton, and Mrs. Thompson, Elma, and four brothers, George at Edmonton, Adam, Regina, James in Vancouver and Charlie at Guelph.

Except Mr. James McKeever, who was unavoidably absent, all the members of the family were home for the funeral, also an uncle Mr. George McKeever, Edmonton; Mr. and Mrs. Ellis, Hamilton; Mr. and Mrs. Matthews, Guelph, and Mr. Wisener of Toronto, were also present.[2]

Gone was one of the great Canadian air aces of the First World War. His life snuffed out way too soon.

EPILOGUE

Sixty-eight years after McKeever's death, his achievements were once again recognized in a ceremony in Listowel on Sunday, October 18, 1987. An Ontario Heritage Foundation plaque, in the town's Cenotaph Park, on Wallace Avenue North, was unveiled in Major McKeever's honour. As well, the Listowel Legion Branch 259 was renamed Major Andrew McKeever Branch 259, Royal Canadian Legion.

Some distinguished guests and hundreds of onlookers were present at a wreath-laying ceremony at Cenotaph Park. Laying the wreath were McKeever's nephews T. Campbell (Cam) Thompson and Andrew McKeever (Mac) Thompson, and Commander Adam Hamilton, Fleet Air Arm pilot in the First World War, a first cousin of Major McKeever.

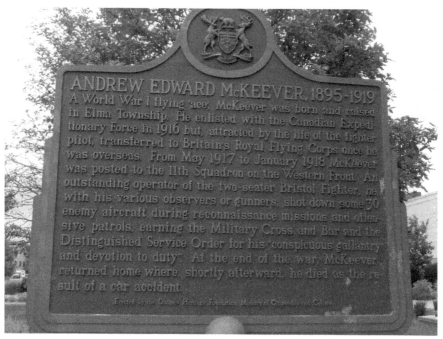

McKeever plaque in Listowel, Ontario.

Another wreath was laid by two Vimy Ridge veterans, William Green and Erskin Jardine, of the 11th Battalion, commemorating the seventieth anniversary of that battle.

The *Listowel Banner* reported on the ceremony:

> At the conclusion of the Cenotaph Park service, a fly-past was performed by two vintage aircraft from the Canadian Warplane Heritage Museum. An Anson, piloted by Bob McKinnon, and a Harvard, flown by Bob Hill made several passes over the park and dropped poppies onto that area of the town.
>
> A ceremony also took place at the Legion. Major-General Morton spoke on behalf of the minister of national defence. Morton said, "McKeever truly deserved the title king of the two seaters."

McKeever's machine gun, as displayed in the Listowel Legion Hall.

Mervyn "Bun" Morley, who had chaired the special committee which organized the recognition ceremony told those in attendance that Andrew McKeever was the second cousin of Dr. John McCrae who wrote the famous poem "In Flanders Fields."[3]

Later that day, a reception was held in the newly named legion's auditorium. Mr. Adam Hamilton presented the toast to the memory of Major McKeever. Joe C.W. Armstrong, a director of the Ontario Heritage Foundation, outlined Major McKeever's remarkable war record. He concluded his remarks with "He was truly a remarkable pilot and a crack shot."

A glass trophy case of McKeever memorabilia can be seen today at the Listowel legion, including his DSO and MC and Bar, his ID bracelet, the Lewis machine gun from his Bristol Fighter and a telescope his observers used. There are also many pictures of McKeever and the planes in which he flew.

The *Listowel Banner* also reported on the unveiling of a plaque at the legion hall itself: "Legion Provincial Past President Mr. William Smith unveiled the Legion plaque and District Commander G. Bridge read the inscription. Mr. Smith remarked after the ceremony that all heroes he talked to said the same thing, 'They said it was something that had to be done. This is a true Canadian dedication on a truly Canadian fall day,' Mr. Smith said of the ceremony."[4]

Andrew Edward McKeever has not been inducted into Canada's Aviation Hall of Fame but most definitely should be!

PART 3

Donald Roderick MacLaren

TWELVE

Don MacLaren's Early Years

Donald Roderick MacLaren was born in Ottawa on May 28, 1893, son of Robert James and Mary Jeanie MacLaren. His grandparents had been original Scottish settlers in the Pembroke area a few miles west of Ottawa. Donald moved to Calgary with his parents when he was a young boy in late 1900. The Fourth Census of Canada, 1901, lists the MacLaren family at that time as Robert, husband, age thirty-six; Mary J., wife, age thirty-six; a daughter, Gabel, age nine; Donald, age seven (at his last birthday); and another son, Roy, age five. Donald attended public school in Calgary and went to the Western Canada College, on 17 Avenue, for his high school years. At that time it was on the very edge of the city.

Donald also learned how to shoot a gun. Donald's father had been taught to shoot a rifle by his father, so he was going to pass down the family skill to his two sons.

His father gave him a small shotgun and set up a trap
beside the river at the back of their house. There the
whole family shot at clay pigeons, and Donald soon
became an excellent shot. It was not long before he
was shooting duck and prairie chickens, and year by
year he developed the keen eye and quick judgment
which were such an essential part of his later success
in the air.[1]

The family left Calgary in 1911, a year before the first Calgary
Stampede, and moved to Vancouver. Donald did not stay there long,
as he applied to and was accepted by McGill University in Montreal in
October 1912. There he studied mechanical engineering for two years to
February 1914. Due to an illness, he had to give up his studies and return
to Vancouver, where he took a surveyors course.

The male members of the family then moved to the remote hamlet
of Keg River Prairie in northern Alberta, over a hundred miles north of
Peace River Crossing, the nearest railway station. There they opened a
fur-trading post in competition with the Hudson's Bay Company and
Revillon Frères. There was so much virgin forest and land to be hunted
that the competition did not matter to the MacLarens. They befriended
the local Cree and Denesuline (Chipewyan) trappers and would travel
with them by canoe in the summer and mush dogs in the winter to get to
the remote traplines to pick up the furs.

Life was tough and primitive in the north, but the three MacLarens
survived and settled into their new life. Isolated in this remote part of
the country, they did not realize that a worldwide conflict had begun
in August of 1914. They continued to live their lives as they had been
doing; Donald and his brother and father trapped for two years, from
1914 to 1916. In the spring of 1916, Donald put his surveyor training
to work and assisted a government party to survey the sixth principal
meridian. When he returned in the fall, he discovered his brother, Roy,
had enlisted in the army.

Lieutenant Colonel George Drew, in *Canada's Fighting Airmen,* describes what the other two did:

Donald and his father soon came to the same decision. It meant a heavy loss, giving up their established business but the following spring, having sold their interests as best they could, they went south to Vancouver and offered their services. R.J. MacLaren, the father, had the figure of a youth, tall, erect, keen-eyed and fit, but in spite of every effort, he was rejected for active service because of his age. He served with the Imperial Munitions Board, however, until the end of the war and did excellent work. Donald enlisted with the Royal Flying Corps.[2]

MacLaren listed on his military record his civilian occupation as surveyor, noting that he had been employed as one from June 1915 to November 1916.

In a speech at a reunion of Canadian pilots in Vancouver in May 1979, Don MacLaren admitted to wanting first to join the navy. "I was eager to join the Navy, the Bell Bottom Navy, but was told their quota had been filled. Then we learned the RFC was establishing in Ontario. I applied and was told to report to Capt. Tweedale at Work Point barracks Victoria, and 3 weeks later boarded the CPR at Vancouver with six others from Victoria some of these you may remember; Bert Crowe, Pinky Walker, and Bill Cutler."[3]

Donald MacLaren travelled by train from Vancouver to Toronto in early May 1917 to begin his flight training.

THIRTEEN

Training to Be a Pilot

MacLaren and his fellow cadets reported to Captain Cooper of the RFC at the Imperial Oil Building in Toronto. There they were accepted, attested, and they filled out other official documents.

MacLaren's attestation papers into the Royal Flying Corps, completed and signed on May 10, 1917, in Toronto, record his age as twenty-four, his height as five feet six inches and his "Girth when fully expanded" as thirty-seven inches. Distinctive marks included "Scar on left side of head" and "Scar on forehead."[1]

One can only speculate how he got these scars. Was he in a brawl in a saloon in northern Alberta? Or did he get into a knife fight with a local trapper? Or was he attacked by a grizzly bear when walking the traplines? In all likelihood it was the latter, as Donald was a teetotaller and never touched alcohol.

They were then fitted out with their uniforms. MacLaren described these as

> the latest style dress for 3rd class Air Mechanics which was the rank we were given as flight Cadets. The tunics and slacks were of coarse khaki, the boots were well made, but on hot days we were mostly uncomfortable.
>
> A walking out dress was issued, the typical RFC tunic of good cloth buttoned up to the neck, known as the maternity jacket, with the Beauchamp and Howe version of British officer breeches, Fox puttees topped and held together by a handsome Sam Browne belt to be worn without the shoulder strap until we became commissioned officers.[2]

The cadets were billeted in the University of Toronto students' residence, close to the parade square and the School of Military Aeronautics (SMA), where they were taught the theory of flight. MacLaren makes the following comments on that experience:

> To keep us from being bored, we were paraded at 6:00 am now and then for inspection — boots and buttons polished — then PT (physical training) by Sgt. Major Figg, a strong voice but not offensive.
>
> The instructors at the school had been pilots on Fe2b and Be2cs but gave us little information on how to attack the enemy. Two weeks at the SMA brought written exams; we all passed and were posted to flight training stations; Mohawk, Deseronto, and Long Branch, and later Armour Heights and Leaside.[3]

Donald MacLaren's initial flight training was at the Curtiss School at Long Branch, twelve miles west of Toronto on the lakeshore. The Curtiss School began operations in 1915 and throughout the war young pilot cadets trained there, learning the basic elements of flight. MacLaren was part of "Y" CRS or Canadian Replacement Squadron. At that time, Captain Sherrin was in command as the chief flight instructor, with Lieutenant Stan Taylor as assistant instructor. S.F. Wise in *Canadian Airmen and the First World War* explains the tests the trainees faced:

> With the exception of the FAI [Federation Aeronautique Internationale] examination at the end of the course, all flying at the Curtiss School was dual. The tests called for three separate solo flights. Two involved flying a series of figures-of-eight around two posts 500 metres apart. In these flights the aircraft's engine had to be cut before or at the moment of landing and the machine brought to a stop not more than fifty metres from a predetermined point. On the third flight the student was required to gain at least 100 metres of altitude and then to cut the engine, gliding down without power to a successful landing. These tests were witnessed by official observers and certificates were issued in the name of the Royal Aero Club of the United Kingdom, which then represented all parts of the British Empire in the FAI.[4]

MacLaren went on his first dual flight on June 18, 1917. It lasted a mere five minutes, during which he flew at eight hundred feet, flying a square around the airfield. His logbook records the landing as "bumpy." He was up again on June 19, flying for thirty minutes, to an altitude of one thousand feet; apparently, the landing was similarly bumpy. His forty-minute flight on June 20 reached four thousand feet. Again it ended in a bumpy landing. He flew twice on June 21, each time for over an hour. He flew only once on June 22.

By 1917 cadet pilots were receiving instruction on the Curtiss "Jenny," JN-4A. Flight training could be quite boring, waiting for your turn to fly. There were many more cadets than Jennys available, so there was much waiting around.

MacLaren's first solo flight was on June 23. It lasted for only ten minutes. Prior to that, he had had only six dual flights and had acquired only three-and-a-half hours of flying time. On the occasion of MacLaren's first flight, Captain Sherrin "climbed out of his seat with the engine turning over gently and shouted to me, ok go ahead and kill yourself."

MacLaren was up again soloing the same day. Writing of that, he commented, "I came in too fast, overshot and ended up in the swamp where the landing gear came off. As I returned to the hangar dragging the wheels with me and reported to Captain Sherrin, he remarked, 'Yes I saw you come in about 90 mph. There isn't that much room around here. But anyway you have to smash up more than one aeroplane before you learn how to fly.'"[5]

MacLaren flew the next day and on June 25 as well. By month's end, he had a total of seven-and-a-quarter hours in the air, three hours and forty minutes of which were solo.

MacLaren flew eleven times from July 2 to July 17, 1917, at which point he was transferred to the newly constructed aerodrome at Armour Heights in north Toronto. There he joined Squadron 90 of the Central Training School.

Canada's method of training new cadets became known as the Armour Heights System, from the location where the training details were worked out. Here, a Canadian instructor's manual was created and instructors were trained in applying it.

MacLaren was at Armour Heights for only two weeks of flying, but was often in the air three or four times a day. The availability of machines was much greater at Armour Heights than at Long Branch. MacLaren was instructed in artillery observation, bombing, and reading Panneau (ground strips), along with wireless training. He also flew figure eights at an altitude of 8,500 feet. On July 19 alone, he was in the air a total of eleven times!

At the end of July, MacLaren was transferred to Squadron 81 CTS as part of the School of Aerial Gunnery at Camp Borden. At the time, Camp Borden had five squadrons in place, squadrons 78 to 82. There, MacLaren was instructed on aerial photography, aerial gunnery, map reading, cross-country flying, and formation flying. Some of the JN-4s were fitted with a camera gun, which would record whether or not you would have scored a hit on the aircraft you were attacking. S.F. Wise, in *Canadian Airmen and the First World War*, describes gunnery training at the camp:

> After a group of officer and NCO gunnery specialists arrived in April, a School of Aerial Gunnery was formed on 1 May at Camp Borden. Its beginnings were small. A first class of eighteen cadets did a limited amount of ground range firing on one of the school's two machine guns. As equipment came in from Britain and new instructors were trained, the school expanded.... Camera guns were received in July. By autumn the course was set at three weeks, and cadets were doing aerial firing with fixed Vickers machine guns after synchronizing gear had been designed for the JN4 so that the gun could be fired forward through the propeller arc.[6]

For aerial gunnery training, some machines were modified so the trainee could fire a machine gun and not hit the propeller. MacLaren explains how it worked and the dangers of such training:

> For the aerial part of the training the pupil was strapped into a bucket shaped seat rigged over the forward cockpit so that he could shoot at whatever target the pilot aimed him at without hitting the propeller. This was sandy dune country and the air close to the ground very bumpy. After two pupils had been thrown from their seats and lost their lives, one of these was our friend Pinky Walker from Victoria. The exercise was changed to evenings and early mornings.[7]

The cadets also practised firing the Vickers machine gun on the ground toward targets, or butts, as they were called. It was hot work carrying the machine guns to the sand-dune target areas of Camp Borden, firing, dismantling, and reassembling the machine guns over and over again.

By August 6, MacLaren has amassed a total of thirty-six hours and forty minutes in the air, of which thirty-two hours and fifty-five minutes were solo. For the balance of August and for the month of September, there are no entries in his flying log. This is because he had been moved to the new station at Leaside to await receipt of his commission.

By August 19 MacLaren had received his pilot's wings. He described what it was like to no longer be a cadet: "We were now 2nd Lts. RFC and could remove the white 'chastity' band from our caps, put up the coveted shoulder strap on our Sam Brownes and practise returning the salutes from whatever lower ranks we met who cared to acknowledge our new found superiority."[8]

After being commissioned as officers, MacLaren and his fellow second lieutenants were given ten days leave. They were then to report to Union Station in Toronto, where they boarded a train bound for Montreal. Waiting for them at the Montreal docks was the SS *Metagama*, the very same ship that had transported Alan McLeod to England in August 1917. MacLaren describes the voyage:

> Nine days it took to cross the Atlantic as we zigged and zagged to avoid submarine attack then dropped anchor in a little south of [*sic*] Ireland harbor called Bere Haven.
>
> After 2 days here we rounded the point one morning to see a sinking ship dead ahead of us; two destroyers threshing around dropping depth charges. Back to the harbor for another night then up the Bristol Channel to Liverpool.[9]

At Liverpool they boarded a train for Euston Station in London. MacLaren stayed at the Queen Mary Club for Officers on Eaton Square. At night they could hear the dull throbbing sound of German bombers and the crash of bombs exploding. It was a sign of things to come.

The next day the second lieutenants reported to the Air Board at Cecil House in the Strand and were met there by Major Baird. He offered them the choice of training in scouts or in two-seaters. It seemed to MacLaren that "the Sopwith Camel looked as if it could take care of itself."[10]

MacLaren and his comrades were posted to the Turnberry Aerial Gunnery Station. There they practised firing a Lewis machine gun at ground targets from the nacelle of a F.E.2b, which was at the front of the machine. In these planes, the pilot was seated behind the trainee. Or they flew in B.E.2cs, firing over the head of the pilot. After about ten days of gunnery practice, they moved on to No. 43 Training Squadron at the Ternhill aerodrome in Shropshire.

Located near the towns of Newport and Market Drayton, Ternhill first opened in 1916 and was equipped with Avro 504 aircraft. These two-seater machines were mainly used for training purposes and were manufactured by A.V. Roe and Company, Ltd., in Manchester. Herris and Pearson, in *Aircraft of World War I: 1914–1918,* give the specifications of the aircraft: "Generating 100 h.p. its rotary engine lifted the aircraft at 50 mph and cruised easily at 80 mph. It had a ceiling of 13,500 feet and a top speed of 88mph."[11]

The Avro 504 was able to perform a steady glide with the engine shut off and the pilot's hands off the controls. It could also get out of a spin without any intervention by the pilot. Flying officer in training Roderick Ward Maclennan described the stability of the Avro as follows: "I flew an Avro for 20 minutes the other day with both hands in my pockets and then only took hold of the stick because it was time to land. Does not this speak well for the stability of the Avro? Even if the engine stops all the machine does is to glide slowly to earth, keeping the correct gliding angle herself."[12]

MacLaren's first flight in an Avro (B3106) was on October 1, 1917. It was a dual flight lasting only fifteen minutes. He had three other dual flights that same day, and soloed for fifteen minutes before the day was out. During the first week of October, MacLaren practised doing loops, stalls, stall turns, spins, and Immelmann turns. The latter manoeuvre, named after the German ace Max Immelmann, involved the pilot beginning to loop his machine, only to stop the loop at the top, and do a half roll to reverse direction.

MacLaren mastered these manoeuvres and impressed his instructors. However, for whatever reason, MacLaren did not get on well with Senior Flight Instructor Captain Mansell.

> Mansell who believed we lacked discipline ordered early morning [practice flights] and accused two of us of being late. We were ordered to sleep in the hangar which we resented as none of us had been late. An appeal to the C.O. [Commanding Officer] got nowhere but assistance from the MO (Medical Officer) was readily furnished by means of a chit declaring that these two officers were unfit to sleep in the hangars.[13]

MacLaren was flying in other types of aircraft than just the Avro. For example, on October 10 he flew a Bristol Scout with a Gnome engine. On October 12 he piloted a Bristol Scout with a Le Rhône engine, and the same day was up in a Nieuport Scout. On October 13 he flew a DH.5 scout. The DH.5 was a curious-looking machine because its upper wing (or plane as it was called) was positioned back from the lower, leading wing; most other biplanes reversed the placement of the two wings, i.e., the upper wing was forward and the lower wing slightly behind the upper one.

Practice was the name of the game and MacLaren continued to perform Immelmanns, loops, and stalls at heights of three thousand to 3,500 feet. He also flew circuits around Ternhill. From October 1 to October 9, he flew a total of eight hours. From October 10 to 13, he logged six hours and twenty minutes, often flying three to four times a day. MacLaren flew DH.5s and Nieuport Scouts the week of October 18–23, logging seven hours and forty minutes. To his bag of aerobatic tricks he added the sharp turn, which he later used successfully in combat to avoid the fire of enemy aircraft. For the week of October 24 to 29, MacLaren flew Bristols, doing circuits and practising formation flying. He also went on simulated bombing runs. He flew for an hour or two hours at a time, logging five hours and forty minutes that week. He ended the month

Second Lieutenant Donald R. MacLaren (left) with a DH.5 aircraft of the Royal Flying Corps, England, 1917.

practising loops, spins, and rolls in a Bristol. MacLaren's total accumulated time aloft was sixty-seven hours forty minutes, of which sixty hours thirty minutes was solo.

In early November 1917, MacLaren was transferred to No. 34 Training Squadron, also located at the Ternhill base. During the first week in that squadron, MacLaren continued to practice loops, spins, rolls, and stall turns, flying the Bristol Scout. In a loop, MacLaren would start by putting the joystick forward to get the nose of the machine down to gain speed. Eighty miles an hour turned into eighty-five miles per hour. At that point, he would bring the joystick slowly back. The horizon fell away and he climbed upward into a blank sky. He could feel the force of the climb pushing him against his seat, tighter and tighter. Then, as he reached the pinnacle of the loop, he was suspended in the air with nothing but his harness holding him into the cockpit. His machine would stall momentarily at the top of the loop. Blood would rush to his head. The opposite horizon would appear from behind him. He would let the stick go slowly forward, and shut off the fuel as the aircraft fell toward the earth in the downward side of the loop. The horizon he had been originally facing would reappear as he finished the loop in perfect fashion.

On November 8 MacLaren had his first solo in a Sopwith Camel, number 6435. Norman Franks, in *Sopwith Camel Aces of World War 1*, describes this aircraft:

> The Camel, a design by Herbert Smith of Sopwith, came together through the efforts of a team of Sopwith men. Designed specifically to house two guns up-front, firing through the propeller, the scout bore some resemblance to the Pup, although the design team decided to have the main mass weight positioned right up front, with the engine, guns/ammunition, pilot, fuel and oil tanks all housed within the first third of the fuselage. This gave it a rather squat, bullish appearance.
>
> Another identifying feature was the wings. The upper-wing, to assist production, was made in one piece, perfectly straight with no dihedral, while the lower wings had increased dihedral. Ailerons were fitted to upper and lower wings, making the whole structure very manoeuvrable, especially with a 130-hp Clerget engine as its power plant. This large rotary engine (that is to say the whole engine went round with the propeller), which rotated clockwise when viewed from the cockpit, together with the mass frontal weight gave the Camel a massive right-hand turn capability.
>
> This in itself was fine for pilots once they had gained experience on the type, but in the beginning it came as a shock, especially to pilots coming off docile training types, or service machines like the Pup. The Camel's nose tended to drop during a steep turn to starboard (with the rotating engine), and for it to rise with a port climbing turn (against the rotating engine). In both cases, the pilot had to put on left rudder.[14]

Like most pilots flying the Camel for the first time, MacLaren struggled. He had to remember to apply a light left rudder most of the time to counteract the twist to the right. If he didn't, the machine would immediately flop into a right-hand spin. Many a trainee pilot met his end this way. One had to constantly fly the Camel. It was so light on the controls that the slightest jerk would result in the Camel gyrating all over the sky. Once the pilot got used to it, though, the sensitivity of the controls became an asset. Camels were very nimble machines. The novices often found them difficult to land, although MacLaren's logbook makes no mention of a rough landing on his first flight in a Camel.

Herris and Pearson provide the specs for this machine: "The Camel could climb to 5,000 feet in no time at all due to its maximum speed of 117 mph. It had a ceiling of 19,000 feet. Its wing span was 28 feet and had a length of 18 feet 9 inches. Its height was 8 feet 6 inches."[15]

On November 9 MacLaren was again in a Camel (6434), practising vertical banks. He flew three different Camels on November 11 — 6434, 6219, and 6435 — doing circuits, fighting practice, and landings. From November 14 to November 18, MacLaren continued to practise his rolls, spins, and dives, all the time in a Camel. Gunnery practice was also part of the training. MacLaren recorded firing five hundred rounds from his dual Vickers machine guns on November 20.

During his time with No. 34 Training Squadron, MacLaren logged a total of twelve hours and thirty-five minutes, of which nine hours and twenty-five minutes were in Camels.

By the time his training was finally over, from June 18 when he was at Long Branch to the end of November in England, five and a half months, MacLaren had amassed a total of eighty-one hours and fifteen minutes flying time, of which seventy-three hours and five minutes were solo.

Donald MacLaren could hardly wait to get to France and be a part of a combat squadron. His wish came true in early December 1917. Initially, MacLaren and his mates were shipped to the Scout Pool at Fienvillers, France, meaning he could be sent to any scout squadron in need of replacements. The morning after his arrival, "a pompous young officer called out my name informing me I was to accompany him to 46 Sqdn. in the usual Crossley tender, where I reported to Major Babington one of the finest officers I ever met."[16]

FOURTEEN

No. 46 Squadron

Donald MacLaren joined No. 46 Squadron just days before its new commanding officer was appointed on December 5, 1917. He was Major R.H.S. Mealing, replacing Major P. Babington, who had been CO since July 14, 1916. MacLaren had taken an instant liking to Babington and his squadron, describing it as

> a cheerful gathering of fine young officers well experienced and enjoying the leadership of a CO worth following.
>
> After dinner Major Babington lost no time recording the silhouette of the new boy. You just sat between a sheet of thin paper and a lamp; the major traced the

outline of your profile on the sheet, filled in the date and you were asked to sign it.[1]

No. 46 Squadron, part of III Brigade, had arrived in France on October 20, 1916, and flew out of Saint-Omer aerodrome. By the time MacLaren arrived, the squadron was stationed at the aerodrome of Le Hameau, nestled in the orchard of Filescamp Farm, a few miles west of the city of Arras. The aerodrome continued to have the heroic spirit of the famous British pilot Albert Ball, who was based there when he perished on a mission in May of 1917.

In November, No. 46 Squadron had begun receiving Sopwith Camels. At that time, the squadron was supporting the operations of the British Third Army before the town of Cambrai, an important rail hub that transported German troops and supplies to the front. It was often a target for Allied bombing raids.

The No. 46 Squadron History describes an incident involving the squadron's Captain A.G. (Arthur Gould) Lee:

> On the 23rd November machines of No. 46 Squadron attached enemy infantry in Bourlon Wood, Fontaine, Marquion, etc. Several officers exhausting their ammunition returned for more, and all brought back valuable information in addition to the exact position of our troops.
>
> In these same operations, Captain Lee, having helped to drive down an enemy two-seater north of Bourlon Wood, dropped four bombs into the wood and then fired at enemy infantry on Fontaine. While temporarily retiring to correct jams in his guns, a shell burst beneath him, forcing him to land so close to the enemy that he was unable to burn his machine and had to run 100 yards under hot machine-gun fire. During his walk back to Cantaing, under the direction of a guide, a shell burst in a house Captain Lee

was passing and he was blown across the road. This officer later got into communication with his squadron and while waiting helped stretcher-bearers to bring in the wounded.[2]

Lee, in his fascinating book *No Parachute: The Exploits of a Fighter Pilot in the First World War*, comments on the arrival of MacLaren: "Two batches of new pilots have arrived during the past few days. They seem a very good lot. Among them are two more Canadians, MacLaren and Falkenburg. Amazing how many Canadians there are in the R.F.C."[3]

MacLaren was assigned to A Flight, under Captain V.A.H. Robeson, MC. And his first flight in a Camel with his new squadron was on December 4. He did circuits for fifteen minutes, getting accustomed to the geography around the aerodrome. On December 5–7, he was up doing firing and flying practice in Camels and Sopwith Pups; he repeated this exercise on December 10 and 12. At no time did MacLaren venture near the front lines — not that he knew where they were.

On December 15, 1917, however, Captain Robeson took MacLaren and the rest of A Flight over the lines for the first time, on a flight lasting two-and-a-half hours. Robeson wanted the pilots to become familiar with the geography at the front. Another flight that day lasted an hour and fifty minutes. On this flight, an E.A., a brightly coloured Albatros scout, flying two hundred feet below them, was spotted over the town of Arras but no combat ensued. Robeson knew his young pilots were not yet ready for combat. They still had a lot to learn.

A Flight was up again on December 19 on an offensive patrol over the front lines. This time two E.A. were spotted and two hundred rounds were fired by the rookie Camel pilots, but they were too far from their targets to score any hits. More flights took place on December 22 and 23. Enemy aircraft were spotted but no combat occurred.

Christmas was celebrated with turkey, oysters, puddings, and other rich foods, all served with champagne. There was a church parade and a Christmas concert. The real celebration was the announcement that three sergeants of No. 46 Squadron had been awarded the Military Medal, recommended by Captain Lee.

Lee described the celebration:

> There was uproar, and everybody was pouring down
> drink without a care, whisky, port, champagne, beer,
> anything that was handy....
>
> At last we pulled clear, and went down to the Mess
> for our own dinner and our own drinks. Then we stag-
> gered up to the hangar again, this time for the concert
> which was excellent, but also for yet more drinks. How
> we got through it all, I just don't know. Almost the only
> one who was sober was MacLaren, who neither smokes
> nor drinks. Because the men knew I'd done the recom-
> mending, they plied me with neat whisky so persistently
> I was reduced to slyly pouring it to the ground behind
> my back. I can't remember much afterwards, except
> joining in a mad jamboree with everybody loosing off
> Very lights regardless.[4]

Captain Lee had to take up a patrol at 8:00 a.m. the next day. It
must have been a struggle for him. MacLaren's flight was in the air on
December 26 as well. He must have been the only one not hungover
from the festivities of Christmas Day. He was as sober as a church mouse.
Four enemy two-seaters were seen on December 26 and eight E.A. sight-
ed on December 28. Firing at long range, no combat ensued. MacLaren
and A Flight closed out the month of December doing fighting and
bombing practice. By the end of 1917, MacLaren had soloed for a total
of 101 hours and 45 minutes, with a total time in the air of 109 hours
and 55 minutes.

MacLaren and A Flight were in the air on New Year's Day, flying near
the German-held town of Cambrai. Flying at fifteen thousand feet, they
spotted six enemy scouts but did not engage them.

On January 3, 4, and 6, A Flight was on COP (Contact Offensive
Patrol). Some days, E.A. were seen, other days no E.A. were seen. Pilots
often went up in their machines to test their guns, since they were

notorious for jamming. MacLaren went up on January 7 for fifteen minutes, specifically to make sure his guns were in order, only to have them jam on a COP on January 9 when he attempted an attack on an enemy aircraft.

More offensive patrols occurred over Cambrai, or the "back country," as the Canadians in the squadron called it, on January 12 and 13. No. 46 Squadron was given the task of protecting a group of R.E.8 reconnaissance aircraft. Some German scouts were seen but they did not attack the squadron.

On January 19, at 11:15 a.m., A Flight leader Captain Robeson led Second Lieutenants Falkenberg, Bulman, and MacLaren on an offensive patrol between Cantaing and Cambrai. At twelve thousand feet they spotted a two-seater Albatros about five hundred feet above them. The flight pulled up toward the enemy and let loose about 350 rounds between them. The observer in the German machine returned the fire. The two-seater then dove on Captain Robeson, who took evasive action. He ended up under the E.A. and was able to shoot fifty rounds at it. That was enough for the Albatros, which made a hasty retreat eastward. A Flight did not pursue the Albatros, as four German scouts came upon them five hundred feet above and two hundred yards to the rear. The Germans were content to just take potshots at the Camels. After following A Flight for a while, they flew off east into the clouds around 12:15 p.m. The combat was recorded as indecisive.

MacLaren and the flight flew most days for the balance of January; however, there was little contact with the enemy. MacLaren was called on from time to time to take one of the squadron's Camels to another aerodrome to exchange for another machine, which he brought back to his squadron on the return trip. In all likelihood, he was exchanging a defective machine for one in total working order.

February was much like the month of January, with few sightings of enemy aircraft and virtually no aerial combats. Some flights were devoted to practising flying in formation, or, as in January, gun practice. Bomb practice took place on a number of days in the last week of February. This was the lull before the storm. The relative inactivity took its toll on the pilots, whose pent-up nervous energy had few releases.

Second Lieutenant D.R. MacLaren, No. 46 Squadron, RFC, Izel-lès-Hameau, France, January 1918.

A highlight of the month of February occurred when A Flight was chosen to compete in the aerial gunnery competition on February 16 at Berck-sur-Mer, near Étaples, on the coast of France. MacLaren describes the event:

> We captured the trophy, a large silver cigar box present-ed by General Sir Hugh Trenchard for competition by all scout squadrons of RFC Lt. Paul Bulman contribut-ed chiefly to our high score by his close in dog-fighting recorded by a 35mm cinema camera fastened to the starboard gun. I was able to win the shoot-off for clay birds with Major Breg Dallas of 41 Sqdn. This is where we lost our little Billy Cutler who had been with [us] all the way from Victoria. He had met a downdraft while diving on a ground target.[5]

In recognition of his performance at the gunnery competition, MacLaren was granted two weeks leave. However, due to poor weather MacLaren cut short his leave and returned to No. 46 Squadron on February 24.

During the last weeks of February and the first three weeks of March 1918, the Germans were building up their forces behind their lines in preparation for the big push that was to be called Operation Michael. The increased German activity was noticed by reconnaissance flights and led to No. 46 Squadron and many other squadrons in the area being or-dered to carry out low-bombing missions on troop concentrations, rail-way yards, and supply areas.

On February 26, MacLaren and the rest of the flight took off for a bombing mission over the Marcoing Canal. At low altitude, between fifty and one hundred feet, they attacked barges on the canal. MacLaren let loose his four twenty-pound bombs on a barge and saw it burst apart.

Around this time, Captain Robeson was promoted to major and took over command of No. 29 Squadron. Captain Marchant took his place as flight commander.

D.R. MacLaren (left) and J. Gilmore of No. 46 Squadron, in front of Nissen hut.

MacLaren recalled receiving a visit at that time from an old friend.

> A visitor from 70 sqdn. landed in a shiny nose Camel
> and out stepped our old friend George Howsam. He
> was the same "up and at em" George and had plenty
> to talk about. They had been tangling with Albatross
> scouts and he demonstrated the methods they were
> using to shoot them down. This demonstration from
> George [words missing in document] … me and many
> successes we had later can be the result of … inspiration
> we got that day from George Howsam.
>
> Right here I should repeat a conviction which I held
> for many years. Had he been able to carry on as he was
> doing when he [*sic*] forced to leave the combat zones for
> a hospital bed, George Howsam would very well have
> the [*sic*] leading Canadian fighter pilot.[6]

The first three months in No. 46 were relatively uneventful for
MacLaren. Apart from the few, dangerous, low-level bombing raids he
took part in, there were not many encounters with German aircraft.
As S.F. Wise explains, "for nearly three months, from 15 December
to 5 March 1918, the only things to distinguish Second Lieutenant
MacLaren from most of the other Sopwith Camel pilots of the Western
Front were his age — he was then twenty-five, old for a fighter pilot —
and the fact that he had not yet shot down an enemy plane or been shot
down himself."[7]

March 6 saw MacLaren get his first victory. A flight, travelling west
of Douai with Captain G.E. Thomson, Second Lieutenant MacLaren
(flying Camel B9153), and Lieutenants Jenkins, Vlasto, and Debenham,
observed three enemy aircraft, all painted a silver grey, flying at thirteen
thousand feet. These were new-type German models, with two horizontal tailplanes. They were probably German Hannover scouts. The flight
report filled out after landing back at the RAF aerodrome and signed by
the five pilots reads as follows:

Keeping the sun behind, we approached the E.A. who were still above. The E.A. on seeing the patrol, dived. Capt. Thomson got on one E.A.'s tail and fired a short burst at very close range. The E.A. turned on its back, when Capt. Thomson fired again. The E.A. went down in a spin. Capt. Thomson left the E.A. at 5,000 feet, he was still spinning. 2/Lt. MacLaren closed on another E.A. and fired a burst of 100 rds. at 100 yds. range. The E.A. stalled and tail-slid and was last seen at 6,000 feet by 2/Lt. MacLaren evidently going down completely out of control. Lt. Jenkins fired about 60 rds. at the third E.A. at 150 yds. range. The E.A. side-slipped, turned on its back and disappeared under him, losing him in the mist. Lt. A.G. Vlasto who was flying above the formation with Lt. Debenham fired about 100 rds. at 200 yds. range at two E.A. who dived away East. Lt. Debenham observed four E.A. approaching from the East of Douai. He flew toward the E.A. and fired about 80 rds. at the nearest one and then all four E.A. turned East.[8]

The report concluded two E.A. were driven down out of control and one was driven down. MacLaren was credited with one of the E.A. driven down out of control.

The next day, MacLaren's flight had a bombing mission. Flying at 3,500 feet, the Camels attacked railway trucks (the term used at the time) at Brebières. The trucks were destroyed. On March 8 another bombing mission was ordered. This time the flight bombed the town of Quéant. These were dangerous missions, as the squadron encountered heavy anti-aircraft fire, also known as flak. The Camels had to fly low enough to be able to hit the targets with some accuracy but that meant the ground fire was more likely to hit them. Upon his return to base, MacLaren noticed his machine had been shot through. MacLaren's Camel B9153 was repaired sufficiently by the next day for him to join the flight in bombing targets at Marquion and shooting at cavalry at Graincourt.

MacLaren's second victory was four days later, on March 10, 1918. He and Second Lieutenant M.M. Freehill were on an early morning bombing mission to Marcoing. Flying over the target at low altitude, the two pilots dropped their bombs on soldiers' billets and made direct hits. They then spotted five Albatros D.Vs west of Graincourt and below them. MacLaren dove on one of the Albatros, firing short bursts of twenty rounds each. The German scout tried to evade by climbing away. This allowed Freehill to dive on it, firing his own short bursts of machine-gun fire. Freehill damaged the tail section of the Albatros. As it continued to pull up, it fired at MacLaren, who manoeuvred his Camel behind the E.A. With the sun at his back, MacLaren dove onto the Albatros and fired a long burst, aiming for the pilot and his engine. The Albatros keeled over and went straight down, completely out of control. As it fell, it broke up into pieces. Both Freehill and MacLaren returned safely to their aerodrome. MacLaren's machine was by then totally out of ammunition.

The Albatros D.V was the mainstay of the German air forces in early 1918. Though it had replaced the D.III model in the summer of 1917, it was outclassed by the Camel. Norman Franks in *Albatros Aces of World War 1* describes the D.V as follows:

> The new fighter did not give the *Jasta* pilots much of a combat advantage over the vastly improving Allied fighters. Indeed, the high command realized that the D V could not hope for the technical superiority its predecessors from Albatros had enjoyed over its foes from mid-1916 through to the spring of 1917. Instead, they hoped that improved construction techniques associated with the new fighter would allow an increased number of aircraft to be supplied to the *Jastas,* who in turn would use these to numerically overwhelm the opposition.
>
> The main recognition feature of the D V was its rounded fuselage and rudder, whilst "under the skin" there were other improvements like aileron cables enclosed in the upper wing. Despite these modifications,

the D V still had a propensity for breaking up when held in a prolonged dive, which created more than a little unease amongst its pilots.[9]

MacLaren and No. 46 Squadron were on bomb patrol again on March 12, with Moevrer as their target. The Camels attacked transport vehicles. The fire from the ground was quite heavy. MacLaren saw one Camel spinning down out of control and in flames. At the end of the mission, pilots Muir and Berg were missing. The next day the squadron bombed Vis-en-Artois. On March 18, MacLaren attacked a German observation balloon at Brebières, but without success.

FIFTEEN

Operation Michael

P lans for Operation Michael were nearing completion. General Ludendorff's sixty-two divisions were to smash through the British Fifth and Third Armies, then wheel northwest to envelop Arras. The attack began on the morning of March 21, 1918, as John Toland describes in his book *No Man's Land: 1918, the Last Year of the Great War.*

> It was 4:40 A.M. and the most massive bombardment in history had begun. Along a front of more than fifty miles, some 6,000 guns, more than 2,500 of which were heavy or superheavy, simultaneously began pounding the Third and Fifth Armies. The bombardment was a carefully orchestrated program devised by Germany's leading

artillery expert, Lieutenant Colonel Georg Bruchmüller, nicknamed "Durchbruhmüller" (Breakthrough Müller). The hellish din was such that when 2,500 British guns answered the additional noise was hardly noticeable.[1]

When the bombardment ceased, it was the German mortar fire's turn to land in the British trenches. As the morning mist cleared, thousands of enemy infantry poured across no-man's-land, taking the British positions and beyond. Both the Third and the Fifth Armies were being overrun.

All available British squadrons flew into the thick of the battle. MacLaren, flying his trusty and reliable Camel B9153, was one of eight pilots from No. 46 Squadron who took off in the afternoon, intending to knock out a long-range gun mounted on a railway car. This particular artillery piece had been firing salvos onto the Saint-Pol rail centre, causing considerable destruction. The two flights of Camels flew behind the German lines in search of the big gun.

The German artillery piece was finally spotted in the area of Brebières, about six miles behind the German lines. The eight Camels came in low over their target, dodging the anti-aircraft fire. Flying in single file, line astern, the first Camel dove onto the target. They could see the great muzzle of the beast poking out from the trees at a rail siding. Arch Whitehouse, in *Heroes of the Sunlit Sky*, describes what happened next:

> The Camels in a tight formation nosed down for the attack. The leader's plane jerked as his rack of bombs went out, but he missed by several yards. MacLaren was next and he tugged his release and put two Coopers smack on the railcar. The Camel bounced off the bolster of concussion and jerked back into a climb. MacLaren banked over hard and came back with two more bombs and nosed down again. He pulled the release and his last two bombs dropped on the tracks just behind the gun. There was another double blast and the flat-bed truck collapsed and the rails were splayed wide. That big gun would be out of action for weeks![2]

Having released his load of four twenty-pound bombs, MacLaren returned toward the lines. Flying at one thousand feet, he spotted a German LVG two-seater below him.* In a diving turn, MacLaren got onto the E.A.'s tail, and fired off one hundred rounds at close range. The E.A. went into a spin. MacLaren saw the two-seater crash on the west corner of the town of Douai. He then climbed toward the lines. At about 4:30 p.m., MacLaren saw a German balloon above Biache-Saint-Vaast at an altitude of about 1,500 feet. MacLaren approached the balloon at top speed so the anti-aircraft guns placed around the balloon would have little time to aim at his Camel. Getting as close as possible, he let loose one hundred rounds. The balloon burst into flames. The observer bailed out and MacLaren could see, below him, the observer's parachute opening. He must have wondered why Allied pilots were not issued parachutes.

On getting over the front lines, MacLaren headed south. He saw another German LVG two-seater, this one painted bright green, below him over the town of Graincourt. The time was about 4:45 p.m. The German pilot and observer had spotted MacLaren, and gave him a burst of machine-gun fire. MacLaren quickly took evasive action and got into position to make a head-on dive on the E.A. Waiting until the last second, he fired fifty rounds straight into the German machine. It turned and dove away, the observer firing at MacLaren as it went down. MacLaren followed, firing three or four more bursts at the stricken aircraft, in all about another fifty rounds. The LVG went into a spin, the pilot mortally wounded. MacLaren saw the LVG crash just east of Marquion. For his efforts that day, MacLaren was credited with three victories: two two-seaters and a balloon. This fine work resulted in MacLaren's being awarded the Military Cross on April 2.

The citation, appearing in the *London Gazette* on June 22, 1918, for MacLaren's Military Cross, from His Majesty King George V, read,

---

* The LVG C.V saw action on the Western Front beginning in the spring of 1918. These were the machines MacLaren encountered in March. Powered by a two-hundred-hp Benz IV engine, it had a maximum speed of 155.3 mph and a service ceiling of 16,500 feet. It was armed with a 0.313-inch forward-facing machine gun and a rear-facing machine gun of similar size for the observer. The LVG C.V was a tough, reliable, manoeuvrable airplane that served with distinction until war's end.[3]

For conspicuous gallantry and devotion to duty. On one occasion, when on low bombing work, he bombed a long-range enemy gun 9,000 yards behind the lines, obtaining from a height of 200 feet two direct hits on the gun and two on the railway track alongside. When returning to our lines he encountered a hostile two-seater machine, which he shot down crashing to earth. He then attacked a balloon, which burst into flames, and finally, observing another enemy two-seater plane, he engaged it and finally succeeded in crashing it to earth. He has set an excellent example of gallantry and skill to his squadron.[4]

By March 21, the Germans had advanced more than a mile and a half into British-held territory; in some places they had penetrated four miles. Trying to halt this advance, No. 46 Squadron was the only single-seater squadron to be used exclusively for low-flying ground attacks. MacLaren recorded in his logbook for March 22, "Dropped bombs on troops in fields E. of Croisilles (W. of Cherisy) Shot down 2 seater."[5] In fact, he was credited with downing two LVGs, brought down near Bullecourt. The Germans, however, were continuing to gain ground.

On March 23 the Germans renewed their advance, making their biggest gains yet against the Fifth Army and the southern flank of the Third Army. S.F. Wise records the activity in the air:

The remainder of the Third Army, however, was more or less holding its own and its overall balance enabled III Brigade, desperately endeavoring to strengthen the southern flank by developing a real air supremacy, to concentrate its machines on the threatened wing and deploy them in their scheduled roles. As the fighter squadrons returned to their proper duties 117 air combats were recorded, nearly triple the number of the previous day, with thirty-seven of them being marked down as "decisive" victories. Twenty-one German aircraft were reported as "crashed." Donald MacLaren was credited with one of them as well as two out of control.[6]

MacLaren started his day on March 23 with a low-level bombing run north of Croisilles at 9:00 a.m. Having completed his run and climbing to gain altitude, he spotted an Albatros two-seater doing a contact patrol (to establish, by aerial observation, the exact location of the advancing troops) at one thousand feet. MacLaren immediately dove onto the un-suspecting German machine and fired off a burst of fifty rounds. He pulled his Camel up, gained a height advantage over the Albatros, and dove on it again, firing fifty rounds dead on target. The E.A. went down in a slow spin, out of control. MacLaren did not see it hit the ground because of the mist and smoke. That was recorded as an "out of con-trol." Minutes later, MacLaren's flight was attacked by another Albatros two-seater. Donald MacLaren counterattacked, firing a hundred rounds at long range, hoping to scare off the enemy machine. In the meantime, Second Lieutenant J.H. Smith got to within 150 yards of the Albatros and fired a hundred bullets from his two Vickers machine guns. Second Lieutenant H.P. Blakely was next to attack the two-seater, getting off sixty rounds, but from a distance of three hundred yards. MacLaren was able to manoeuvre into a position only fifty yards away and fired once more on the outnumbered Albatros, which was seen to do a half roll then go down in a slow spin, smoking and out of control. MacLaren was credited with a "driven down out of control" shared between himself and Second Lieutenants Blakely and Smith.

In the early afternoon that same day, MacLaren was on another low-altitude bombing run — the target, troops at Pozières. Having com-pleted the run, he noticed an Albatros two-seater above him. It had blue wings and a red fuselage with light blue underneath. MacLaren pulled his Camel into position below the Albatros and fired a hundred rounds from a hundred yards. The E.A. turned over and went into a spin. MacLaren followed it down and saw it crash into a hundred pieces. This encounter with the enemy was described as a "decisive combat."

MacLaren was not the only pilot of No. 46 Squadron involved in action on March 23. Others were engaged with German scouts in dogfights.

> On the 23rd March seven Camels of No. 46 Squadron when returning from low-bombing reconnaissances [*sic*] met seven enemy scouts, four of which were triplanes. In the general engagement which followed one E.A. crashed to the ground, two were driven down out of control and two more were driven down. This is a memorable day in the history of the squadron. Altogether about sixty hours were flown, ten hours on escort duty and the remaining fifty on low-flying work, yet the squadron had over thirty combats in the air, in which seven E.A. were totally destroyed, and ten others driven down out of control.[7]

The RFC was flying ground-support operations as never before in the war. The amount of rounds fired at ground targets was immense — so too was the tonnage of bombs dropped. S.F. Wise gives us an indication of the magnitude of the attack: "On 21 March some 28,000 rounds were fired at ground targets by the RFC and fifteen-and-a-half tons of bombs were dropped during the day and night. The next day, 41,000 rounds were fired and twenty-one tons of bombs dropped; on the 23rd, 44,000 rounds and thirty-three tons of bombs were expended. But on the 24th the expenditure of ammunition rose to 82,000 rounds, although the tonnage of bombs dropped only increased by three-and-a-half tons."[8]

The Germans had difficulty countering this ground-support activity by the RFC, for a number of reasons. First, they had taken a defensive role in the air over the Western Front. Second, the German aerodromes were now farther away from the front as the Germans advanced, and third, if some German squadrons did move forward to new airfields, their efforts were not coordinated with the German army. In addition, "The standard German fighters in the spring of 1918 (Albatros D-V and Pfalz D-III) could stay aloft for only one-and-a-half hours as against two-and-a-half hours for the equivalent British machines (SE5a and Sopwith Camel)."[9]

MacLaren was out again on bombing patrols on March 24 and 25. On the second day he was bombing enemy troops who had advanced to the town of Albert. Upon his return to base, he encountered an LVG two-seater flying at one thousand feet. MacLaren attacked from above and behind the E.A., pouring seventy-five rounds into it from a distance of seventy-five yards. The LVG spun to the ground and crashed while MacLaren watched its demise.

The German drive toward Albert came virtually to a standstill, and pressure was shifted southward. On March 25 the Germans began to align their main effort along the Saint-Quentin–Amiens axis, pushing hard against the junction between the Fifth Army and elements of the French Third Army now taking over the southern end of the Fifth Army's front. By nightfall on March 25, after five days of fighting, the Germans had gained more than four hundred square miles of territory and their advance showed no signs of flagging. S.F. Wise describes the extent of the activity:

> In the air, however, they had now lost their initial advantage. On the Fifth Army front, after five hectic days, the tempo of German air activity was reported as "normal" on the 25th....
>
> All the low-flying offensive patrols took full advantage of the opportunity presented them by the slackening of German activity.... One hundred and thirty-one sorties were flown and because they were less threatened from the air, RFC pilots were able to wreak even more destruction on the ground.[10]

No. 46 Squadron continued to carry out bombing patrols for the remainder of the month. On March 26 MacLaren and his flight were bombing German troops near Montdidier. There he fought an Albatros scout, but with no result. Later that day, he chased four E.A. north of St. Pol. On his third flight of the day, MacLaren's logbook mentions shooting down a German two-seater. However, he did not file a combat report for that kill. There is a combat report, though, for March 27, 1918. After his bombing run that day, he encountered a strange-looking German two-seater; the type unrecognizable to MacLaren. It had an unusually short and deep fuselage and a small tail. It was a Junkers model. This E.A. was below MacLaren at an altitude of one thousand feet. He dove on it but from the side, firing seventy-five rounds at one hundred yards. The Junkers dove to the right and spun down out of control. MacLaren did not see it crash due to mist and cloud. Nonetheless, he was credited with a "decisive combat."

Donald MacLaren, because of his exploits in the month of March, was promoted to captain and given command of a flight of his own, C Flight, effective April 6, 1918. MacLaren was just the type of pilot all squadrons were looking for. He was a great marksman and had mastered the art of deflection shooting, knowing where his bullets would hit after they left his machine gun. MacLaren had also mastered his machine, and in his hands it could perform to its maximum capability.

Taylor Downing, in *Secret Warriors: Key Scientists, Code Breakers and Propagandists of the Great War*, gives us a sense of the qualities needed in a pilot: "Becoming a flying ace involved more than just mastering the science of aeronautics. As well as being a supremely good pilot who was totally at home in his aircraft, an ace had to have several special qualities. He usually only attacked when he knew he had the upper hand, either through a superiority in numbers or in approaching the enemy unseen. And he needed to have an obsession with attacking enemy aircraft, a quality that was more than an aggressive impulse but verged on a sort of addictive compulsion."[11]

Donald MacLaren had all of those qualities.

Ronald Dodds's *The Brave Young Wings* and Christopher Shores, Norman Franks, and Russell Guest's *Above the Trenches: A Complete Record of the Fighter Aces and Units of the British Empire Air Forces 1915–1920* both mention MacLaren shooting down a balloon on March 24. However, MacLaren's logbook entry for March 30 states, "Shot down Balloon in flames. Queant." This author could find no combat report for the claim of a balloon on either March 24 or March 30. In the heat of battle, especially one like Operation Michael, perfect documentation may not have been a priority, so it's not surprising that there were gaps or contradictions in the records.

By March 27 the Germans had pushed their attack to within fifteen miles of Amiens. On that day, all available squadrons from I, II, III, V, and IX Brigades conducted ground-support missions all along the battlefront where the Germans were advancing. Included in the air attacks was Alan McLeod of No. 2 Squadron. It was on this fateful day that McLeod and observer Hammond were shot down, as is described in Part 1. On that day alone, the RFC discharged thirteen thousand rounds of machine-gun fire and fifty tons of bombs on the enemy.

With the battle still raging, MacLaren was back in the air. Now captain of C Flight, MacLaren led his patrol on March 31 on an offensive mission. Flying at ten thousand feet, they spotted seventeen Albatros and Pfalz scouts eight hundred feet below them. Squadron No. 46's *Combats of the Air* describes the encounter:

> Capt. MacLaren dived [*sic*] on one firing about 100 rds. at 50 yds. range. E.A. turned on its side and went into a wide slow spin, and went down in this way for 5000 or 6000 ft. Was not seen to crash owing to presence of other E.A. but was obviously out of control. This was confirmed by other pilots of the patrol.
>
> Lt. Yeates dived [*sic*] on the tail of a Pfalz scout firing about 100 rds. at about 200 yds. range and tracers were seen to enter the fuselage but owing to gun trouble, Lt. Yeates had to pull out and did not see the E.A. again.
>
> Capt. MacLaren attacked another E.A. who had half rolled and was trying to dive underneath him. He fired 200 rds. at 50 yds. range but E.A. had disappeared while Camel was turning and was not seen again.[12]

MacLaren was credited with one "decisive combat," the one seen to be out of control and witnessed by other members of his flight. For his recent victories, MacLaren was recommended by his squadron commander, Major R.H.S. Mealing, for a bar to his Military Cross. In the month of March, MacLaren had shot down eleven German machines and one, maybe two balloons. A remarkable feat for a pilot who had joined the squadron only four months prior.

On April 1, in the early evening, MacLaren was on an offensive patrol near Caix. He spotted three Albatros below him, flying west. As he had the height advantage, he picked out one and dove toward it. At a distance of one hundred yards he fired off one hundred rounds from his twin Vickers machine guns. The Albatros went down in a spin, apparently out of control. MacLaren lost sight of the E.A. as it fell into a bank of cloud. He then attacked the remaining two Albatros machines. They turned to try to gain height. MacLaren followed them but they dove east and escaped. MacLaren was given credit for a "driven down out of control."

April 1, 1918, is significant in the history of the British air war, as that was the date the Royal Naval Air Service merged with the Royal Flying Corps to become the Royal Air Force.

The next day, MacLaren and four other pilots of No. 46 Squadron were on a midday offensive patrol over Courcelles. Flying at five thousand feet, they encountered a German two-seater reconnaissance machine. It had a mahogany-coloured fuselage and camouflaged blue wings, and was flying west about a thousand feet above the flight of Camels. Captain S.P. Smith fired fifty rounds at long range, two hundred yards. The German E.A. then turned east and dove for safety, the Camels hot on its tail. Many of the Camel pilots took shots at the two-seater from various ranges, between fifty and one hundred yards. They shot 750 rounds at it. The two-seater suddenly dove vertically. All but MacLaren overshot their prey and pulled up. MacLaren continued the chase and shot one hundred rounds from fifty yards. The German two-seater received many direct hits and was seen by MacLaren to fall out of control and crash south of Courcelles. That victory was recorded as a "decisive combat," with the machine "destroyed." It was a shared victory between MacLaren and the other members of the flight.

On April 3, while flying with J.H. Smith on an early afternoon patrol east of Albert, MacLaren spotted a German observation balloon.

He dove onto it, firing a burst of a hundred bullets from two hundred yards. The ground crew had time to hurriedly pull the balloon down. MacLaren's machine guns jammed at that time, as well. Clearing the jam, MacLaren and Smith flew on to the next balloon. Both pilots attacked it, each pouring a hundred rounds into the gasbag from about one hundred yards. Both pilots saw the German observer jump from his balloon as it started to sag badly, then crumple up and fall to the ground. MacLaren and Smith shared credit for the balloon.

By April 3 the German advance had stalled, both on the ground and in the air, as S.F. Wise explains:

> British battle reports ... make fewer references to German air activity each day, until, by 3 April, the attack south of Arras had ground to a complete halt, both on the ground and in the air. Enemy planes were still over the battlefield in substantial numbers on occasion, but they had largely reverted to their practice of the first days of the battle, flying in massed formations at high altitudes, where they caused little inconvenience to British aircraft which were intervening in the ground operations. Rarely did the enemy choose to seek combat.[13]

General Ludendorff cut his losses at Arras and attacked next between the British First and Second Armies. Known as the Battle of the Lys, it began on April 9, 1918, with an offensive directed at the northern flank of the First Army. Knowing the battle was about to begin, a number of squadrons were transferred to reinforce the British First Army. Two fighter squadrons with III Brigade had been earmarked for transfer once the attack began. These were Nos. 46 (Camel) and 64 (S.E.5a), and they moved to the 10th (Army) Wing, I Brigade, on April 11. No. 46 Squadron still flew out of Le Hameau. By April 10 the Germans had expanded their attack to include the British Second Army sector. The British forces were in retreat. On April 12 the commander-in-chief of

Captain D.R. MacLaren wearing a flying helmet in front of Sopwith Camel.

(below) Interior view of the cockpit of Donald MacLaren's Sopwith Camel.

all the British forces, General Haig, issued his famous "back to the wall" order. The Germans continued to make advances, but by April 25 the Ludendorff offensive was spent.

April 20 was the first time MacLaren officially led C Flight as its captain. No enemy aircraft were spotted. The next day, however, he came across a number of Albatros D.V scouts near the town of Lens. MacLaren dove at one, which had separated from the group. He fired a hundred rounds at a hundred yards as the E.A. was pulling up to attack MacLaren. The Albatros turned over on its back and began a slow spin, out of control and trailing smoke as it descended. MacLaren lost sight of the German machine as it entered a bank of clouds, still spinning at only four thousand feet.

Other Albatros scouts were gaining altitude to attack so MacLaren beat a hasty retreat and escaped from the enemy by diving away. Then he spotted a German sausage balloon tethered at four thousand feet, just above the clouds. He dove onto the balloon and fired one hundred rounds into it. He did little damage as he was firing normal bullets, not Buckingham incendiary ammunition. MacLaren saw the balloon's observer jump out and deploy his parachute. MacLaren spotted another balloon, which he also attacked. The observer jumped out of the balloon as it was being pulled down, and MacLaren could do no more damage to it. MacLaren was given credit for the one Albatros shot down.

MacLaren had no decisive victories for the balance of April. He attacked two two-seaters on April 22 but had engine trouble so he left the fight. He then attacked a Pfalz, but his guns would not fire. He had to return to the aerodrome. On a number of missions late in the month no enemy aircraft were seen. On April 25 MacLaren and C Flight went out on a bombing patrol to Lestrem. The anti-aircraft fire was very heavy. After the flight returned to base, MacLaren went over his machine, B9153, and found that his left-hand lower wing was all shot up from anti-aircraft fire. Due to the problems MacLaren was having with his machine guns, he took his Camel up on a number of occasions just to test the guns and to practise firing. The month ended on a sad note. While MacLaren and his flight were doing "low work," attacking ground targets on April 29, Second Lieutenant Smith went down in flames just east of Vimy.

SIXTEEN

May, June, July 1918

May was to be a very memorable month for MacLaren. The number of victories he would accumulate would be absolutely astounding.

On May 3 MacLaren, in Camel B9153, led C Flight on a mission south of Bailleul. There they met with pilots from No. 41 Squadron. He spotted an enemy LVG two-seater on a reconnaissance patrol north of the front lines at twelve thousand feet. He attacked by diving, getting as close as he could before firing. He let loose a burst of seventy-five rounds from fifty yards. The LVG half rolled underneath MacLaren, made a slight turn, then fell into a spin. It was then seen to burst into flames. This was confirmed by pilots in No. 41 Squadron.

Later, MacLaren and his flight came across two Halberstadt two-seaters at fourteen thousand feet northwest of Don. He dove on one from the rear, putting fifty bullets into the enemy machine from fifty yards. Second Lieutenant V.M. Yeates fired fifty rounds from 150 yards at the enemy, as well. Meanwhile, the other Halberstadt was attacking a Camel, which quickly dove away from it. Upon seeing this, MacLaren dove down upon that German machine, pouring fifty rounds into it from a distance of fifty yards. The Halberstadt's right-hand wings came off and the E.A. plummeted to earth.

That day MacLaren was credited with two decisive victories, one he shared with Yeates. They did not come without a cost, however. Second Lieutenant Skinner went missing, probably a victim of the second Halberstadt.

The Halberstadt C.V two-seater was the best German short-range reconnaissance and artillery-spotting type during the war's final months. As Herris and Pearson explain, "It had a wing span of 44 feet 8 inches, was 22 feet 8 inches long and measured a little over 11 feet in height. It was powered by a 220 hp. Benz engine and had a fixed-forward firing .313 inch machine gun and a similar but flexible rotating machine gun for the observer."[1]

On May 4 MacLaren led Second Lieutenant McConnell and Lieutenant H.L.M. Dodson on an offensive patrol over the River Scarpe. Flying at fourteen thousand feet, they saw six Albatros scouts flying below them north over Bullecourt. The patrol dove onto the unsuspecting Germans, scattering them in all directions. Five managed to escape, but the lone remaining E.A. was fired on by the entire patrol, which got off three hundred rounds from a distance of one hundred yards. The Albatros seemed to stall, then turn over, and go into a very fast spin with the engine on at full power. It went down completely out of control. As they watched the crippled Albatros descend, MacLaren's patrol was set upon by nine other Albatros scouts, which had observed the original encounter from above. They dove on the Camels, but MacLaren and his fellow pilots managed to get away from the attackers by diving at a greater speed than the Albatros scouts could manage. The Albatros eventually gave up the chase and returned over their own lines. MacLaren, McConnell, and Dodson shared credit for the victory.

Captains MacLaren and C.J. Marchant, along with their respective flights, left their aerodrome on an offensive patrol over Saint-Venant on May 6, 1918. Captain Marchant spotted a DFW two-seater flying east. He approached the German machine and opened fire on it from fifty yards. At the same time, Captain MacLaren dove at the E.A. head-on and a little to the right. He let loose a burst and continued to fire until he was forced to zoom up so as not to collide with the German machine. Marchant climbed up to gain height for a dive on the E.A. He dove on to the enemy's tail, firing his machine guns at close range. The observer was seen to collapse in his cockpit. MacLaren also dove on to the E.A.'s tail. The E.A. climbed vertically, as if to loop, then stalled and fell over on its back. To avoid colliding with the mortally wounded E.A., which fell and went into a spin, Marchant had to take evasive action. As it fell, black smoke trailed from the crippled German machine until it crashed to earth and shattered. MacLaren, Marchant, and other pilots in the engagement shared credit for the kill.

The DFW C.V was a tough, reliable, and manoeuvrable opponent and difficult to bring down. Herris and Pearson provide the specifications of this machine: "The DFW had a wingspan of 43 and a half feet, was 25 feet 10 inches long and was 10 feet 8 inches high. Powered by a 200 hp. Benz inline piston engine, it had a top speed of only 97 mph. It had a forward firing 0.312 inch machine gun and a similar sized Parabellum machine gun in the rear for use by the observer."[2]

MacLaren was curious to see the downed DFW so he landed near it to investigate the extent of the damage. It must have been a gruesome sight. Years later, after the war, MacLaren wrote about his experiences. Many of his friends would ask him if he ever felt any remorse for the men in the aircraft he shot down. MacLaren replied,

> The first time I saw two Germans being carried away from their machines which we had brought down behind our lines, I did feel it very keenly. But the feeling that was uppermost with us was a great love for our own fellows, and we knew well that every Hun who got away might kill one or more of our comrades later on. We had not asked for the war, and we were there for one purpose — to kill

the Hun.... Fortunately in the air you do not see your opponent's face. It is like shooting a bird, and the personal aspect does not affect you. It was my experience that our bravest air fighters, those who always fought to a finish, were the most courteous to captured airmen, and the most deeply grieved when one of their own men was killed. Those who were at all squeamish about the Hun were usually comparatively indifferent to the death of a comrade.[3]

On May 8, 1918, MacLaren and the rest of C Flight, Lieutenant Vlasto, and Second Lieutenants Yeates and McConnell, were on an evening offensive patrol. They came across five Albatros scouts flying northwest over Laventie. MacLaren dove from out of the sun on one of the E.A., firing a burst at it from point-blank range. The Albatros immediately stalled, turned over onto its back, and then fell completely out of control. The Albatros was last seen at five thousand feet spinning erratically. No one saw the German machine crash, as eight other Albatros scouts were flying above C Flight.

The fight with the remaining four Albatros scouts continued, with Lieutenant Vlasto firing a salvo of about seventy rounds at an E.A. It started to spin downward but was seen to flatten out later and head east under control. Yeates and McConnell fired several bursts at two of the other Albatros machines. However, they soon disengaged and C Flight, not wanting to tangle with the eight Albatros machines above them, dove for home, chased part of the way by the eight German machines, which dove after them. The Germans could not catch the Camels, however, as they had too much of a lead, so they gave up the chase and flew east. MacLaren was credited with a decisive victory. The attacks by the others of C Flight were deemed to be indecisive.

The next day, May 9, saw MacLaren take his flight members Lieutenant Dodson, Lieutenant J.H. Smith, and Lieutenant McConnell (both Smith and McConnell had been recently promoted to lieutenant from second lieutenant) on an offensive patrol at midday south of Lestrem. MacLaren's C Flight was part of a sweep of flights from No. 46 Squadron over this area of the front. The combat report filed by MacLaren and his pilots after the mission reads as follows:

Whilst on O.P. Capt. MacLaren's patrol which was the top patrol of the sweep was attacked by two Fokker triplanes. One of the E.A. got onto Lt. McConnell's tail and fired a burst which shot both spars through and a centre section wire. In order to entice the E.A. down Lt. McConnell let his machine fall as though out of control swerving aside however each time the E.A. dived and fired. This ruse having succeeded Lt. Dodson attacked the E.A. firing 150 rounds and 50 yards range. E.A. pulled up, stalled and went into a spin. After a 1000 ft. or so E.A. came out of spin and then went into another as though his controls had been shot away. He went down spinning, recovering and then again spinning till he attempted to land ... but turned over and crashed hoplessly [*sic*] in doing so. Lt. Smith also fired 50 rounds at the same E.A. as he passed the lower patrol going down out of control. The other Triplane dived steeply away east before he could be attacked.[4]

Dodson was credited with the victory over the Fokker triplane.[*]
MacLaren took Lieutenant Vlasto with him on an evening patrol,

---

* At this time in the war Baron Manfred von Richthofen's Flying Circus were flying Fokker triplanes, as were other Jastas (squadrons) in his Geschwader (wing). Von Richthofen himself had been shot down and killed just days before on April 21, 1918. The Fokker triplanes had been painted all the colours of the rainbow. Richthofen's was a solid red colour, others were painted green and yellow while still others were blue or mottled camouflage colours.

"The Fokker design was entirely original ... the Dutch designer (Anthony Fokker) using a cantilever wing structure... The wings were built around two box spars coupled together, and ailerons were fitted only to the upper wing, eventually modified into aerodynamically balanced (extended) ailerons. The lower two wings were of basically equal chord, although each was of slightly shorter span than the wing just above it.

These three wings were supported by what looked like one interplane strut each side, but each strut was in two pieces — not one large strut passing through from upper to lower wing. These struts were supports for the cantilever design, and were added to increase wing rigidity.

Armament consisted of two synchronized Maxim LMG 08/15 'Spandau' machine guns fitted in front of the cockpit, and set to fire through the propeller arc."[5]

later on May 9, north of the town of Béthune. Flying at seven thousand feet, they encountered twelve Pfalz scouts flying north of Laventie. After manoeuvring into position, MacLaren and Vlasto dove onto a formation of seven of the Pfalz scouts. The enemy machines were unaware of what was about to hit them.

MacLaren fired two quick bursts of machine-gun fire from thirty and twenty yards. His tracer bullets were seen entering the pilot's cockpit. The injured Pfalz half stalled, rolled over on its back, then began to spin quickly as it descended with the engine full on. It fell toward earth completely out of control. Meanwhile, Vlasto had picked out a target and dove on another Pfalz. As he tried to get on to the E.A.'s tail to get a shot in, the Pfalz took evasive action and went into a climbing turn to the left. Vlasto, in his agile Camel, followed on the tail of the Pfalz and fired his machine guns as the E.A. was at the top of its turn. Two blasts of one hundred rounds were fired at sixty and then at twenty yards. The Pfalz turned upside down, then fell sideways and started to spin, quite out of control.

Five of the original twelve Pfalz scouts, not wanting to be the next victims of these two Camel pilots, escaped eastward back to their base. The remaining five Pfalz machines attacked MacLaren and his formation from above. The Germans fired short bursts from long range before heading east. Although they did not see the two they had shot down crash, both MacLaren and Vlasto were convinced the E.A. they attacked were both shot down out of control. The squadron commander gave each pilot credit for a decisive combat.

Between May 9 and May 15, MacLaren's flights were uneventful. No enemy aircraft were seen. He had trouble with his Camel (D6418) one day, with the links to the engine belts broken. The machine was repaired and MacLaren was back in the air on May 15.

Along with Vlasto and Yeates, MacLaren took off around midday on an offensive patrol around the French town of Armentières. At the target area, they ran into a formation of eleven Pfalz scouts and Fokker triplanes. The enemy aircraft gave no indication that they had noticed the oncoming Camels, so MacLaren, Yeates, and Vlasto climbed so their backs would be to the sun when they dove upon the unsuspecting Germans. MacLaren picked out a Pfalz D.III to the left side of the

Fokker Dr.I Triplane No. 102/17, flown by the German First World War aces Werner Voss and Manfred von Richthofen, France.

German pilots meeting in Berlin.

formation and fired fifty rounds at point-blank range. The Pfalz dove to the right to escape but then was seen to stall, turn on its back, and go into a spin, completely out of control. After his attack on the first Pfalz, MacLaren made a climbing turn, then dove on the leader of the formation, another Pfalz D.III, which immediately turned underneath him. MacLaren, expertly manoeuvring his plane, performed a stall-turn, getting himself on the tail of the German leader. He fired fifty rounds at very close range, nearly hitting the German with his undercarriage. The German machine immediately went into a spin, descending very quickly to the ground, completely out of control.

Vlasto's first run at the enemy was on a Pfalz to the right of the formation. He fired a long burst of seventy-five rounds at point-blank range. The Pfalz went down, smoking badly, then turned into a very low flat spin, out of control. Vlasto then picked out another E.A. and fired about seventy-five rounds at very close range. The German pilot fell forward against his control stick, pushing his machine into a vertical dive.

Yeates, meanwhile, had fuel-pressure problems. That did not stop him from diving on a Pfalz, which had turned under him after he fired on it from long range. The Pfalz was seen to go down vertically, turning erratically, out of control. The rest of the German formation broke up and escaped eastward. Five enemy machines had been destroyed on this outing.

MacLaren had another mission later that day. He chased two two-seaters but without success. During the week from May 16 to 19, MacLaren and his flight members saw E.A., but only from a distance and were not in a position to attack. Number 46 Squadron moved on May 16 from Le Hameau north to Estrée-Blanche, near the town of Liettres, northwest of Béthune.

On May 20 Captain MacLaren, along with Lieutenants Chapman, Yeates, and Cote, left their aerodrome in late afternoon on an offensive patrol. The *Combats of the Air* report filed and signed by MacLaren and Chapman reads as follows:

> Whilst leading his patrol Capt. MacLaren saw an E.A. 2 seater working North of LA BASSEE which appeared to be doing a shoot on BETHUNE. E.A. was flying South towards patrol which was 2000 ft. above, but then turned East. Capt. MacLaren and Lt. Chapman immediately dived on his tail firing several bursts to within very close range. E.As. Observer fell back into his cockpit. Just after this E.A. put his nose down in

a very steep dive whilst smoking heavily eventually bursting into flames and went down vertically. Flying North Capt. MacLaren saw two balloons South of STEENWERCKE one at 7000 ft. and the other at 4000 ft. He dived on the higher one three times firing several bursts from long to close range, the Observer jumping out after the first dive. The balloon crumpled up smoking and then fell in flames. Capt. MacLaren then saw another balloon 2000 ft. below him. He dived on this twice, as before the observer jumped out immediately, his parachute however half opened and then collapsed. After the second dive the balloon burst into flames.

Lt. Yeates and Lt. Cote also fired at the first balloon.[6]

The two-seater MacLaren shot down was a DFW. He shared that victory with Lieutenant C.R. Chapman. MacLaren bagged a two-seater and two kite balloons in a single mission. He was quite a marksman.

Missions took place on May 21 and 22 but either no enemy were seen or E.A. were chased from the sky without knocking them down. However, on May 23 MacLaren had a better result.

For most of May MacLaren flew Camel D6418 and May 23 was no exception. He flew an early morning offensive patrol with Lieutenant Vlasto. They were flying at over fifteen thousand feet, south of Armentières when, below them, they saw seven German Pfalz aircraft and Fokker triplanes. Having the advantage of height, both MacLaren and Vlasto dove onto the enemy aircraft. MacLaren picked out a Pfalz and poured fifty rounds into it from fifty yards. The Pfalz faltered, stalled, and then went down in a slow spin, completely out of control. Vlasto had picked out his own victim, another Pfalz, and shot off two bursts of seventy rounds each at the E.A., which then stalled and dove vertically. As it dove away it seemed to be under control. The remaining five German machines attacked the two Camels, which took evasive action and escaped, returning to base.

MacLaren was given credit for the downed Pfalz, which was piloted by Lt. Hans Oberlander of Jasta 30. He was wounded, but somehow managed to land behind his own lines.

In the late afternoon of May 26, 1918, MacLaren went up on his own, as a lone wolf, on an offensive patrol over Laventie. Flying at six thousand feet, he spotted an Albatros two-seater flying west over Estaires, a thousand feet below him. MacLaren was flying east, so he dove head-on at the Albatros. He unleashed a burst of fifty rounds at it when he was at one hundred yards. The two-seater immediately took evasive action, turning and diving away. MacLaren did not let it get away. Now on the enemy's tail, he fired about fifty bullets from a distance of seventy yards. The two-seater stalled and went down underneath MacLaren in a slow spin. He watched it plummet to earth and crash.

On May 27 MacLaren received a bar to his Military Cross, based on the squadron commander's recommendation of March 31. The citation, published in the *London Gazette* on August 16, 1918, stated: "For conspicuous gallantry and devotion to duty as a fighting pilot. He has recently destroyed no less than nine enemy machines, and proved himself a brilliant fighting pilot against enemy aircraft often far superior in number. He has done magnificent service, and set a splendid example to his patrol."[7]

The award of a bar to a decoration meant that the recipient had already won the decoration at least once. A silver bar was affixed to the medal ribbon.

The next day, MacLaren and his flight were on a late-afternoon mission north of Laventie, near Sailly-sur-la-Lys. MacLaren, ever watchful of the sky around him, spotted ten Albatros scouts and a solitary Pfalz flying below, attacking a French Bréguet machine. He dove onto one of the E.A., firing about fifty rounds from a hundred yards. The German machine turned below Captain MacLaren, who then did a half roll to get on the enemy aircraft's tail and fired another fifty rounds at close range. The Albatros went down into a slow, flat spin, then into a fast spin, falling out of control. Lieutenant Yeates later confirmed he saw the crippled Albatros still going down out of control at five thousand feet. MacLaren and the rest of the flight then drove off the rest of the enemy machines, saving the French Bréguet aircraft. MacLaren was credited with a decisive victory over the stricken Albatros.

On an evening offensive patrol on May 30, MacLaren and his C Flight, composed of Lieutenant M.M. Freehill and Lieutenant P.M.

Tudhope, were accompanied by another No. 46 Squadron flight, led by Captain D.W. Forshaw, which included Lieutenants D.H. Robertson, W.T.A. Burkitt, and G. Hudson. The two flights were at eight thousand feet over Estaires when they encountered E.A. The combat report, made after their encounter with the enemy, a somewhat lengthy report, and signed by all participants, read as follows:

> Whilst on O.P. at 7.30 pm Capt. Forshaw leading his patrol saw a formation of eight E.A. scouts below them. He dived on an Albatross scout firing 50 rds. at 150 yrds range, E.A. turned on his back and went down out of control giving out clouds of smoke, Lt. Burkitt saw this E.A. burst into flames practically on the ground. Lt. Robertson dived on a Pfalz scout painted black and white and orange firing 200 rds at 150 to 50 yds range, E.A. stalled and went down falling in all directions absolutely out of control. Lt. Burkitt confirms this E.A. as crashed hopelessly on the ground just N of ESTAIRES. Lt. Hudson dived on another E.A. firing 100 rds at 150 yds range E.A. did a stall turn to the left and went down in a very slow eractic [*sic*] spin and was confirmed by Capt. Forshaw as out of control. Later Lt. Burkitt saw this E.A. crashed on the ground by the first one N of ESTAIRES. Lt. Burkitt fired 200 rds at 100 yds range at another E.A. then had to leave the combat owing to pressure failure but stayed the formation [*sic*] trying to regain his height. Capt. Forshaw then saw an E.A. diving on a Camel's tail below him. He half rolled and dived vertically on to the E.A. firing a short burst at point blank range. Pulling out to avoid collision he lost sight of E.A. Lt. Freehill saw a triplane going at 9,000 ft S. of ESTAIRES. He dived on it firing 50 rds. at 40 yds. range. E.A. dived followed by Lt. Freehill who fired another fifty rds. at close range. E.A. stalled and went down in a slow spin obviously out of

control. Lt. Freehill last saw this E.A. still going down out of control at 3,000 ft. Lt. Tudhope saw two Pfalz Scouts going North behind the triplane. He turned and dived on the leader from the front firing 100 rds. at 100 yds. to point blank range. E.A. turned to the right enabling Lt. Tudhope to get on its tail. Lt. Tudhope again dived firing another burst at very close range and E.A. turned on its back. Lt. Tudhope pulled out to avoid collision with E.A.'s undercarriage and then lost sight of it. Capt. MacLaren saw this E.A. burst into flames and go down ... Capt. MacLaren attacked the second E.A. firing 75 rds. at point blank range. EA. stalled and went down completely out of control in a flat spin which later became a fast irregular vertical spin. Capt. MacLaren watched this E.A. down to about 1,000 ft. but here lost sight of it. Lt. Hudson confirms this E.A. completely out of control.[8]

For their efforts that day, the two flights of Camels were credited with six decisive combats and two indecisive combats. MacLaren was given credit for one of the Albatros scouts. In the month of May alone, MacLaren had managed to shoot down fifteen German aeroplanes and two German balloons! Quite a feat, shooting down an enemy machine every other day of the month!

June paled in comparison. It was a relatively tranquil month. In June the skies were practically clear of German aircraft. It was as if they were taking a break from flying to rest and recuperate. By this time in the war, the British blockade of Germany was taking a tremendous toll on the German military machine and on the people of Germany as a whole. Food was in short supply and so too were oil and gasoline, key to keeping aircraft in the air.

On June 2, 1918, MacLaren's flight did manage to encounter seven Albatros scouts flying south over Laventie. MacLaren climbed to get into an attacking position but by that time the enemy aircraft had spotted the Camels and had turned in the opposite direction. MacLaren turned with them and dove onto the nearest Albatros D.V. He unloaded a burst of machine-gun fire from his twin Vickers. Fifty rounds from one hundred yards hit their mark. The E.A. turned underneath MacLaren, so he half rolled and fired another burst of one hundred rounds from a distance of fifty to one hundred yards. The Albatros stalled and turned over sideways. It then went into a spin, out of control. MacLaren could not watch it crash as he was in the middle of a dogfight with the other six Albatros machines.

Lieutenant Preston dove onto an Albatros scout, pouring 150 rounds into it from one hundred yards. He saw his tracer bullets enter the pilot's cockpit and witnessed the pilot lurch back in his seat, killed instantly. The Albatros fell to the left, spinning out of control. Lieutenant Watt attacked one of the German Albatros, firing 150 rounds from one hundred yards to point-blank range. The enemy aircraft turned over on its belly then plummeted earthward. Donald MacLaren was able to observe these two combats because he had removed himself from the fight due to his machine guns' malfunctioning. He could confirm the victories of Preston and Watt. Lieutenant Cote meanwhile attacked an Albatros, firing one hundred rounds from one hundred yards. It too stalled and went down into a spin. Cote then pulled out of his dive and fired on another Albatros, shooting about one hundred rounds from a close distance of seventy yards. The Albatros D.V went into a slow, flat spin, mortally wounded.

At no time during the dogfight were the Albatros machines able to get into position to fire on the British Camels. That speaks highly to the flying ability of MacLaren and his pilots of C Flight. The flight was credited with three decisive victories, one of which was given to MacLaren.

Between June 2 and June 7, no enemy aircraft were spotted. On June 7, however, while MacLaren was on a late-morning patrol near Armentières, he spotted a German two-seat Rumpler two thousand feet above him. It was doing reconnaissance over the lines. MacLaren attempted to gain height to chase the Rumpler but the German machine spotted him and flew off. MacLaren then noticed a flight of seven Pfalz scouts crossing the lines from the west by Béthune. MacLaren joined another British patrol in the area and together they attacked the German machines. MacLaren picked out a Pfalz two thousand feet below the others and dove onto it, firing one hundred rounds from only fifty yards. The E.A. rolled over and spun down out of control. MacLaren saw it crash just south of Armentières.

No enemy aircraft were seen on MacLaren's patrols from June 8 to June 13. The skies were clear. On June 15, on an early evening offensive patrol, MacLaren and his flight encountered an Albatros two-seater flying west over Estaires. MacLaren waited until the E.A. was just over the front lines before he turned to attack. The two-seater, seeing the Camel, took evasive action, diving across MacLaren's path. As it did so, MacLaren fired off about fifty rounds from one hundred yards. The Albatros turned and dove in a steep angle but MacLaren was able to get in another burst of fifty rounds from seventy-five yards. The Albatros kept diving and went over, past the vertical, and was seen to turn at the same time. MacLaren lost sight of the German machine as it entered some clouds, diving out of control. MacLaren was credited with a decisive combat.

This victory and those of June 2 and 7 were the only successful combats MacLaren was to have in the entire month of June. On June 17, 1918, No. 46 Squadron moved again, this time to Serny.

July brought better results, starting with July 1. That morning, MacLaren and his flight took off and flew to Neuve Chapelle. Flying at five thousand feet, they spotted six German two-seaters painted with silver-grey camouflage. They had finished their reconnaissance mission and were just west of the front lines. MacLaren was the first to dive at one of the two-seaters. He waited until he was almost on top of the E.A. before firing about fifty rounds. The two-seater turned and passed under MacLaren, who then half rolled and got behind the German machine, firing his twin machine guns again. The two-seater faltered, then went into a flat spin, out of control. It seemed to recover but then lost control again and crashed to earth just east of Neuve Chapelle. MacLaren was credited with a decisive combat.

MacLaren's offensive patrols from July 2 to July 5 were uneventful. On July 6 MacLaren led Lieutenants Freehill, Aldridge, and McConnell on a mission to Fromelles. Flying at twelve thousand feet, they noticed a new type of enemy aircraft, the Fokker D.VII biplane. Two of these Fokker biplanes were flying at the same altitude. The German machines had not spotted MacLaren's Camels so they climbed to gain altitude. With their backs to the sun, they dove on the two unsuspecting aircraft. MacLaren fired fifty rounds into one of the Fokkers, which immediately turned underneath MacLaren. Both Fokker machines dove, attempting to escape, but the Camels were in hot pursuit. When they came out of their dive, MacLaren fired at one of the E.A., pouring fifty rounds into it at point-blank range. It half rolled and sideslipped to try to get away, but MacLaren was in a position to fire a further twenty rounds at the E.A. The Fokker stalled, went over on its back, then started to fall to the ground. It spun one way, recovered, then spun in the other direction. The German machine was completely out of control down to three thousand feet. MacLaren did not see it crash. The second Fokker D.VII was later seen circling a spot on the ground, presumably its destroyed colleague. Freehill dove onto the second Fokker biplane, firing fifty rounds at it. The Fokker turned underneath Freehill and dove away, but Freehill noticed that its propeller was only just turning, as if its engine had been hit. Aldridge and McConnell followed it down and also fired on the Fokker, which eventually recovered and escaped. MacLaren was credited with a decisive combat over the Fokker D.VII.

MacLaren described the Fokker D.VII in the following manner:

> A new type of German fighting-machine appeared, the Fokker Biplane Scout. It was much the best machine the Huns had ever had, and as they appeared in great numbers we began to have a lively time of it. They patrolled in formations of from fifteen to thirty machines. On bright days they would fly as high as possible, and on dull days one would meet them on the fringe of the mist. After one or two brushes with them, it could be seen that the German flying corps had regained the offensive spirit, and were fighting with a ferocity that they had never equalled in the past. It was their last bid for supremacy, and, provided they were in large numbers, they fought furiously — but always on their own side of the line.[9]

242

MacLaren described his first encounter with a Fokker D.VII as follows:

> The first Fokker I had seen had shown himself two months previous to this, and we had enjoyed some good sport at the time. He was the leader of the White Tail Squadron (although his own machine was entirely black), and one day, while flying alone, I spotted him, evidently on the same quest as myself, out for a small and quiet scrap. At ten thousand feet we met, but when I made towards him, he turned across my front. I had not seen a Fokker before, so I turned to have a good look at him, climbing at the same time. He seemed enormous in size, and looked very grim in his dull black with white crosses. The colour of his machine was, I suppose, his expression of German psychology.
>
> When he saw that I was alone he swung away from me, but I put my nose down and started to close up with him. He looked back at me once, and then went straight down; but I followed. When we flattened out of our dive I found I was being fired at from the ground, and also that his speed was superior to mine. I let loose a few rounds from my guns, but, try as I would, I could not get closer to him; so, giving it up, I climbed again. I had not gone far when, to my amazement, he began climbing after me.
>
> Evidently this was a Hun of some kidney!
>
> In a few minutes we were at it again, but when I approached him he would dive towards the ground before a burst could be got in on him; and when I climbed to a few thousand feet, up he came too. After this had happened several times, and each of us had missed the other by inches, I thought I should like to show my appreciation of his sportsmanship by flying alongside and waving. I was on the point of doing this, when the

memory of what some of their chaps had done altered
my decision; so I went after him again, and this time he
flew straight for home and never looked back.

It was the last time I saw a Fokker alone, and, to
the best of my knowledge, the last time that a German
airman showed that he loved the game and was ready to
take on any passing adventurer for the zest of a fight.[10]

The Fokker D.VII was one of the best machines the Germans produced. Hundreds of these aircraft were made in the last year of the war.
Herris and Pearson, in *Aircraft of World War I: 1914–1918*, describe the
specifications of this machine: Powered by a 185 horsepower BMW IIIa
six-cylinder inline piston engine, the Fokker D.VII had a top speed of
127 miles per hour. It could climb to 22,900 feet and was armed with two
0.313 inch machine guns. It was twenty-two feet eight inches long, was
nine feet six inches high, and had a wingspan of a little over twenty-nine
feet. The Fokker D.VII "could out-climb all opponents, had a higher
ceiling, and finally gave the Germans a fighter with speed competitive
with the SE.5a and SPAD XIII."[11]

On July 8 MacLaren and Lieutenant Sawyer were escorting two DH.9
reconnaissance machines from No. 103 Squadron, which were crossing
the front lines at Merville. They were attacked from the south by seven
Fokker D.VIIs. The lead Fokker singled out one of the DH.9s and shot at
it. MacLaren dove head-on at the lead Fokker, pouring seventy-five rounds
from fifty yards. The Fokker made an evasive turn to the left but could not
outmanoeuvre MacLaren, who quickly got onto the Fokker's tail, firing
another fifty rounds at very close range. The E.A. went into an immediate spin, mortally wounded. MacLaren returned to the DH.9s, joining
Sawyer in combat against the remaining Fokker D.VIIs. Sawyer fired a
burst of fifty rounds at one of the Fokkers at long range, which immediately retired from the combat. The remaining five German Fokkers retreated
east, refusing further combat. MacLaren chalked up another victory.

July 10 and 11 saw MacLaren and his flight on a bombing run to
Bac-Saint-Maur. On July 14 he shot at a two-seater but did not bring the
E.A. down. MacLaren was up again the same day and chased a Rumpler

over Gravelines but had to cut short the chase as he was fired on by his own British anti-aircraft batteries. On July 15, however, he successfully brought down a German DFW. On July 17 MacLaren's flight escorted British bombers, which bombed the German aerodrome at Haubourdin.

No. 46 Squadron received notification of some German balloons south of Estaires causing the British troops and artillery batteries grief. Observers in the balloons could contact German artillery and give them the precise location of British forces. MacLaren volunteered to go and shoot the balloons down. The combat report of his attack on the balloons on July 19, 1918, read as follows:

> At 3.00 pm. South of ESTAIRES Capt. MacLaren saw a balloon below him in the mist. Waiting for a gap in the clouds he dived down and fired about fifty rounds at long range, but clouds drifted between him and [sic] balloon. He then climbed above the clouds and short- ly after observed two others near ESTAIRES. He dived down through the clouds at one of them but came out too far away so took the next one firing fifty rounds at 100 yards range. The fabric of the balloon ripped open and immediately the balloon burst into flames. The ob- server had previously jumped out.[12]

The report concluded that one of the balloons had been destroyed but the other attack had been indecisive.

On July 22 MacLaren and his flight were on an offensive patrol over Estaires and Bailleul. Flying at eleven thousand feet, the flight spotted below them and to the south four Albatros scouts with white tails flying in a westerly direction toward Merville. Hermann Goering was known to fly an Albatros with a white tail, spinner, and undercarriage, black fuselage, and brown and green wings. The Albatros scouts were getting into a position to make their own attack on a flight of British S.E.5s. MacLaren dove on an Albatros, which was diving to attack an S.E.5. He was on its tail when he let loose a burst of fifty rounds from close range. Flying past the German machine, MacLaren performed a turn and roll and attacked the Albatros again. He fired twenty rounds at point-blank range. The German aeroplane turned to the left and went into a flat spin, then dove irregularly. Parts of the Albatros were seen to break off before it crashed to the ground.

MacLaren, returning to the aerial combat, witnessed two other Albatros diving on the tail of an S.E.5. MacLaren saw one Albatros break off the attack, so he immediately went after it, pouring fifty rounds into it at close range. The enemy aircraft, mortally wounded, went down, falling from side to side. MacLaren, following it down, saw the Albatros regain control at one thousand feet. But it then spun into the ground, breaking into pieces.

In the meantime, Lieutenant McConnell, one of MacLaren's flight members, was continuing the fight against the remaining Albatros scouts. He rolled his Camel over, diving onto the tail of an Albatros, firing fifty rounds from a distance of between seventy-five and fifty yards. The Albatros immediately went into a flat spin downward. McConnell followed the injured machine to about four thousand feet. It was still spinning out of control. McConnell disengaged from this Albatros and climbed toward the remaining Albatros. He fired seventy-five rounds from one hundred yards.

Two of the S.E.5s were attacking the outnumbered Albatros from closer range. Lieutenants Sawyer and Skevington from MacLaren's flight also fired on the German Albatros, each firing seventy-five rounds. Outnumbered five to one, the enemy machine took evasive action, spinning and diving to the ground as fast as it could. It was seen to flatten out as it reached almost ground level, still pursued by one of the British S.E.5s. MacLaren and his flight returned to base out of ammunition and almost out of fuel. They had accounted for three destroyed Albatros and one indecisive encounter. MacLaren was credited with two of the Albatros scouts.

From July 23 to 29, MacLaren and his flight did not encounter any E.A. He test-flew Camel B2953 to see it was airworthy. Back in his tried and true Camel D6603, MacLaren, along with Lieutenant Lamburn and Second Lieutenant Bruce, were on a wireless interruption mission against German reconnaissance aircraft. Over Estaires, at five thousand feet, Lamburn saw three two-seater Hannovers* flying in formation. Lamburn and Bruce crossed the lines at Merville and turned to come at the Hannovers from the east. Pulling up under the tail of the rearmost machine, Lamburn fired off a burst of eighty rounds from a distance of one hundred yards. Bruce fired eighty rounds at it at the same time but had to pull away when his machine guns jammed.

Meanwhile, MacLaren had crossed the lines at La Bassée, getting into position to attack from out of the sun. He dove onto a fourth Hannover, firing fifty rounds from the two-hundred-yard range. MacLaren's Aldis sight had fogged up, causing him to miss. Lamburn dove onto the same E.A., but he too was having trouble with his Aldis sight. His tracer fire passed in front of the Hannover, which made an evasive turn. MacLaren dove twice more onto the Hannover, firing one hundred rounds in all. The E.A. put its nose down and dove to escape. The other Hannovers were shooting at MacLaren, so he turned his attention to them and did not see whether the Hannover he had just attacked had crashed or not.

In the meantime, Lamburn had spotted a DFW flying west of Paradis. He dove onto it head-on, letting loose one hundred rounds from 150 yards. The DFW dove to the ground. At one thousand feet, Lamburn lost it in the mist and cloud cover. Both E.A. Lamburn and MacLaren attacked were categorized as indecisive combats.

The next day, MacLaren flew a special mission. The air combat report, signed by Captain MacLaren and approved by Major O'Hara Wood, made no mention of the nature of the special mission. O'Hara Wood had taken over No. 46 Squadron on July 25, replacing Major Mealing, who returned to Home Establishment. MacLaren's combat report of July 31 reads as follows:

> Whilst on Special Mission at 4 p.m. Capt. MacLaren
> saw 3 Halberstadt two seaters making E. for the line

---

* The Hannover CL.III was a tough and reliable two-seater that could manoeuvre as well as any Allied aircraft. On a par with its companion aircraft the Halberstadt, the Hannover was powered by a 160 hp Isotta-Fraschini V.4B inline piston engine. It had a maximum speed of only 102.5 mph but had a ceiling of over 19,600 feet.[13] A distinctive feature of the CL.III was its biplane horizontal tail, with a lower element in the conventional position and a second element on the top of the fin.

at 8,000 ft. E. of ESTAIRES. He dived on the leader firing 50 rounds at 200 yards range. E.A. turned and the Observer started to fire at Capt. MacLaren. The other two E.A. fired at him with their front guns. As Capt. MacLaren got down to their level following the first E.A. who was diving E. the other two Observers opened fire. The Observer in the first machine stopped firing as though hit. Capt. MacLaren then heard firing from behind his tail and looking up saw 2 more Halberstadts diving on him. He immediately pulled out and started to climb. The E.A. also climbed up firing at intervals, but the Camel outclimbed them. The E.A. all went E. Capt. MacLaren waited nearly an hour over ESTARIES, but saw no more E.A.[14]

The month of August was to be a turning point in the war for the Allies. It signalled the beginning of the Allied victory campaign.

SEVENTEEN

Amiens

The Battle of Amiens was the beginning of the end for the German forces. It was the start of the last one hundred days of the war. The British air forces would play a pivotal support role leading up to and during the Amiens offensive, as S.F. Wise describes:

> On 1 August General Salmond [head of the RAF] submitted proposals to Haig for the employment of the air force. In the preparatory phase the RAF's principal task was to help maintain security for the forthcoming operation. This meant preventing German reconnaissance

of the allied positions, as well as patrolling behind the Fourth Army front in order to report on any abnormal movement which might also be visible to the enemy. Bad flying weather during the first week of August, however, greatly restricted German air reconnaissance and even when they were able to fly, German pilots and observers saw little to arouse their suspicions. They reported active traffic behind Fourth Army lines on 1 August but considered it normal.[1]

On that very same day, MacLaren was on a mission against German reconnaissance flights over the British lines. He attacked and shot down a two-seater over Estaires and followed it down to watch it crash near Armentières. In this combat with the two-seater, although MacLaren was the victor, the German pilot and observer managed to shoot through one of his struts holding the upper plane or wing to the lower plane. MacLaren quickly got it repaired and went on a special mission, also on August 1, looking again for German reconnaissance aircraft. He attacked five Halberstadts over Estaires, scattering them and forcing them to fly east to their own lines.

MacLaren must have then taken a fortnight's leave as there is a gap in his pilot's logbook with no entries for the period August 2 to August 22 inclusive. He was recommended for the award of a Distinguished Flying Cross on July 23, and it was confirmed in the *London Gazette* on August 21, 1918. The citation announcing the award to the decoration read as follows:

Accompanied by two machines this officer attacked four enemy aeroplanes; all of these were destroyed; he himself fought two down to 200 feet of the ground, destroying both. The two pilots that were with him each account-ed for one of the remaining two. It was a well-conceived manoeuvre ably carried out, reflecting credit to all con-cerned. This officer in 4 1/2 months has accounted for 37 hostile aircraft and six balloons, displaying great resolu-tion and exceptional tactical ability.[2]

The Distinguished Flying Cross was established in June 1918 to recognize acts of valour and courage. It was a silver cross composed of four airplane propellers, surmounted on the horizontal axis by two wings. The cross terminated in the horizontal and base bars with bombs, the upper bar terminated with a rose. At its centre was a roundel within a wreath with the letters "RAF" thereon. At the top of the wreath was the Imperial Crown. The ribbon consisted of alternating diagonal white and violet stripes.

The Battle of Amiens began in the early hours of August 8, 1918, with a devastating bombardment by Allied artillery on the German lines all along the front. A creeping barrage was followed by the advance of British, Canadian, Australian, and other Allied forces. The advance was so successful that the Germans in the first line of trenches were taken completely by surprise. In the air, nineteen Camel squadrons joined the offensive, including No. 46 Squadron, under the command of Major A.H. O'Hara Wood, flying out of Serny. RAF aircraft bombed and machine gunned enemy positions. Some eight hundred aircraft were available to support the attack. By the end of the day, the Canadians had advanced eight miles, others had advanced between three and seven miles. Over five thousand German soldiers had been taken prisoner. General Ludendorff described it as the "black day" for the German army. For the Allies, it was the most successful day of the war so far. The next day, German defences stiffened, but the Canadian forces were able to advance another four miles, a deeper penetration than any other Allied advance that day.

From August 5 to 11 the RAF claimed 276 German aircraft and balloons destroyed or brought down. This amounted to the highest number of claims for any comparable time in the entire war. The RAF lost only ninety-three machines.

On August 10 and 11, the RAF attacked the railway stations at Péronne and Équancourt. No. 46 Squadron's history states, "did much low-flying work, dropping a large number of bombs, and firing many thousands of rounds of [sic] ground targets, which included the railway stations and dumps (later in the battle) at Hendecourt and Epehy, St.Quentin and vicinity."[3]

The Battle of Amiens continued until August 14. The Allied forces had advanced more than fifteen miles into German-held territory and, as

Tim Cook in *Shock Troops: Canadians Fighting The Great War 1917–1918,* Volume Two, states that "the almost 30,000 prisoners lost to the Allied forces could be seen as nothing other than an indication that rot had set into the army. The Kaiser viewed Amiens in equally bleak terms: 'We have reached the limits of our capacity. The war must be terminated.'"[4]

The German Air Force (GAF) had also sustained considerable losses during the battle of Amiens as S.F. Wise explains:

> Their casualties take no account of machines flown back to bases (their aerodromes were so close to the bridges that they could often glide down to them right out of the battle) so badly damaged that they could not fly again without major repairs or replacement. The forty-eight airmen that they lost contained an inordinate proportion of the pilots from the élite *Jagdgeschwadern* that had borne the brunt of the battle. When the Richthofen wing moved to Bernes on 11 August, it had been reduced to a quarter of the strength with which it had entered the battle three days earlier; and, unlike its opponents, it was virtually impossible for the GAF to make good its losses in men or *matériel*.[5]

On August 23 the British Third Army, under Sir Julian Byng, began its offensive toward the town of Bapaume in what was to become the Battle of Albert. Farther south, the British Fourth Army, under General Rawlinson, advanced as well, and by August 24 had made good progress toward Bray. Over the next eight days, the British forces had pushed the Germans back behind the east bank of the Somme River and had captured some 34,000 prisoners and 270 guns.

On August 24, on a special mission flying alone just east of Bray, MacLaren spotted a German DFW over Bray at 1,500 feet. He had the advantage of height and dove onto the E.A., firing sixty rounds at point-blank range. The DFW half rolled to the left and went into a slow spin, out of control. MacLaren could not follow it down to see it crash as it entered a bank of mist and was lost in the smoke of the battle raging below. MacLaren was, however, given credit for a decisive combat.

The next day, MacLaren led his flight on a bombing mission to Gueudecourt. They were providing air support for the advancing British armies by coming in low over the town and releasing their twenty-pound bombs from a height of just a few hundred feet. The threat of ground fire from the enemy was constant. Everywhere they could see German troops clogging the roads, in retreat. Returning from their bombing run, MacLaren and Lieutenant P.F. Paton observed a DFW flying west over the Albert to Bapaume Road. The two Camel pilots dove onto the German machine, its black crosses clearly visible. MacLaren attacked the DFW from head-on, pouring seventy-five rounds into it from fifty yards. The E.A.'s observer was seen to be hanging over the side of the two-seater's fuselage, mortally wounded. The German pilot took evasive action, diving down toward the Delville Wood. Paton and MacLaren followed it down, firing one hundred rounds at it as it tried to escape. The DFW pilot tried to land his machine but it crashed into shell holes and burst into flames. MacLaren and Paton were given shared credit for the destroyed two-seater.

On August 27 MacLaren took his patrol up for an offensive mission. Leaving the aerodrome in the early morning, they flew toward Hendecourt. Gaining altitude to four thousand feet, they saw above them eight Fokker biplanes (Fokker D.VIIs) painted spotted yellow and brown. At the same time, MacLaren's flight encountered anti-aircraft fire. Black explosions appeared near an enemy two-seater to warn it of the approaching Camels. For some reason, the Fokkers dove past the Camels and away from the archie, toward the two-seater, which they must have mistaken for an Allied aircraft. MacLaren's flight, realizing the tactical blunder of the German machines, dove onto their tails. They were joined by a flight of S.E.5s that was approaching the Fokkers as well. MacLaren attacked the rearmost Fokker, firing a burst of one hundred rounds from about 150-yard range. He saw the Fokker D.VII turn onto its back then go down in a spin, completely out of control. Lieutenants Viall and Buchanan saw the crippled Fokker break up in the air, losing an entire wing during its descent.

After the war, MacLaren, in his *Chambers Journal* article, "The Last Three Months of the War in the Air," described the above-mentioned encounter, or one similar to it, as follows:

My first big encounter with these new people [Fokker D.VIIs] occurred shortly after the battle of Amiens, when our troops held a line running roughly from Bray to Bapaume. Our aerodrome was then at Bertangles, a long distance from the fighting, so that it took twenty minutes to reach our patrol area.

It was a dull morning, with the clouds about four thousand feet from the earth, and the air was very cold. We had passed over Albert and that horribly devastated area east of it, and were making our way towards Bapaume, when I espied several machines in the distance hanging about in the mist. As we drew closer several more appeared, and I made them out to be Fokkers — about twenty in number. Our artillery were putting over a heavy barrage opposite Le Transloy, and the Huns were evidently on the look-out for some poor old British artillery machine that might be observing for the guns.

True enough, there was the old "Harry Tate" cruising up and down our side, waiting for the Hun to go away, or for some help, so that he could get on with his job.

We were in single flight formation (seven machines), so we were outnumbered; but a large formation like theirs is rather clumsy to manoeuvre in a mist, and as our machines were smaller, we could keep in close formation without risk of collision.

It was a case of watching for some of the enemy to become isolated, dash in and attack them, and dash out again — tactics, incidentally, which were laid down in that music-hall ditty some ten years ago:

> He walked right in,
> And he turned around,
> And walked right out again, &c.

We climbed into the edge of the mist and waited. Presently a rift in the cloud appeared, and it occurred to me that we might get into this rift, climb a bit, and watch for anything that might cross below us. This was quickly done, and hardly ten seconds had passed before four of the machines emerged from the mist and began to cross the lane.

Then I noticed that they had white tails. This was luck. They belonged to one of the crack *Jagdstäffel*, and we had certain scores to settle with these gentlemen.

I dived steeply at the leader, and when within twenty yards of him started shooting into his "shop-windows." I doubt if he knew what happened. There was hardly time to get fifty rounds into him ere I had to "zoom" to avoid ramming, but when I turned to see what had happened he had begun his fall, the smoke from his engine showing he had been unable to shut it off. My right-hand man had succeeded in sending one of the enemy spinning to the earth, but the remainder had escaped by diving east.

It was with a great feeling of elation that we realized that, small as it was, we had scored out first victory in the Allied push, and that we had accomplished the turning of at least one cog in the great Foch* machine. But caution was necessary; we had to get past the cloud, and at any moment we might meet more of the enemy. We had just passed through a thin layer of haze when our suspicions received sudden confirmation.

Five Huns were coming right at us!

Our plan of action had to be decided in a matter of seconds. We could not pass over them, as our heads were against the ceiling; if we turned they would give us a broadside at close range which would hit some one surely; and if we dived — well, that wasn't done. They

---

* French Marshal Ferdinand Foch was the supreme commander of all the Allied forces.

would be right behind us, shooting all the while, and over German territory. Diving was neither good sportsmanship nor good tactics.

Fritz, however, spared us any further brain-ache for he decided for us. His formation quickly spread. The leader opened fire on me, and I let fire a string of bullets, which seemed to be put right into his radiator. One of his shots hit my centre section with a "click," and in a fraction of a second I pulled back the stick and swooped up into the clouds; but as I did, he shot by underneath, on his back.

It was a disagreeable situation. I was in the cloud, and hardly knew whether I dared emerge from it or not. My compass kept turning round and round, and suddenly I learned from my speed-indicator that the machine was travelling at one hundred and twenty miles an hour that wouldn't do — we must be diving. I decided to climb, so, gently easing the stick back, I watched the dial. All at once I was almost sent out of my belt, and the next thing I knew I was spinning — a most uncomfortable sensation, and a very bad exhibition of flying.

Instinctively I shut off the motor, and as the earth appeared below me, straightened out and raced for the others. They were just in front of me, and I could have yelled with delight — when I received a shock. A little way ahead of them a veritable swarm of Huns appeared. This time it was a case not of ethics but of dire necessity. We dived straight for our lines, the Huns doing the same thing, and sending smoke-tracer bullets singing all about us. Luck was with us, however, and no one was hit.

We got safely over our lines, and had started to rise, when we were over joyed to see a whole squadron of S.E.5's coming down from the north toward the Fokkers. It looked as if there was going to be a battle-royal, when the enemy turned tail and dived east. It must have been a great disappointment to the British squadron commander, for it would have been a splendid fight; but the Hun never relished a scrap unless he was much superior in numbers.

So, after all this ado, we went home, and I wrote my report.[6]

To get closer to the front lines, Squadron No. 46 moved to an aerodrome at Poulainville in late August. MacLaren completed that month doing ground-support bombing runs to Saint-Quentin and chasing Fokkers west of Péronne. On the ground, the British, Canadian, and Australian armies continued their advance against the German infantry. General Sir Henry Horne, using the Canadian Corps as a spearhead, pushed his forces eastward. Bapaume fell to the Allies on August 29 and Péronne was captured from the Germans on September 1.

MacLaren describes the role of ground support, which, Squadron No. 46 was involved in, as the British Army advanced:

At the time I have in mind our troops were making an effort to cross the Somme at Péronne and Brie, and when the mist was not too low we lent them what aid we could by attacking the enemy troops, flying very low and dropping twenty-pound Cooper bombs among them, as well as peppering them with machine-gun bullets. In every case it was a hot reception they gave us, and a great many of our best pilots had been killed or wounded, leaving a feeling of depression which we were unable to shake off.[7]

The first few days of September were rainy, so the squadron was grounded. MacLaren and his comrades made the most of the lull in the air war by taking a car and visiting Abbeville. It was hoped this diversion would get their minds off the many comrades who had fallen recently.

They managed to find an *estaminet* that served chips and eggs. It was said that if the owner of the establishment took a liking to you he might even find some steak for you to eat.

On another day they visited Amiens and toured the ruins caused by German shelling only a couple of months before. The town had been battered constantly by high-explosive shells and little remained of the original town. MacLaren and his fellow pilots did manage to find an *estaminet* still operating. They feasted on fresh bread, eggs, and goat, washed down by champagne and red wine. Being the teetotaler in the group, MacLaren drank water or milk and drove the fellows back to base. The others had drowned their sorrows and were in a happy state of euphoria, breaking into song all the way home.

MacLaren, flying Camel number F1974, led his flight on further ground-support operations on September 6, bombing the town of Hargicourt, just behind enemy lines. Each of the Camels was armed with four twenty-pound Cooper bombs. By that date MacLaren had logged a total of 390 solo hours in the air. The next day they bombed Saint-Quentin station. On the way home they were chased by six Fokker D.VIIs, but the German machines could not catch the speedy Camels. On September 8, MacLaren and Lieutenant McConnell, flying at fifteen thousand feet, encountered a German Rumpler on a reconnaissance mission over Havrincourt. They dove on the E.A. and quickly shot it down.

For the next few days, MacLaren's Camel suffered from defective machine guns. He had them repaired, then spent a few days testing them to see if they were faultless. It was the worst situation possible, to have your guns jam or malfunction in the middle of a dogfight with the enemy.

MacLaren's machine-gun trouble continued, so he could not join his flight on the offensive patrol on September 15. The ground crew mechanics finally got his guns in working order so MacLaren took off, trying to catch up to his flight. As he reached the lines at fourteen thousand feet, MacLaren spotted a British balloon west of Havrincourt on fire. Diving to investigate, MacLaren found six Fokker D.VIIs circling the crippled balloon. MacLaren attacked one from the front, pouring fifty rounds into it from one hundred yards. The German E.A. spun out of control. MacLaren did not see it hit the ground as he was set upon by one of the other Fokkers, which positioned itself on MacLaren's tail. The rest of the Fokkers were above, waiting to pounce. By means of some very adept flying by MacLaren and because the Germans had spotted some British S.E.5s approaching, they did not complete their attack. MacLaren quickly escaped to the east. He was credited with a decisive combat.

The next day, on an evening patrol over Cambrai, MacLaren, along with Lieutenants Skevington, Sawyer, Viall, and Paton, came upon a flight of ten Fokker biplanes attacking a group of S.E.5s. The Fokkers were of a garish camouflaged green, brown, and spotted grey colour. They were also adorned with two black, sloping bars in an inverted *V* shape. Two of the Fokkers dove on an S.E.5. MacLaren's flight came to the rescue. The report of this combat read as follows:

> The patrol attacked these two. Capt. MacLaren fired 80 rds. at one within 100 yards range. This machine turned underneath him. Lt. Skevington followed it down and fired 50 rds. at under 100 yds. range when he came out of his spin. Was unable to observe result owing to other E.A. Capt. MacLaren then dived on the second E.A. firing 50 rds. at under 100 yds. range. At the same time Lt. Sawyer fired 75 rds. at about the same range. This machine half rolled and Lt. Viall then fired 50 rds. at under 100 yards range at it. As Capt. MacLaren turned round he saw this machine go down in flames and immediately afterwards saw another Fokker go down completely out of control. Lts. Viall, Paton and Saunders [Sawyer] also saw this machine falling out of control. Lt. Paton also saw the other machine in flames. Four Fokkers dived down and fired at long range at Lt. Partridge. Lt. Paton turned and fired 100 rds. at long range. One E.A. went down East in a slow dive, turning as he went. Lt. Usher-Somers last saw this machine several thousand feet below still going down.[8]

MacLaren was given credit for one of the downed Fokkers and shared the other victory with Lieutenants Viall and Sawyer.

MacLaren describes a similar encounter to the one cited above, referring to it, however, as a morning flight.

> One fine, bright morning we took off as a squadron for the first time on this front, and, in conjunction with an S.E. squadron, started towards Roye to see what we could see. We crossed the line at twelve thousand feet while the S.E.5's well above us, covering every manoeuvre. We went a good way over the lines, and were swinging up towards Péronne when a large formation of Fokkers became visible, flying towards us from the east. They were slightly above us, and by the way they flew, it looked very much as if they meant business. Right over the top of us they came in good formation, thinking, of course, that there was no one else in the sky but themselves and us. They turned and swooped down on us, but as they did so the S.E.5's were on them.
>
> I had turned to meet them as they attacked us, and they seemed to be in utter confusion. Some of them began to spin, others were doing extraordinary half-rolls, and over to my right one was in flames. Then, quite suddenly, there was a deal [*sic*] of smoke-tracer about, and looking to its source, I got a shock.
>
> It was my friend of the black Fokker making quick flat turns and firing in every direction.
>
> This time I determined that the air wasn't vast enough for both of us, and I gave him a heavy burst. He did not wait, but, up to his old tricks, put his nose down and made straight east. I had just started off after him, when I noticed a white-tailed Fokker to my right, about my own level, and about one hundred yards away. He did not seem to know what was happening, so I opened out, going under him, then pulled up, giving him a good

burst from underneath at very short range. He turned over, made one large curve, and burst into flames.

But my grim enemy had managed to get clear away again. He was an undoubted adept [*sic*] at extricating himself from hot corners; but the Fates had in store that we should meet once more, for the third and last time.

None of us had suffered any damage, and we knew that there would be no more Fokkers on that patrol. When we returned home I found that the S.E.5's had shot down three and we had accounted for two.[9]

At midday on September 17, MacLaren flew with a fellow Canadian, Second Lieutenant Gilpin-Brown, along with Captain Odell, Lieutenant Tudhope, and Second Lieutenants Sawyer, Skevington, and Taylor. They were on an offensive patrol over Cambrai at an altitude of twelve thousand feet when they were attacked by twelve Fokker D.VIIs from above. With that large a formation of attackers there was always a danger of enemy machines colliding with one another. Two of the Fokkers dove upon Gilpin-Brown, who immediately made a diving spin to try to escape. Tudhope fired seventy rounds from a distance of just twenty-five yards at one of the attackers as it sped across his line of fire, but to no effect. The two German machines followed Gilpin-Brown down to an altitude of six thousand feet at which point one of the Fokkers veered away, letting the sole Fokker pursue Gilpin-Brown. It continued to be right on the tail of Gilpin-Brown, who could not seem to escape its clutches. Down they both flew, the Fokker firing burst after burst at the Camel. Finally Gilpin-Brown managed to effect a tight turn, ending up on the Fokker's tail. In a moment's notice the tables were turned. The hunter became the hunted. Gilpin-Brown then fired off several rounds into the Fokker at point-blank range. The E.A. had had enough and beat a hasty retreat east. Gilpin-Brown, now at only fifty feet above the ground, flew his crippled machine homeward, badly shot about.

In the melee with the other ten Fokkers, MacLaren and his fellow pilots had their hands full. Two Fokkers had the same target in mind as they dove close together. Too close, in fact. Taylor witnessed the left wing of one hit the right wing of the other, causing one of the Fokkers to break apart and fall tail first for about a thousand feet. Taylor took his eyes off the two damaged Fokkers in order to take evasive action from other D.VIIs that were attacking him. Then, in an instant, the air was clear of Fokkers; they had disengaged and flown home.

Later on the same patrol, MacLaren's C Flight attacked head-on a German two-seater flying at an altitude of ten thousand feet west of Bourlon Wood. MacLaren was the first to fire. He shot ten rounds at it but his guns jammed. Next, Sawyer fired three bursts of fifty rounds each from one hundred yards, raking the E.A. from side to tail. Skevington and Odell each fired on the German two-seater, which at first dove away and then climbed to twenty-one thousand feet, west of Saint-Quentin, out of reach of the pursuing Camels. They could not fly as high as the two-seater could.

Each of the pilots on that patrol, including MacLaren, shared in the victory over the two Fokkers that had collided and perished.

As that battle showed, enemy and Allied aircraft faced the risk of a mid-air collision. On September 19 MacLaren's flight was on an offensive patrol. Flying in formation at fifteen thousand feet, pilots Bruce and Partridge flew too close to one another and collided. The two machines fell together locked in a fatal embrace. It was a sad day for No. 46 Squadron.

Flying Camel number F2137, MacLaren and his flight on September 21 went looking for German reconnaissance two-seaters. They spotted one south of Saint-Quentin at ten thousand feet, and attacked it. The E.A. had noticed them just as they started their pursuit and climbed to gain altitude. MacLaren fired from a distance but the German machine could climb above the maximum ceiling of a Camel so his flight had to return to base.

On September 24 MacLaren took Second Lieutenants C.R. Sawyer and A.K. Allen with him on an offensive patrol over Gouzeaucourt. Flying at ten thousand feet, they observed a German two-seater below them so they dove upon it from the front. All three Camel pilots fired short bursts at the E.A. from point-blank range. The two-seater escaped by diving into the cloud.

MacLaren's patrol then spotted two formations of Fokker D.VIIs containing eight to ten machines each. The Fokkers were about to attack two British Bristol Fighters that were doing low-level photography work. MacLaren's Camels, although outnumbered, entered the fray and drove off the two formations of Fokkers. In all likelihood, the Fokker pilots were quite new to air combat, since they dispersed with little prodding.

In September, Squadron No. 46 received orders to move from Poulainville to Cappy, an aerodrome closer to the front. MacLaren describes the life of the pilots at Cappy, when they were not in the air:

> When finally settled in our new quarters — although they could hardly be termed luxurious — we became more of a happy family than we had been for some time.
>
> Our C.O. was not one who supported the idea that the flying-man must drink and dissipate to enjoy his spare time; in fact, he heartily discouraged such things. He did encourage sport, though, and we used to play every kind of game in our odd leisure hours. In the evening we had an orchestra that was a godsend, composed of a violin, a mandolin, a flute, and, of course, a piano. I shall never forget the hours that orchestra helped to pass.
>
> They were happy days during that dull weather, for, though we knew that not many of us would be alive after the offensive, every one was full out to do his best for a comrade on the ground, as he was ready to do it in the air. They were the most-likeable fellows one could meet — unselfish, hospitable and in good spirits all the time....
>
> We had a large number of Canadians in the squadron at the time, and our C.O. showed his appreciation of them in many ways. No nationality or national temperament has all the flying faculty, but he felt (as I do) most sincerely that the Canadian has the flying instinct, combined with the fighting spirit, to a high degree. Let me admit frankly that I may be biassed [*sic*] in this matter. At any rate, we thought we were the best airmen in

the world, and this is not a bad cargo to carry with you when you meet the Hun at fifteen thousand feet.

The aerodrome which we were occupying then had been used by the famous Richthofen, and there were numerous evidences that he had been there. One souvenir which I took was a sign warning pedestrians against aerial firing taking place on the aerodrome. It bore Richthofen's signature.[10]

MacLaren rose early on the morning of September 26. He and Second Lieutenants Sawyer and Skevington grabbed a quick breakfast of fried eggs and bread, washed down with a hot mug of coffee. By seven the ground crew had Sopwith Camels F2137, F3101, and F3230 ready to fly. The three pilots took off into the mist and low-hanging cloud. Their destination, the air above Épehy. By 7:40 a.m. they were east of Gouzeaucourt, flying at four thousand feet. MacLaren had excellent eyesight. He saw a German LVG below him. The patrol fired at it from long range with no apparent result except to warn the E.A. of the approaching Camels. It tried to dive away but MacLaren was on its tail firing one hundred rounds from one hundred yards. Sawyer fired seventy-five rounds from farther back and Skevington fired on the LVG as well. The German two-seater continued to dive into the mist and clouds and disappeared. This encounter was ruled by Squadron Major O'Hara Wood an indecisive combat.

Greater success would be achieved that evening. MacLaren, along with Lieutenants R. Viall and R.F. McRae (a fellow Canadian from Niagara Falls, Ontario) and Second Lieutenants J. Taylor and A.M. Allan (of Toronto) went on an offensive patrol near Havrincourt. At about 6:15 p.m., MacLaren spotted six Fokker D.VIIs flying at the same altitude as the Camels, twelve thousand feet. One of the Fokkers had a red fuselage and tail, another was black all over and another had a yellow tail and pinkish camouflaged fuselage and wings. A further sixteen Fokkers were seen flying above them. MacLaren was the first to attack, flying head-on against the nearest oncoming enemy aircraft. He fired twenty rounds from ten yards. Each bullet found its mark. The Fokker immediately went over onto its back; it hung there as MacLaren pulled up above the stricken Fokker. It then fell into an erratic spin, out of which it did not recover. It crashed near the village of Havrincourt. Viall saw it smoking as it plummeted to earth.

Lieutenant Allan (who had been flying operationally only since September 5) fired forty rounds from fifty yards at another approaching Fokker. It went into a dive and was not seen again. At that moment a Fokker got onto Allan's tail. McRae chased it off without firing a shot. In the meantime Taylor had manoeuvred underneath the Fokker that had, just moments before, been on Allan's tail, and fired a burst of fifty rounds from one hundred feet with no apparent result.

Nine of the sixteen Fokkers from the formation above joined in the action by diving onto MacLaren and his flight. One of the Fokkers manoeuvred into position behind a Camel but McRae half rolled onto the E.A., firing one hundred rounds at point-blank range. This Fokker turned over but was not seen going down as MacLaren and his fellow pilots had their hands full fighting the remaining Fokkers. The Camels managed to extricate themselves from the dogfight just as the Fokkers had had enough and turned east. MacLaren was credited with a decisive victory.

MacLaren took two days off and was back in the air on September 29, 1918. He along with fellow captain Odell; Lieutenants McRae, Moxon, and Skevington; and Second Lieutenant Sawyer, took off to escort a low-level bombing mission toward Le Cateau. The combat report of the flight reads as follows:

> While escorting low bombing flight Capt. MacLaren's patrol saw 4 Fokkers at 2,500 ft. Capt. MacLaren fired 50 rds. at 100 yds. range head on and from above at one E.A. on Lt. Skevington's tail. This E.A. half rolled and spun and was lost sight of. Lt. Sawyer fired 75 rds. at 100 yds. at same E.A. Result was unobserved owing to other E.A.
>
> Capt. Odell leading bombers chased E.A. off Lt. Moxon's tail, fired 50 rds. at E.A. who half rolled and

went E. Capt. Odell was then attacked, turned on E.A. chased this E.A. away then saw another E.A. on a Camel's tail firing at it. Turned on this E.A. and fired 75 rds. at 75 yds. This E.A. was jerked quickly on to its back and went down vertically from a height of 800 ft. Result was unobserved as he was then re-attacked by E.A. Four E.A. were seen at the beginning, only two were seen to leave by Lt. Sawyer and Capt. MacLaren.

Lt. McRae fired 80 rounds at E.A. on Camel's tail. No result observed. This fight took place at 4:40 pm. S. of BEAU REVOIR on the road to LE CATEAU with a patrol of about 8 Camels E. and above the fight who did not observe the E.A. and took no part in the contest, and allowed 2 Fokkers to fly off E. immediately beneath them.[11]

MacLaren shared a victory with Sawyer, one of two decisive combats on that patrol. The combat report points out clearly the need for pilots to be ever vigilant during a fight, since one moment a pilot might be attacking a foe and then the next instant he might be on the receiving end of an attack by the enemy, which meant that he had no time to see whether the machine he had just attacked went down out of control or not.

September proved to be a successful month for MacLaren, who bagged seven victories. S.F. Wise elaborates:

Both British and German air forces reduced their activities through the middle of September, with indifferent weather conditions and the American attack in the south, at St. Mihiel, taking much of the pressure off the British front for a while. Only three top-scoring British fighter pilots still flying on the Western Front — the South African Beauchamp-Proctor of 84 Squadron, Raymond Collishaw, commanding No. 203, and Donald MacLaren, now leading a flight of No. 46 — were able to record any number of victories during the last half of the month. Collishaw claimed two Fokker D-VIIs over Bourlon Wood on the 24th and two more over Lieu St. Amand on the 26th, while MacLaren was credited with his second D-VII on the 15th, a share of two more on the 16th, another on the 26th, and his penultimate victim on the 29 September, for a total of forty-seven credited victories in 201 days of service in an operational squadron.[12]

This was a remarkable feat, and, including the balloons he shot down, his score was at fifty-two.

He scored two more in October, not one, as S.F. Wise referred to in the quotation above. On October 1, MacLaren, along with Captain Odell and Lieutenant Sawyer, were on a midday offensive patrol south east of Saint-Quentin. Flying at 7,500 feet, they spotted a German LVG two-seater doing reconnaissance. MacLaren dove onto it and fired one hundred rounds at one hundred yards from behind as the LVG tried to escape by diving away. Sawyer fired seventy-five rounds from the same range and Odell fired off seventy-five rounds, as well, at the escaping German machine, which did evade the attackers. It was last seen still diving eastward at three thousand feet.

The next day, MacLaren and three other captains, H.W. Odell, H. Lawson, and J.L. Leith, led their respective flights on an offensive patrol near Morcourt. Flying at twelve thousand feet, they saw four Fokkers below them and ten Fokkers above them at fifteen thousand feet. Suspecting that if he dove on the four German machines below them, the other ten would pounce on the Camels from above, MacLaren and the others took their chances and dove onto the Fokkers. MacLaren singled one out, getting in a twenty-round burst of machine-gun fire, which hit it broadside. Captain Leith fired at the same E.A., unleashing seventy-five rounds from 150 yards. Lieutenant Sawyer fired 125 rounds from seventy-five yards at the same Fokker D.VII, which fell out of control between Morcourt and Homblieres. Many Camel pilots on the patrol saw it fall hopelessly out of control.

In the meantime a Camel, at very low altitude, was seen being attacked by three German machines. MacLaren, Sawyer, Skevington, and

Leith went down to help but by the time they were at attacking distance, the three Fokkers had riddled the Camel with machine-gun fire. The ten Fokkers above now dove into the combat. Leith was attacked by a Fokker from the rear. It was Lawson who came to his rescue, firing a burst at one hundred yards distance. The Fokker peeled away.

It was a mad scramble with Camels and Fokker D.VIIs manoeuvring all over the sky trying to get in and out of danger. Captain Odell attacked one of the Fokkers, firing about 50 rounds at it from a distance of one hundred yards. It went into a diving spin, coming out of it lower down and away from the combat. F.A.H. Dorris entered the action, attacking a Fokker head-on, firing a burst of machine-gun fire from one hundred yards. The German machine dove underneath him. Dorris continued on, getting another Fokker within his sights. He fired fifty rounds from one hundred yards but the enemy aircraft promptly dove away. In the meantime McRae came to the rescue of a Camel being attacked from behind by a Fokker. McRae fired forty rounds from one hundred yards and the Fokker disengaged and flew off toward the east. Thus ended the dogfight, with MacLaren, Leith and Sawyer sharing the one decisive victory.

Again, such battles showed how crucial and how difficult it was to maintain proper position in the air.

For the past number of weeks, MacLaren had been annoyed with his squadron leader, Major O'Hara Wood. As MacLaren put it in a speech long after the war, in 1979,

> He had a fixation. He was out to be a real squadron leader — to get as much of the action as possible. As senior flight commander I had developed a formation of the three flights at different levels of about 100 ft. apart, led by C Flight on the lower level. Major Wood insisted on flying on my right to get a piece of the action if there was any, but I had to head him off from attacking our balloons. One day he decided to lead the squadron leaving me to guard the upper flank.
>
> I had explained to him that his habit of continuous twisting and turning in formation made it hazardous

for other pilots as there was serious risk of collision. After half an hour on the line the squadron surrounded me and I noticed that Major Wood was missing. On landing at the station I learned that Major Wood had collided with his right wing man and that they had both crashed.[13]

The collision occurred on October 4, 1918, at fourteen thousand feet near Saint-Quentin. Number 46 Squadron had taken off from von Richthofen's old aerodrome at Cappy. Both O'Hara Wood and Saunders were killed. In his *Chambers Journal* article, MacLaren described this fateful event in the following way:

And now came a tragedy that cast its gloom over every man in the squadron. It meant promotion for me, but that was a mighty small compensation for the sorrow I felt. The incident I refer to left us all determined to fight to the end whenever we were engaged in a scrap.

Several new pilots had been with us for some time, and had now been judged fit to fly over the lines. Our C.O. accordingly expressed his intention of leading them over on their first trip. I, for my part, took two with me, and when we arrived at the lines I remained east of the main formation in order to act as a bait to any Huns that might be tempted to dive on me.

After a time eight Fokkers, who thought we should be easy prey, came swinging down on us, but as they approached we plunged underneath the C.O.'s formation. The Fokkers saw what was up, and drew away immediately — except one who, believing himself more skilful than his fellows, came straight in among us and attacked my right-hand man. He was so close to me that I could see him leaning forward, looking along his sights and shooting wildly. Before I could get my sights on him he turned. My left-hand man crossed behind me and shot this fellow down. It was a quick bit of work, especially as this pilot had been in France only a few weeks.

Our main formation, however, seemed to be very much agitated, and, as I picked up my two partners, the others came and joined us. They seemed to have no leader, and I could not see the C.O.'s machine among them. I knew they had not been attacked, as they had been in sight all the time; so, greatly puzzled, I took them back, and we landed. Then I learned the truth.

Our C.O. had been killed.

He had had a collision with one of the new pilots, and both machines had been hopelessly smashed. There wasn't an officer or man who hadn't loved him as only men can love a brave and gallant gentleman.[14]

One of the flight commanders, Captain J. Leith, who was flying on O'Hara Wood's left, had seen him make a sharp left turn. Leith followed him. O'Hara Wood went right into the path of the oncoming Saunders's Camel. The collision happened so quickly neither could avoid the other. Both officers were admitted to Casualty Clearing Station 37 but were dead on arrival. MacLaren went up on a search mission to find the crash site but was unsuccessful.

MacLaren was placed in temporary command of the squadron until a replacement for O'Hara Wood could be found. The day of the tragedy, MacLaren and a fellow by the name of Robson visited the aerodrome at Athies, which was to be the new home of No. 46 Squadron. MacLaren organized the move, and it took place on October 6. The new aerodrome, wrote MacLaren,

pleased us all, as it would help us to forget some of the bad events of the previous weeks, and in fresh surroundings I should have a chance of putting into practice some ideas I had always cherished.

Our new aerodrome had also formerly been used by the Huns, and the officers' quarters had been built by them as well. The quarters were warm and comfortable, and although somewhat garishly calcimined within, were preferable to tents.[15]

MacLaren spent the next few days getting used to his new role of running a squadron. The weather was inclement so flying was impossible. He had to think of some way to keep the pilots occupied.

I had several targets put up against a bank, and a Vickers machine gun mounted on a tripod, so that the pilots could get as much practice as possible. I also kept them well supplied with pistol ammunition, and they spent most of their time competing with each other for stakes.

I think it is generally conceded that good shooting in aerial warfare plays a much greater part than freak flying. At least, I have always been convinced of this fact. A pilot, by extraordinary freak flying, may be able to place himself in an excellent position to shoot down an enemy, but if he cannot hit him when he does get there, what is his advantage? He may be able to get away when he is in a tight position, but it is much safer to bring the other chap down instead.[16]

No. 46 Squadron was taken over by Major G. Allen on October 8, 1918, and this officer continued to command it until early in 1919. MacLaren described Allen as "a Sandhurst type who had flown DH2s in France in 1915."[17]

* * *

Early on the morning of October 9, MacLaren's C Flight took off from Athies.

> It was a dull day when we recommenced work, and as we approached the lines we found Bohain and many villages to eastward on fire. Why the Huns set fire to these pretty little places I have never been able to figure out, unless from pure vandalism. As we were directly over Bohain a huge mine exploded, sending up showers of burning embers, earth, and dust; and as we followed the railway line towards Busigny, another large mine went up. It all made a very picturesque scene, and I dropped lower to get a better view of it, when I noticed a German balloon below, unusually close to the line. We went down at him, one behind the other. When he filled my sights I let fire, and a white parachute appeared below. As the last of us passed there was a small flame, then a huge blaze, and a lot of black smoke. One more "Drachen" destroyed!
>
> Meanwhile their "Archies" were paying us the most complimentary attention. They had a nasty bark (they always did when one was trying to get back to one's own territory), and were throwing little balls of phosphorus, eight in a row. However we returned without mishap.[18]

At that time in the war, the Germans were in full retreat and were employing a scorched earth policy, destroying everything that would be in the path of the advancing British Army. S.F. Wise elaborates on this point as follows:

> By 5 October 1918 the British line in the south had advanced to the outskirts of Montbrehain and Ponchaux, the Third Army was in Crevecoeur and Proville, and the First Army through Tilloy, so that Cambrai was now threatened from both flanks. The RAF

reported that "all enemy airfields west of the railway St Quentin-Bohain-Busigny-Le Cateau were evacuated and that the great ammunition dumps at Fresnoy le Grand and Brancourt-le-Grand were empty." In the north, where the Second Army's attack in front of Ypres had met with less resolute resistance, the British had taken Dadizeele, were through the Gheluwe switch line, and in Comines and Armientières by 3 October.[19]

MacLaren's final victory occurred on October 9. He and C Flight were on a low-bombing mission east of Le Cateau. They joined up with an S.E.5 and attacked a two-seater Hannover CL.III. MacLaren was the first to dive onto the German machine, pouring in one hundred rounds at fifty-yard range. The two-seater turned to try to escape but then went into a spin and crashed west of Ricqueval Wood.

That same day MacLaren took his flight on another low-altitude bombing run. He picks up the story:

> One afternoon, after several days of bad weather, we were detailed to do a low bombing show on the road east of Le Cateau. Reports had been received that this road was congested with retreating German troops, and it was up to us to destroy them. By that time the Allied offensive was developing so furiously that the Hun was staggering like a man in the ring who knows that if he cannot get a rest he must go under to his opponent's anvil blows. The British policy of "sweep the Hun from the air" we now had to apply to *terra firma*. We were to do our best to complete the disorganization of the Boches as they retreated.
>
> On a scout machine is fitted a small bomb-rack, at the bottom of the fuselage, between the struts of the undercarriage, and for jobs of this character this rack carries four twenty-pound Cooper bombs, or "man-killers," which can be released by pulling a flexible wire when the

machine is over the target. Being very fast and easy to manoeuvre, scout machines, carrying such bombs, can drop down on troops in a road, let fall their eggs, open fire with their guns, and cause a great deal of damage in a few minutes.

One can spot troops on the move, drop down close to the ground a mile or so away from them, then fly over fields fringed with trees, and come right on top of them before they even know you are in the vicinity.

This afternoon we spotted the enemy on the road quickly enough — there were hundreds of them. Getting well east of them, we dropped down below the tops of the trees and came towards them, skimming the surface of the fields. When we were almost on them I rose up over the trees and flew along the road, the others stringing out behind me in single file. It is hardly possible to miss a target at that height, and as we dropped our bombs we turned and swept the road with machine-gun fire. As our guns fired at the rate of eleven hundred and fifty rounds a minute, it can be easily realized what confusion resulted among the Germans. They stampeded in all directions, but we could see every move, and followed them wherever they went. It was a weird sight: a wagon lying dismantled in one spot, with its horses killed — a lorry, without its occupants, standing stolidly in the road — a group of men huddling in a ditch — men and horses wildly running everywhere.

It is impossible to state how many were killed. What my squadron was doing, others were doing all along the line; and I am convinced that these raids on the roads were a tremendous factor in bringing the Prussian bully to his knees.

When, however, a few Germans managed to keep their heads, especially if there were machine-guns with them, it was a very dangerous pursuit, and many a good chap went West* in these last stage raids.[20]

His view of the benefits of ground strafing and low bombing described above is quite different than what he said in 1979, in a speech at a reunion of the First World War pilots in Vancouver, British Columbia: "We had been low bombing retreating troops at daybreak but after losing two pilots Muir who was killed and Falkenberg who suffered a broken leg; I protested to our Brigadier Ludlow Hewitt that this was a useless exercise and scouts should be relieved from the operation. This was generally agreed to."[21]

Perhaps initially MacLaren could see the benefits of low-bombing operations, but when they resulted in the death or injury of pilots for which he was responsible, he changed his tune.

MacLaren and his flight continued their ground support on October 10, bombing the crossroads at Fontaine. On October 11 the flight was on an offensive patrol again. MacLaren describes it in the following way:

> The next day I met the black Hun again.
>
> The clouds were very high, and there was little wind, so, climbing to sixteen thousand feet, we approached the line opposite St Quentin. In this light it is easier to spot enemy aircraft than on clear days, and we soon perceived several Fokkers, slightly below us, who were attacking a British two-seater. This was a De Havilland Liberty 9, and he was putting up a splendid fight. The Huns seemed afraid to approach him too closely, probably hoping to force him to the ground on their side of the line.
>
> They did not see us until we began to fire, and then they tried to climb towards the east. When I got close to the leader I saw that his machine was all black.
>
> It was my psychological German of the dark Fokker.

---

* Meaning they perished.

This time I had him. He was still shooting at the two-seater when he filled my sights, and I let loose a burst into him. Down he went, turning and twisting from side to side, so that it seemed certain he was hit. Following him down to make sure he was not tricking me again, I saw him crash close to the bank of the river Oise, his black planes and fuselage a grim wreck of matchwood.

In the meantime one of our "Camels" had fought cleverly, and a Fokker burst into flames, going down to its end. The rest of them got away, and we drew off in close formation to avoid a straggler being caught.[22]

It is a mystery why this combat was not recorded in MacLaren's logbook. Nor is there a combat report of the engagement signed by MacLaren. He writes of it in the *Chambers Journal* article and yet there is no official record of it.

The "black Hun" was undoubtedly Eduard Ritter von Schleich, also known as the "Black Knight." A Bavarian, he had received in 1917 the Bavarian Military Max Joseph Order, becoming a noble — hence the title Ritter, or Knight. Schleich flew an all-black Albatros D.Va and later an all-black Fokker D.VII, both of which he had marked, on the side of the fuselage, with a Bavarian lion. At the beginning of December 1917, Schleich received the Pour le Mérite and by March 1918 he was appointed chief of the newly formed *Jagdgruppe* Nr. 8. By October 1918, JG 8 had been reinforced and redesignated JG 4. Flying out of Fleures near Charleroi, Schleich, on a solitary mission, surprised six Camels over Auchonvillers and shot down three of them in five minutes. Schleich had a total count of thirty-five Allied machines and survived the war.

No E.A. were seen on MacLaren's patrol of October 17, 1918. However, MacLaren's last patrol was on October 18, and then there was much action. MacLaren picks up the story:

Shortly after this we had one more real battle in the air, and it proved to be my last.

Fifteen of us left the aerodrome one fine afternoon, flying east of Le Nouvion, when eight Fokkers came at us from out of the sun. After a brisk scrap, I managed to send the leader down in flames, when the rest of the Fokkers dived. As they did so, one of my chaps, by a smart bit of work, shot down a bright-yellow Fokker. It was fine manoeuvring and quick thinking.

Although tempted to follow them, I was afraid it was part of a plan, and that something was above us. Looking around to determine our plan of action, I saw about twenty Fokkers circling about, preparing to attack us. We were caught. There was nothing for it but to use every subterfuge we knew, and trust to luck for some opening.

Picking up our formation, we turned and dived westward towards our lines. Our middle flight was well above and west of me, so that the Huns would have to attack the lower flight first. Without any hesitation, three of them swooped down on my rear man, but as they came close I made a stall turn and flew towards them. One of them turned across my front, and I put a burst into him, but apparently without doing any vital damage, for he dived east, evidently unhurt. One of my fellows had succeeded in getting on a Fokker's tail, and as I watched them the Hun turned over quickly and went down spinning. The remaining Hun of the three began to shoot from behind, his bullets striking my top plane; but one of my rear men gave him a burst, and he disappeared, although the machine was still under control.

Meanwhile the remainder of the enemy formation, in coming down to aid the first three, had been splendidly attacked by our two top flights, as one of their number had gone down in flames.

Suddenly the whole enemy formation turned to the east, and flew on; but as we turned south they flew parallel with us for a while. We turned to the north next, with the same result. Coming up towards Le Cateau, they followed us a short distance, and then dived for the east.

And that was the last time I saw the Hun in the air.[23]

The victory MacLaren claims on his last flight is not confirmed in his logbook, and again the author could find no combat report made out and signed by MacLaren for that encounter.

The war ended for MacLaren in a rather inglorious way. He injured his leg in a wrestling match with another officer, in the mess, around the end of October. By that time, he had accumulated a total of 454 hours, 5 minutes of solo flying time.

MacLaren described what appears to be a conspiracy of sorts to get him out of France and back to England. "I had fractured a bone in my ankle and although not serious my friend the Wing MO [Medical Officer] conspired through the Wing Commander the famous Louis Strange to fasten some sort of label on me that would get me out of France. This they did by inventing a malady called 'Flying Sickness' printed it on a document and by Nov. 1st I was given a farewell and a sendoff to Kitchener Hospital at Brighton."[24]

This was nothing more than a conspiracy — to get MacLaren out of the war and to eliminate any chance of his being shot down. His squadron mates wanted to ensure he ended the war alive with his aerial record and his skin saved. From the beginning of 1918 to the armistice, the RAF on the Western Front suffered total casualties of over seven thousand, of which more than 3,700 were due to combat.

It was a tearful goodbye, leaving his mates at No. 46 Squadron because of an ankle injury and orders to be hospitalized, as MacLaren describes:

It was mighty hard luck, and I missed the last few days of the war as a result. On the day I was to go away the Hun shelled the aerodrome early in the morning, but was good enough to desist during breakfast.

It was a very hard tug to leave the squadron, and I felt wretched as I climbed into the car after breakfast. There were a few last words to be said to the flight commanders, a few last good-byes, and then the old, wonderful wish, "Good-bye and good luck." As the car drew away, the fellows — the best in the world — gave me a cheer, and the Hun speeded the parting guest by dropping a few odd shells on the aerodrome.[25]

MacLaren was credited with fifty-four victories, including six balloons, all while piloting Sopwith Camels: nineteen victories in Camel B9153, eighteen victories in Camel D6418, eight victories in Camel D6603, and nine victories in Camel F2137. He ranked third among the Canadian pilots of the First World War, next to Billy Bishop and Raymond Collishaw. He was the RAF's fifth highest scoring ace, behind Major Edward Mannock (seventy-three victories), Colonel William A. Bishop (seventy-two victories), Major Raymond Collishaw (sixty victories), Captain James McCudden (fifty-eight victories), and tied with Captain Andrew Beauchamp-Proctor (fifty-four victories).

France made MacLaren a Chevalier of the Legion D'Honneur and awarded him the Croix de Guerre avec Palme, on July 15, 1919. After the war, on January 9, 1919, by army orders by General Sir H.S. Rawlinson, Commander Fourth Army, MacLaren was decorated with the Distinguished Service Order. He was gazetted on February 8, 1919. The citation read as follows:

> Bold in attack and skilled in manoeuvre, Captain MacLaren is conspicuous for his success in aerial combats. On 24th September he and his patrol of three machines attacked a formation of six enemy scouts, although the latter were protected by sixteen other enemy aircraft at a higher altitude. Firing a burst at point-blank range, this officer shot down one in flames. In all he has accounted for forty-eight enemy machines and six kite balloons.[26]

Donald MacLaren was credited with more victories in a Sopwith Camel than any other pilot in the First World War. In terms of victories he was No. 46 Squadron's most successful pilot.

He was revered by those who flew with him. One of the American pilots in his flight had this to say about him: "MacLaren, our flight commander, was absolutely terrific.... He took wonderful care of his flyers in the air, and on the ground ... I just cannot say enough for MacLaren. He was a friendly sort of chap and was an absolutely uncanny pilot in his tactics."[27]

MacLaren's flying days were certainly not over. A new chapter of flying was about to begin. He pondered his future as he made his way back to England.

EIGHTEEN

The Canadian Air Force

MacLaren was admitted to 14 General Hospital in France on November 4, 1918, and by November 7 he had arrived at Kitchener Hospital in England. The following day, the attending medical officer wrote in his Medical Case Sheet, "Patient states that he feels fit in every way but that he has been in France flying for 12 months and feels he needs a rest ... looks and feels well."[1] MacLaren was granted four weeks of leave for convalescence.

MacLaren's ankle injury did not impede him from enjoying the armistice celebrations in London. MacLaren celebrated the end of hostilities along with his brother. With two bottles of champagne under their arms, they walked down the Strand among the throng of Londoners, all ready to party. There were hoots and hollers of joy. The women were kissing every soldier in sight. Everyone was in a celebratory mood. They wanted the party to last forever to make up for four long years of war. By daybreak the two MacLarens ended up in Piccadilly Circus. The champagne was gone, with Donald not having touched a drop. He could not recall who had. MacLaren and his brother returned to the Royal Air Force Club, where they had been staying while in London, tired but in good spirits. The war was finally over, so was the death and destruction. It was time to move on and rebuild.

MacLaren returned to the hospital from his leave feeling quite fit. By December 18, 1918, MacLaren was on leave again. On December 28, 1918, using the Queen Mary Club for Officers' letterhead, he wrote to the hospital.

> Dear Sir,
>
> Having reported to the Air Ministry I find I have been posted to No. 1 Canadian Squadron, Hayford and have been instructed to report to that place on the expiration of my leave, instead of returning to the hospital.
>
> Yours respectfully
> Donald R. MacLaren
> Capt. R.A.F.[2]

MacLaren had heard that the Canadian Air Force (CAF) had been formed and was looking for officers. He put in his application at Oxford Circus, was accepted, and was appointed a flight commander, No. 1 Squadron, stationed out of Upper Heyford, Oxford. His commander was none other than Listowel, Ontario's Major Andrew McKeever, the subject of Part 2 of this book.

McKeever was pleased to have MacLaren as part of his team of flight commanders. The other two were G.O. Johnson, MC, and C.F. Falkenberg, DFC and Bar. All three captains had superb operational records. No. 1 Squadron was a fighter squadron, flying Sopwith Dolphins. McKeever had wanted Sopwith Snipes for his squadron, while Captain

Walter B. Lawson, No. 2 bomber Squadron commander, had wanted Bristol Fighters. He was provided with DH.9s, instead.

As was referred to in Chapter Ten, Home Establishment and the Canadian Air Force, the morale of both the officers and the other ranks of squadrons one and two was not good. The squadrons lacked the equipment and supplies to operate. There was friction with those in the RAF who commanded them. Leave was denied, pay was late, and there was a lack of organizational and administrative structure in the CAF. S.F. Wise explains how fragile things were at this time:

> The CAF's position was precarious. No overall command and administrative structure had been established. The CAF itself was nothing more than two squadrons of the RAF that happened to be all-Canadian. No thought had been given to equipping the squadrons for service in Canada rather than for the Western Front, nor had the financial implications of maintaining them for any considerable period after the Armistice been faced. The CAF continued to exist because the RAF was willing to co-operate and the Canadian government had not made up its mind. But all concerned with it knew that its future was clouded, and they manifested their awareness in a variety of ways. For battle-hardened pilots the transition to peacetime conditions, and to the very different challenges of organization and administration, was difficult enough. The task of formulating a policy that would persuade the government to maintain the CAF was one for which most of them were not equipped.[3]

This situation was partially addressed on March 31, 1919, when the CAF moved to its new home, Shoreham-by-Sea. Both CAF squadrons now formed 1 Canadian Wing under the command of former RNAS pilot Major Robert Leckie, by decision of the Canadian Air Board, the governing body of the CAF.

In addition, a Technical and Supply Branch was established and its members began the task of acquiring technical data from the RAF for future use in Canada. All these measures were taken by authority of the Overseas Military Council.

As part of the organization of the CAF, on May 15, 1919, MacLaren was appointed the liaison officer, with the rank of acting major.

A number of questions still remained unanswered. Should the CAF be equipped with aircraft identical to the RAF's? Or should they be adapted to the rigours of the Canadian climate? What should the role of the CAF be? Should it act in concert with the RAF in time of war? Or should it be a distinctive Canadian force carrying out a civil as well as a military role?

These questions were answered when the British government decided to present to its Dominions a gift of surplus RAF aircraft, as S.F. Wise describes:

> On 4 June the Colonial Secretary cabled to Ottawa that "His Majesty's Government have approved of [a] proposal of Air Council that a gift of aeroplanes not exceeding 100 in number should be made to any Dominion requiring machines object of His Majesty's Government being to assist Dominions wishing to establish air forces and thereby develop defence of the Empire by air."
>
> The Canadian government spent some time in careful examination of this gift horse, and rather more in some picayune bargaining over what aircraft it would be pleased to receive. Eventually Ottawa agreed to accept 62 Avro 504s, 12 DH9s, 12 SE5s, 10 DH4s, two H16 flying boats, two Bristol Fighters, and a Snipe. In addition, Canada received at least six non-rigid airships, some kite balloons, a large amount of tools, spare engines, and other equipment, and three hundred vehicles of various types. The total value of this gift was approximately $5 million; the only cost to Canada was that of shipment. This, it was later remarked, was "a sum greater than that which the Canadian government spent on aviation during the four years 1919–20 to 1922–23."[4]

In a letter dated October 17, 1919, from the Headquarters of the CAF to the British Air Ministry both Squadron Leader Leckie and Squadron Leader MacLaren were formally released from the RAF to continue working with the CAF. The letter read, in part, as follows:

> In the interview with General Trenchard, it was pointed out by him that no objection would be raised by the Air Ministry to the releasing of these two officers for the purpose of doing duty with the Canadian Government, either in Ottawa or in this country.
>
> As Colonel Leckie has been appointed Superintendent of Flying Operations in Canada, it is requested that he be loaned to the Canadian Government without pay and allowances for the period of three years for the purpose of carrying these duties.
>
> It is also requested that Squadron Leader MacLaren be permitted to continue in his duties as Director of Air Services, Canadian Air Force, and as Canadian Liaison Officer at Air Ministry, with a view to being loaned for a period of three years for the purpose of continuing liaison duties at the Air Ministry. This appointment is created by Canadian Air Board for a request to be put forward to the Air Ministry for the loan of this officer.[5]

The gifted aircraft and equipment were shipped to Canada during the summer and fall of 1920. MacLaren acted in the capacity of liaison officer, or "chief scrounger," as he later described the role. When the shipments arrived in Canada, former RNAS pilot Nick Carter was there to receive and distribute them.

By this time the CAF was just a ghost of its former somewhat tenuous self. Officers had received permission to return to the RAF, and many did. What was left at Shoreham were those like MacLaren who managed the shipping of aircraft and equipment to Canada, the last function of the fledgling CAF. MacLaren resigned his permanent commission with the RAF on December 1, 1920.

Left to right: Captains W.G. Claxton, D.R. MacLaren, and Lt. Staffanson, Upper Heyford, Oxfordshire, 1919.

Captain D.R. MacLaren, DSO, MC and Bar, DFC, about 1919.

Major D.R. MacLaren with Sopwith Snipe aircraft, Upper Heyford, Oxfordshire, May 1919.

D.R. MacLaren.

Left to right: Capt. D.R. MacLaren, Major A.E. McKeever, unknown, and C.F. Falkenberg.

NINETEEN

Civil Aviation

B y war's end, the Canadian Air Board turned its attention to domestic uses of aircraft and decided to offer air services in the early 1920s to other Canadian government departments for the performance of such activities as "forestry patrol to control forest fires, fishery patrol to control illegal fishing, aerial surveying and map making from air photographs (which) was to prove of immense value to the prospector and explorer, leading to the opening of many remote regions."[1]

In the spring of 1921, MacLaren was back in his hometown of Vancouver, having resigned from the RAF. At that time, commercial aviation centred around aerial exhibitions and barnstorming. It was not until the mid-1920s that aircraft would be employed in other business activities. In 1924 MacLaren purchased a Curtiss JN-4 and in 1925 formed Pacific Airways Limited in partnership with Ernest Rogers, vice president of the B.C. Sugar Refinery. Pacific Airways was one of two coastal aviation companies. The other was Dominion Airways Ltd., under E.C.W. Dobbin. MacLaren served as executive officer and chief pilot of Pacific Airways until 1928. Chris Weicht, in *Trans Canada Airway: An Aviation History*, describes the evolution of Pacific Airways:

> On June 14, 1926, Pacific Airways purchased a surplus Curtiss HS-2L from the U.S. Navy, registered as G-CAFH, and at S/L Earl Godfrey's suggestion, MacLaren began petitioning the federal government to allow private enterprise the opportunity to bid on the Fishery patrols. The company was based at the Jericho Beach Air Station and was soon successful in doing all the Fishery's flying requirements.
>
> In 1928, Pacific Airways sold out to a new competitor, Western Canada Airways, who continued to operate from a base at Jericho beach on English Bay, but began to acquire new aircraft — a Boeing B-1D, G-CASX, and later a B-1E, G-CATY named "Petrel," as well as leasing two Vickers Vedettes from Canadian Vickers, G-CASW and G-CAUT. W.C.A. itself became part of Winnipeg-based Canadian Airways in 1930, and that company continued operations on the B.C. Coast from Vancouver until it became part of Canadian Pacific Air Lines in mid-December 1941.[2]

In 1928 MacLaren was appointed superintendent of the Pacific Coast Division of Western Canada Airways, with headquarters in Vancouver. As Mary E. Oswald, editor of *They Led the Way: Members of Canada's Aviation Hall of Fame*, explains, "He expanded the air operations into the Yukon using the latest available aircraft, on which he became qualified. Pilots under his command in the sub-Arctic, the Yukon and throughout

D.R. MacLaren with Curtis JN-4A aircraft G-CAEP of Pacific Airways Ltd., Vancouver, B.C., 1925.

British Columbia included N.G. Forester and S.R. McMillan.… In 1929 he and H. Hollick-Kenyon … flew the experimental airmail service between Regina and Moose Jaw, Saskatchewan, and Medicine Hat, Lethbridge and Calgary, Alberta."[3]

Major Donald MacLaren, along with Colonel J.M. Rolston, was instrumental in the establishment of the Vancouver Municipal Field, which replaced the old Lansdowne Field. On their own initiative, having been rebuffed a number of times when they asked the mayor and council to build a municipal airport, they convinced the local farmers who owned land on Sea Island to sell it at $150 per acre. In 1929 the city finally agreed to purchase the land for $350,000. Chris Weicht tells us more:

> In 1930, Bill Templeton began to draw up plans for the new airfield on Sea Island, comprising 462 acres of land. The main runway was 2,350 feet long and 100 feet wide, but a grandiose plan also called for five runways

converging on a 1,000-foot circle, as well as large hangars and recreational facilities, with a total cost to the taxpayers of $600,000 — a hefty sum for the depression era. Local citizens began referring to the airport as "The Folly on the Marsh," but construction went ahead starting in May 1930, albeit on a much more conservative level....

The new Vancouver Municipal Field ... officially opened on July 22, 1931.[4]

With the purchase of Western Canada Airways in 1930 by Canadian Airways out of Winnipeg, owned by James Richardson, it became the Western Canada Division of Canadian Airways Limited. MacLaren was named the assistant general manager for British Columbia and the Yukon, a position he would hold until 1937.

In 1930 Canadian Airways received the contract from the Canadian government to deliver mail from Winnipeg to Calgary and from Regina to Edmonton via Saskatoon, formalizing the Prairie Air Mail service. Frank H. Ellis, in *Canada's Flying Heritage,* tells us who piloted this service: "Ten veteran pilots were assigned to the job: Winnipeg to Regina, W.J. Buchanan and G.A. Thompson; Regina to Calgary, F.R. Brown, A.H. Farrington, A.E. Jarvis, and H. Hollick-Kenyon; Regina to Edmonton, M.E. Ashton, Paul Calder, W.N. Cummings, C.M.G. Farrell and D.R. MacLaren."[5]

In an interview MacLaren gave on his civil aviation career (date of interview unknown), he wanted to play down his war experience, saying any discussion of the war "didn't belong in this era at all." He did discuss his work in civil aviation in the 1930s and '40s. MacLaren described the budding airmail service in this manner: "I was one of the pilots on that for a while, to get it started, to get some experience on this. Well it was a straight bush operation, you know. You had no aids to navigation (just) little lanterns every 15 miles on posts, on steel towers. When the sun rose, they'd go out. When the sun went down, they'd come on."[6]

In addition to the beacon lights along the route, each of the city airports involved had a revolving searchlight that indicated the destination. The Regina to Edmonton route, via Saskatoon and North Battleford, was a day run. A final leg of the route was added in January 1931 between Calgary and Lethbridge. Hollick-Kenyon flew the inaugural trip on January 15.

It should be noted that on December 23, 1931, MacLaren was appointed honorary aide-de-camp to the governor general. The previous April he had been made an honorary wing commander on the non-permanent reserve list of officers with the Royal Canadian Air Force.

The prairie airmail routes continued until almost 1932 when they were discontinued due to government cutbacks as a result of the Great Depression. MacLaren was not at all pleased with this decision. "[S]uddenly the Conservative government cut the whole bloody thing off in 1931. And left everybody sitting with no compensation what so ever. No encouragement what so ever. Just $650,000 a year was what it was costing the government for these, they called them experiments. So they just dropped the thing ... it was too much money."[7]

Commercial passenger service in the early 1930s was in its infancy, with Donald MacLaren playing a major role, as Chris Weicht describes:

> Canadian Airways Ltd. purchased a twin engine 10 passenger Sikorsky S-38C amphibian, CF-ASO, for use on its Vancouver-Victoria route. This company operated from an office at Coal Harbour in Vancouver at the foot of Cadero Street, and provided an excellent service, which was flown by E.P.H. "Bill" Wells, backed up by Pacific Division Manager Major Donald R. MacLaren. Unfortunately, two years later, on May 19, 1934, the popular amphibian had developed corrosion so bad from its continual use in salt water than [sic] it had to be withdrawn from use and was replaced by a Fairchild 71 and a Fokker Super-universal, then much later by a twin engine de Havilland DH-89A.[8]

The de Havilland DH-89 Rapide CF-AVJ began daily service from Vancouver to Seattle in 1936. Billy Wells continued as the pilot. Canadian Airways was in direct competition with United Airlines, which flew the

Boeing 247 airliner. The de Havilland biplane looked like an antique beside the sleeker, more modern, all-metal two-engine 247 monoplane. Quoting from Chris Weicht's *Trans Canada Airway: An Aviation History*,

> C.A.L. had acquired the airmail contract from Vancouver to Seattle and at the insistence of the Canadian Post Office, whose policy was to "buy British," the de Havilland "Rapide" had been pressed into service. Shortly afterwards, however, the Post Office reversed its edict and by August 1936 C.A.L. had ordered a new Lockheed 10A "Electra" CF-AZY, which was flown to Vancouver from the factory at Burbank, California, by Herbert Hollick-Kenyon and Don MacLaren.[9]

It was Canadian Airways Limited's plan to become the first Canada-wide airline. Owner and president James Richardson, along with his partner in this venture, Canadian Pacific Railway, began negotiations with the federal government in late 1936 or early 1937.

In 1936, Ottawa had merged the Department of Railways and Canals and the Department of Marine to form the Department of Transport under its minister, American C.D. Howe, who had quickly laid the groundwork for the formation of Trans-Canada Air Lines.

MacLaren believed Howe was "a man that was dynamic ... he was an engineer and he'd been a professor at Dalhousie University, teaching. An American, of course. He had ideas of getting things done."[10] MacLaren was directly involved in the negotiations with Howe and the government on behalf of Canadian Airways. He worked tirelessly during the summer of 1936 in Ottawa, trying to convince Howe and his bureaucrats of the merits of Canadian Airways' vision for a trans-continental airline. MacLaren got wind of a proposal to C.D. Howe from the Vickers Company, which was manufacturing airplanes in Montreal, to use their aircraft and to let them run the proposed new airline. MacLaren felt there was not a single aircraft from that company that was any good. He had to figure out a way to convince the government of the perils of going with the Vickers plan. MacLaren and his negotiations team needed someone on the political side to support them, so they contacted Gary Turgeon, the deputy whip of the Conservative MPs. MacLaren's lobbying efforts and the lengths he and his team went to make the Conservatives aware of Canadian Airways interests are fascinating.

> Gary Turgeon, who was a smooth little fellow ... A hell of a smart little politician, and as smooth as oil. Well, of course, he showed us right away what we had to do. It took us 2 ½ weeks of hanging around that hotel, going to his room every night and him going to talk to every bloody member of Parliament, himself. Then he'd hold a party; he'd bring a lot of them out, French-Canadians, and we'd sing French songs. I had known a lot of French songs and made friends of these members of Parliament and tell them about Canadian Airways you see. And the minister was at some of these parties, then you could see what was happening. We were making friends. And the next thing you know, the minister said we'll throw this thing out; you fellows know what you are talking about. And we got a chance to talk to him and his deputy, Colonel Smart, who had been one of my professors at McGill University, mechanical engineering. He had a suite in the Chateau Laurier and he had a six-inch lathe up there and a small drill press ... and the oil from this lathe was spinning around and going through the floor.
>
> He was a delightful old guy ... well he was our friend. So we stipulated in our plan ... and we went ahead and made a plan. But we made it too fast; we made a great mistake there. They stuck to this 10A Lockheed, and I didn't like that at all. Lockheed was making a new airplane with bigger engines, called the 14. I didn't like that either, but that was the only thing we could think of having performance over the mountains.[11]

Howe accepted Canadian Airways' plan in principle but wanted a government representative on the board of the company. Since the Canadian government was going to spend lots of money on building runways, providing weather services, navigation systems, and much more for the company, Howe wanted a government representative to oversee all of this. MacLaren did not object, but the partners in the project, the Canadian Pacific Railway, did. Sir Edward Beatty, CEO of CPR did not want to get "boxed in by government." MacLaren could not convince him otherwise. Neither could he convince James Richardson to put pressure on Sir Edward to come around.

Months dragged by. There was talk that Prime Minister Mackenzie King favoured the creation of a government-run airline. Talks broke down between Canadian Airways and the government, and on March 16, 1937, Canadian Airways Ltd. withdrew their proposal.

On April 10, 1937, Trans-Canada Air Lines came into existence, by an Act of Parliament, as a wholly owned subsidiary of Canadian National Railway, which itself was a Crown corporation.

MacLaren was destined to play a pivotal role in the formation and operations of Canada's first airline. He had come to know C.D. Howe during the negotiations with him and Canadian Airways and C.D. was impressed with this young, capable man. MacLaren describes what happened next:

> Well I had been seeing C.D. Howe a lot, you see, during that summer of 36 … in and out of the office, seeing his deputy and so on. So when he did get the thing going … he created it by an Act of Parliament, he called me … I guess this would be March, on the telephone and asked me to go down and report to Mr. Hungerford, president of the Canadian National Railway, because they were going to hold the stock in this new company, Trans Canada Air Lines.
>
> Well, I had to get on the blower right away to Mr. Richardson and ask his permission to do this. I said I want to do this, but I can't do this without your

permission. I'm working for you. Well he reluctant-ly said yes. But I knew it was very reluctant. He hated C.D. Howe, you see. He said he was an engineer and he built elevators for me; he didn't know how to run a government ... that was just the kind of an attitude he took to him. Well I couldn't get around that. So I said all right, with your approval, permission, I'm off. So I went down there.[12]

MacLaren was hired by TCA as its first employee, in the position of assistant to the president, Mr. Hungerford. MacLaren was installed in an office in Montreal on McGill Street at CNR's headquarters. The first thing he was asked to do was to draw up an operations plan for the new airline. MacLaren realized the magnitude of the task ahead, and knew he needed technical assistance. P.G. Johnson, head of United Airlines, offered his help. C.D. Howe and Hungerford were pleased with this de-velopment, since United Airlines could provide the planes for the fleet, and the new Canadian company could benefit from the whole standard of operations that United had developed under Johnson.

The first order of business was to make a survey of the routes the airline would use.

A little Lockheed 12 was made available. With Jack Tudhope at the controls; MacLaren; Dan McLean, assistant controller of civil aviation; and Mr. Colyer, vice president of operations for United, piled into this eight-passenger plane and flew first to Princeton and Cranbrook, then on to Lethbridge, Calgary, and Edmonton. There they stayed over-night. The next day they travelled to Regina and Winnipeg, where they stayed overnight. The next leg of the trip took them to North Bay and on to Toronto, which did not even have a landing field. They touched down on the grass field of the Aero Club, which saw only little Tiger Moths land there, normally. Finally they flew to Ottawa and their final destination, Montreal.

MacLaren drew up the plan for routes and operations with the help of one of the CNR executives and presented it to the minister of trans-port. How was it received?

Wonderful, we had a meeting with his officers. Every one of them agreed. We also specified, we had met statins at certain places. And we wanted forecasters at certain places, at Kapuscasing we were right up near the Arctic Circle almost … at least for weather, you were. There was all kinds of bad weather up in that direction. We had to have a forecaster up in there.

Well, they finally agreed to everything we put in there, and away we went.[13]

P.G. Johnson became the head of Trans-Canada, with Donald MacLaren as his assistant. Mr. Colyer went to Winnipeg to set up the operational headquarters for the airline. There he rented a hangar from Canadian Airways. Two Lockheeds were used for training. Bill Straith, a Canadian, and Slim Lewis were hired as pilot trainers. MacLaren was to hire the pilots necessary for a Canada-wide operation.

Another thing I had to do was deal with the lists of pilots who were writing in from Canadian Airways and wanting to be accepted. I had to send this list back to Canadian Airways. Now here's the list of people who are applying … how many of these can you release? Well, they first of all said they wouldn't release any. Well I coaxed him into remembering they are going to quit on you if you don't. We're not offering them anything as long as they are working for you. But if they quit we will offer them; we will accept applications from them.

Well, they finally softened on it anyway and gave us a list of the ones they wanted to keep. Well, we got a large number of them. There was the cradle of our pilotage, was Canadian Airways. That's where we got the best of the lot that formed the whole strength of Trans-Canada Air Lines. The boys who came from there.

Well, there wasn't one of them though that could fly instruments. Out of the 14 or 15 that we first took

on, maybe 18, there were four who could … fly instruments. Went nervous. People I knew very well too.
Good pilots in the bush, good judgement. But simply
couldn't stand the feeling of trying to fly an airplane
on instruments.…

Slim couldn't understand why it was, but Slim had
never done any bush flying. So anyway we started to
build the thing up, and then we had these Lockheed 14s
we had to get ready. We were not going to carry passengers for a year. It was very wise. But we were going to
run training flights on schedule all the way through to
Montreal. When we could get all the facilities arranged.
We were going to be given mail to help pay the costs.
The post office agreed to that. And express as well.[14]

Canadian Airways offered to TCA the Seattle route, which the latter
readily accepted. Chris Weicht describes the transition for some pilots:
"Canadian Airways' pilots had been flying the Vancouver-Seattle route
until the end of August 1937 when, upon the last flight of that month
at Vancouver, pilots Billy Wells and Maurice McGregor were informed
they now worked for Trans Canada Airlines. The two 'Electra's' were
quickly repainted and on September 1, Trans Canada Airlines made its
first flight to Seattle."[15]

When it came to the building of hangars, one each in Winnipeg,
Lethbridge, and Montreal, MacLaren encountered problems. No one had
ever built in Canada the size of hangars TCA wanted. MacLaren, with his
mechanical engineering training from McGill, helped design them, and
the Austin Company of the United States came up and built them in
three months, using amounts of steel no one had ever imagined would be
needed. MacLaren was criticized for not using Canadian companies, but
explained to his detractors that Mr. Howe and Mr. Johnson had made the
decision in this regard. MacLaren knew his critics were probably right.

Other tasks given to MacLaren included determining what make of
gas truck to purchase. He personally drove and tested a number of manu-
facturers' models and settled on the White company, only to be told that

the CNR board of directors decided to purchase GMC models. It was a political decision, made by the government.

The decision on what make and model of radios to use landed on MacLaren's desk. He oversaw the development of specifications for a new ten-channel system with the help of Western Electric.

Trans-Canada Air Lines started flying passengers on April 1, 1939, but at that time they did not have their own sales department. MacLaren argued for one independent of CNR's.

> The Canadian National told us we didn't need one. We've got all the sales department that you need. And I asked them at the board that day how many of your sales managers believe in aviation. You've got lots of good ticket offices. But if anybody walks into your office and says he wants to fly to Vancouver would anybody there try to sell him an airline ticket? I said we can't have the two together. We can have a stock of tickets in some of your offices, but we will have to have our separate offices, our separate faith and belief in this thing. And people who will do nothing else but concentrate on pushing it.
>
> Well the vice president said the board of directors had authorized a traffic department. Well, that's what we wanted to know, and it was all the help we wanted. Then the legal department, they gave us a lot of help. And the insurance department. And the dining car department helped us design food and purchase it; it was rather elementary, in boxes you know, cold stuff. And they gave us a man to act as kind of a supervisor of food and catering. So they were a great deal of help. And we started hiring trained nurses as stewardesses. And that was a good move, because those girls could cope with anything. It's a lot different today.[16]

As can be seen in these examples of MacLaren's leadership and management style, he was a man who knew what he wanted. He set his mind to creating the very best airline possible, and through all his efforts he accomplished that goal. He was not shy to speak his mind whether to his president, to the board of directors, or to ministers of the government.

TCA was quickly taking shape and all the needed elements for a fully functioning airline were falling into place, some more easily than others. If flying over sixteen thousand feet (the planes were not pressurized at that time) the pilots and passengers had to be issued and wear oxygen masks. Some were reluctant to do so, as MacLaren describes:

> And you would come across some guys oh I don't want these, some pilots of some kind. Boasting I don't want any oxygen, and he'd probably pass out. Coming across from Toronto to Winnipeg one time this little fellow didn't want oxygen, and he passed out, and the little stewardess thought he was dead. Heck he was blue all over. She put a blanket over him. Well the first officer said I've never seen a man dead like that; I'll go down and have a look at him. Shook him and he woke up again.[17]

The fleet of aircraft soon expanded to include twelve Lockheed 14H-2 ten-passenger machines, and six Lockheed Lodestars, each seating fourteen passengers. The original flying personnel included fifty-one captains, forty-nine second officers, and thirty-six stewardesses (at the time, all flight attendants were women and their official title was "stewardess"). The entire complement of staff totalled some 1,200 individuals.

Within three years of joining TCA, MacLaren was made superintendent of stations and director of passenger services. "I had the job of director of stations, the operation of the stations, the personnel of the stations, all the way through the system. Keep them manned, keep them running, keep the dispatching system co-ordinated … we had a lot of trouble with that. Holding examinations for pilots, and things like that. That was kind of working right in to be operations manager. Oh well we have a great organization today."[18]

In 1941 MacLaren formed the first Air Cadet squadron, in Winnipeg, Manitoba. He later became the provincial chairman and then attained the presidency of the Air Cadet League of Canada. Air Canada designed the D.R. MacLaren Trophy in his honour, an award given annually to the most proficient Royal Canadian Air Cadet Squadron in British Columbia.

TCA had planned to have, by 1941, Douglas four-engined DC-4s, called the North Star. They proposed to use the Canadair plant in Quebec to assemble them with Rolls-Royce engines. MacLaren was opposed to this idea. "Well immediately when I heard this ... the same old thing, trying to make racehorses out of mules.... We should have said no to that, because along came the Lockheeds with their 149s [a new, long-range version of the Lockheed L-049 Constellation]. They had 23 of them all ready to sell, $200,000 apiece, pressurized, 60 passengers or more ... everything you could expect in a modern four-engine airplane. And they were going to deliver them right away."[19]

MacLaren's view did not prevail.

In a reorganization of TCA in 1948, MacLaren was named executive assistant to the president, Pacific Area, working again out of Vancouver. Gordon McGregor was the president at that time and MacLaren did not want to go back to Montreal.

> I had had enough of the turmoil. I had organized the passenger service department and catering, frozen food and design of galleys. Our system of galleys was copied by other people. The unit system.
>
> I figured I had had enough of that. I didn't want to go back to Montreal. So I proposed to the president that I could come out here (Vancouver) and represent him as executive assistant to the president. He readily agreed, and so did the board of directors ... I said why don't you make Sandgate your man in Winnipeg. And Walter Fowler your man in Halifax, which they did. So when those things were created, they filled the same job in the east.
>
> I kept in touch with everybody in British Columbia. Called on businesses and other Boards of Trade. Watched anything that was going on, like the building of Kitimat and Kemano. I kept them fully aware of what was going

on in the way of business. And I enjoyed it. Took no executive responsibility. But I was a lot of help to them and others, because they knew what they were doing. You had some friction between your sales department and your operations department; it had been going on all over the system. I knew this. Well I set to work to cure that. And we did ... very easily.

We came back to live here (Vancouver) and it was like coming back to paradise. 1949 we came out here. I was 57 years old then.[20]

MacLaren saw, during his time at TCA, the development of newer and more powerful airplanes like the Super Constellation, a four-engine aircraft of 3,600 horsepower. The Viscount entered the airline field in the early 1950s. It had Rolls-Royce turbo engines, had great performance, and was very quiet inside. MacLaren made sure TCA acquired Viscounts for their fleet. Next came the Vanguard, the next size larger than the Viscount. With its Dart engine "you could run them 6,000 hours without touching them," stated MacLaren.[21]

He retired from TCA in 1958. Reflecting back on his time there, he stated,

But I think it was one of the grandest experiences that anybody could possibly have to have been in on the beginning. Not that you got any reward yourself. But you were one of the people. And that's what makes me so happy.

I don't want to be shown up as important, any more than anyone else because during the war everybody had to pull together very closely. And that's what they're doing today.[22]

MacLaren was not out for personal aggrandizement or glory or recognition. He received satisfaction from being a part of a team, a team which was working well and making a contribution to the cause, be that the cause of freedom in the First World War or the cause of providing fast,

D.R. MacLaren (left) with Paul Martin Sr. at a 1978 presentation.

safe passenger air transportation for Canadians. He was modest about his accomplishments and his contributions, satisfied just to be a part of it all.

In 1977 Donald R. MacLaren was inducted into Canada's Aviation Hall of Fame. His induction citation reads, "His exceptional success as a wartime aviator in the cause of peace, coupled to a succession of civil pioneering achievements as a first generation bush pilot and his dedication to purpose in fostering the growth of the Air Cadet league of Canada, despite adversity, have been of outstanding benefit to Canadian aviation."[23]

Don MacLaren passed away in Vancouver on July 4, 1988, at the ripe old age of ninety-five.

The last words of this book go to Major D.R. MacLaren, DSO, MC and Bar, DFC, CLD'H, CdeG:

When we take the time to look around us at what we have here in this country we call Canada, and the people who live within our boundaries, we can see that there is in the words of our prime minister "the shared belief in the overwhelming importance of human equality and dignity."

We in the aviation business assume great responsibility when we undertake the transportation of people both at home and across borders. As we fly we see no borders, no walls no fences. We are conscious of the fact that the most precious cargo we carry is the human mind. How vital to the welfare of our country and the whole world to increase and encourage the meeting of minds.

As apostles of aviation we look down to see this earth as one country and mankind as One family. We do not see our fellow man as black, yellow, brown or red. We know that aviation can bring the greatest benefits to all mankind and can serve as the most useful bridge to world peace, if only all mankind will agree to remove the barriers he himself has set up. And now we can have the satisfaction of knowing that as we have earnestly and actively spread the aviation gospel, we are surely helping to make this earth one country and to keep this country one Canada.[24]

Acknowledgements

My heartfelt thanks go out to my darling wife and fellow researcher of this book, Diane Elizabeth Gunn. She and I were together in the National Archives in Kew, London, when we looked up all the material available on McLeod, McKeever, and MacLaren. She dove deeper into the records than I, and quite enjoyed the hunt for material. The staff of the National Archives are to be thanked as well.

In Canada, the staff of the Library and Archives Canada in Ottawa are to be thanked, so too is Carol Reid and the library staff of the Canadian War Museum. Ottawa is also the location of the Directorate of History and Heritage, which Diane and I visited. The DHH staff were very helpful. I thank them for allowing me to print many of the pictures that appear in this book. Thanks also go to the staff at the Stratford-Perth Archives for their assistance in gathering information on McKeever. Diane was also my helpdesk in all matters computer-related and technical in nature. Her assistance was invaluable.

I would also like to acknowledge Alan McLeod for his prolific letter writing and Helen McLeod for providing them to the Canadian

War Museum's library in Ottawa. Thanks go to Alan Adams, McLeod's nephew, for his assistance, and to Philip Hayes, an Alan McLeod enthusiast and artist. I would also like to thank Leanne Stewart of McLeod House in Stonewall, Manitoba.

To those at Dundurn, including Kathryn Lane and Carl Brand, I thank you for believing in me and in the merits of this book.

Notes

INTRODUCTION

1. *History of No. 11 Squadron Royal Air Force*, National Archives, London, file: AIR 1/163/15/124/10.

CHAPTER ONE: The Early Days and Flight Training

1. George Drew, *Canada's Fighting Airmen* (Toronto: MacLean Publishing, 1931), 216.
2. "Alan McLeod," George Metcalf Archival Collection, Canadian War Museum, Ottawa, file: 58A1 51.6.
3. C.W. Hunt, *Dancing in the Sky* (Toronto: Dundurn, 2009), 113–16.
4. Jack R. Lincke, *Jenny Was No Lady: The Story of the JN-4D* (New York: W. W. Norton, 1970), 40.
5. Ibid., 38.
6. Hunt, *Dancing in the Sky*, 83.
7. Ibid., 120.
8. Ibid., 121–23.

CHAPTER TWO: Off to the Old Country

1. Anna Malinovska and Mauriel Joslyn, *Voices in Flight: Conversations with Air Veterans of the Great War* (Barnsley, UK: Pen & Sword, 2006), 14.
2. Joseph A. Phelan, *Aeroplanes and Flyers of the First World War* (New York: Grosset & Dunlap, 1966), 30.

CHAPTER THREE: In France with No. 2 Squadron

1. Mike O'Connor, *Airfields and Airmen: Arras*, Battleground Europe (Barnsley, UK: Pen & Sword, 2004), 106.
2. "Combats in the Air, Squadron No. 2," National Archives, London, file: AIR 1/692/21/20/46.

CHAPTER FOUR: McLeod's Last Three Months at War

1. "Combats in the Air, Squadron No. 2," National Archives, London, file, AIR 1/692/21/20/46.
2. Raymond H. Fredette, *The Sky on Fire: The First Battle of Britain, 1917–1918* (Washington, DC: Smithsonian Institution Press, 1991), 183.
3. "Combats in the Air, Squadron No. 2."

CHAPTER FIVE: McLeod's Last Flight

1. Leslie Roberts, *There Shall Be Wings: A History of the Royal Canadian Air Force* (Toronto: Clarke, Irwin, 1959), 12.
2. Peter Kilduff, *Richthofen: Beyond the Legend of the Red Baron* (New York: John Wiley & Sons, 1994), 15.
3. Norman Franks and Greg VanWyngarden, *Fokker Dr I Aces of World War 1*, Aircraft of the Aces 40 (Oxford: 2001), 68.
4. "Alan McLeod," George Metcalf Archival Collection, Canadian War Museum, Ottawa, file: 58A1 51.3.
5. Ibid.
6. George Drew, *Canada's Fighting Airmen* (Toronto: MacLean Publishing, 1931), 230–31.

7. "Alan McLeod," file: 58A1 51.7.

8. Ibid.

9. John D. Clarke, *Gallantry Medals & Awards of the World* (Somerset, UK: Patrick Stephens, 1993), 72.

10. Drew, *Canada's Fighting Airmen,* 232–33.

11. "Alan McLeod," file: 58A1 51.5.

12. Ibid.

13. Molly Billings, "The Influenza Pandemic of 1918," accessed 7/8/2015, virus.stanford.edu/uda.

14. "Alan McLeod," file: 58A1 51.5.

15. Arthur Bishop, *Our Bravest and Our Best: The Stories of Canada's Victoria Cross Winners* (Toronto: McGraw-Hill Ryerson, 1995), 94.

16. "Alan McLeod," file: 58A1 51.7.

17. Ibid.

18. Mike O'Connor, *Airfields and Airmen: Arras,* Battleground Europe (Barnsley, UK: Pen & Sword, 2004), 107.

CHAPTER SIX: The Listowel Boy Joins the RFC

1. W.T. Barnard, *The Queen's Own Rifles of Canada 1860–1960* (Don Mills: Ontario Publishing Company, 1960), 116.

2. "A. McKeever," National Archives, London, UK, file: WO 339/809, 72.

3. Ibid., 35.

4. "McKeever — Canadian Air Ace: Andrew McKeever, the Greatest Two-Seater Pilot Ever," *War Monthly Magazine,* April 1979 Stratford-Perth Archives, file: "Andrew Edward McKeever."

5. John H. Morrow, *The Great War in the Air: Military Aviation from 1909 to 1921* (Washington, DC: Smithsonian Institution Press, 1993), 235.

CHAPTER SEVEN: No. 11 Squadron, RFC

1. Jon Guttman, *Bristol F2 Fighter Aces of World War 1,* Aircraft of the Aces 79 (Oxford: Osprey, 2007), 20.

2. *History of No. 11 Squadron – Royal Air Force*, National Archives, London, UK, file: AIR 1/163/15/124/10.

3. Mike O'Connor, *Airfields and Airmen: Arras*, Battleground Europe (Barnsley, UK: Pen & Sword, 2004), 68.

4. David L. Bashow, *Knights of the Air: Canadian Fighter Pilots in the First World War* (Toronto: McArthur, 2000), 88.

5. Guttman, *Bristol F2 Fighter Aces*, 12.

6. Leonard Bridgman and Oliver Stewart, *The Clouds Remember: The Aeroplanes of World War I* (London: Arms and Armour Press, 1972), 85.

7. Aaron Norman, *The Great Air War: The Men, The Planes, The Saga of Military Aviation: 1914–1918* (New York: Macmillan, 1968), 160–61.

8. Jack Herris and Bob Pearson, *Aircraft of World War I: 1914–1918* (London: Amber Books, 2010), 141.

9. "Combats in the Air, Squadron No. 2," National Archives, London, file: AIR 1/1219/204/5/2634.

10. Ibid.

11. Arthur Gould Lee, *Open Cockpit* (London: Grub Street, 2012), 66–67.

12. George Drew, *Canada's Fighting Airmen* (Toronto: MacLean Publishing, 1931), 278.

CHAPTER EIGHT: August and September 1917

1. "Combats in the Air, Squadron No. 2," National Archives, Kew, UK, file: AIR 1/1219/204/5/2634.

2. Jon Guttman, *Bristol F2 Fighter Aces of World War 1*, Aircraft of the Aces 79 (Oxford: Osprey, 2007), 23.

3. John Norman Harris, *Knights of the Air* (Toronto: Macmillan, 1958), 138–39.

CHAPTER NINE: October and November 1917

1. George Drew, *Canada's Fighting Airmen* (Toronto: MacLean Publishing, 1931), 279.

2. "Combats in the Air, Squadron No. 2," National Archives, London, file: AIR 1/1219/204/5/2634.

3. S.F. Wise, *Canadian Airmen and the First World War: The Official History of the Royal Canadian Air Force*, vol. 1 (Toronto: University of Toronto Press in co-operation with the Department of National Defence and the Canadian Government Publishing Centre, Supply and Services Canada, 1980), 441.

4. Ibid., 445.

5. John Norman Harris, *Knights of the Air* (Toronto: Macmillan, 1958), 135.

6. Drew, *Canada's Fighting Airmen*, 282.

7. Christopher Shores, Norman Franks, and Russell Guest, *Above the Trenches: A Complete Record of the Fighter Aces and Units of the British Empire Air Forces, 1915–1920* (Stoney Creek, ON: Fortress Publications, 1990), 276.

8. "McKeever's Score by Bde Summaries & RFC Communiques," Directorate of History and Heritage, Ottawa, file: "Andrew Edward McKeever."

9. Norm Shannon, *From Baddeck to the Yalu: Stories of Canada's Airmen at War* (Ottawa: Esprit de Corps Books, 2005), 61–62.

10. Arthur Gould Lee, *Open Cockpit* (London: Grub Street, 2012), 191.

CHAPTER TEN: Home Establishment and the Canadian Air Force

1. S.F. Wise, *Canadian Airmen and the First World War: The Official History of the Royal Canadian Air Force*, vol. 1 (Toronto: University of Toronto Press in co-operation with the Department of National Defence and the Canadian Government Publishing Centre, Supply and Services Canada, 1980), 608.

2. Ibid., 609.

3. Ibid., 611.

4. Ibid., 612.

5. Ibid., 613.

CHAPTER ELEVEN: A Tragic Ending

1. "Great Canadian Soldier Answers Last Call, Major A.E. McKeever, D.S.O., M.C., with Bar, D.F.C., Croix de Guerre, Died on Christmas Night," *Listowel Standard*, January 3, 1920, Stratford-Perth Archives, file: "Andrew Edward McKeever."
2. Ibid.
3. "Hundreds Pay Tribute to Town's WW1 Flying Ace," *Listowel Banner*, October 21, 1987, Directorate of History and Heritage, Ottawa, file: "Major A.E. McKeever."
4. Ibid.

CHAPTER TWELVE: Don MacLaren's Early Years

1. George Drew, *Canada's Fighting Airmen* (Toronto: MacLean Publishing, 1931), 185.
2. Ibid., 187.
3. "Notes from a Speech May 1979 of D.R. MacLaren," George Metcalf Archival Collection, Canadian War Museum, Ottawa, file: 58A1 32.

CHAPTER THIRTEEN: Training to Be a Pilot

1. "Short Service (for the Duration of the War) Attestation of Donald Roderick MacLaren, Royal Flying Corps, May 10, 1917," National Archives, London, file: AIR 79/650.
2. "Notes from a Speech May 1979 of D.R. MacLaren," George Metcalf Archival Collection, Canadian War Museum, Ottawa, file: 58A1 32.
3. Ibid.
4. S.F. Wise, *Canadian Airmen and the First World War: The Official History of the Royal Canadian Air Force*, vol. 1 (Toronto: University of Toronto Press in co-operation with the Department of National Defence and the Canadian Government Publishing Centre, Supply and Services Canada, 1980), 39.
5. "Notes from a Speech May 1979."
6. Wise, *Canadian Airmen and the First World War*, 85.
7. "Notes from a Speech May 1979."

8. Ibid.

9. Ibid.

10. Ibid.

11. Jack Herris and Rob Pearson, *Aircraft of World War I: 1914–1918* (London: Amber Books, 2010), 55.

12. Roderick Ward Maclennan, *The Ideals and Training of a Flying Officer* (Manchester: Crecy, 2009), 66.

13. "Notes from a Speech May 1979."

14. Norman Franks, *Sopwith Camel Aces of World War 1,* Aircraft of the Aces 52 (Oxford: Osprey, 2003), 7.

15. Herris and Pearson, *Aircraft of World War I*, 142.

16. "Notes from a Speech May 1979."

CHAPTER FOURTEEN: No. 46 Squadron

1. "Notes from a Speech May 1979 of D.R. MacLaren," George Metcalf Archival Collection, Canadian War Museum, Ottawa, file: 58A1 32.

2. "No. 46 Squadron, Royal Air Force, Outline of History Since Proceeding Overseas 20-10-1916," National Archives, London, file: AIR 1/692/21/20/46.

3. Arthur Gould Lee, *No Parachute: The Exploits of a Fighter Pilot in the First World War* (London: Arrow Books, 1968), 275.

4. Ibid., 289.

5. "Notes from a Speech May 1979."

6. Ibid.

7. S.F. Wise, *Canadian Airmen and the First World War: The Official History of the Royal Canadian Air Force*, vol. 1 (Toronto: University of Toronto Press in co-operation with the Department of National Defence and the Canadian Government Publishing Centre, Supply and Services Canada, 1980), 484.

8. *Combats of the Air, Squadron No.46,* National Archives, London, file: AIR/1/1223/204/5/2634.

9. Norman Franks, *Albatros Aces of World War 1,* Aircraft of the Aces 32 (Oxford: Osprey, 2003), 30.

CHAPTER FIFTEEN: Operation Michael

1. John Toland, *No Man's Land: 1918, The Last Year of the Great War* (New York: Doubleday, 1980), 15.
2. Arch Whitehouse, *Heroes of the Sunlit Sky* (Toronto: Doubleday, 1967), 222–23.
3. Jack Herris and Rob Pearson, *Aircraft of World War I: 1914–1918* (London: Amber Books, 2010), 150.
4. RG150, Box 7015 National Personal Records Centre, Library and Archives Canada, Ottawa, file:1992-93/166, Box 7015.
5. *Pilot's Flying Log Book, D.R. Maclaren,* George Metcalf Archival Collection, Canadian War Museum, Ottawa, file: 58A 1 31.2.
6. S.F. Wise, *Canadian Airmen and the First World War: The Official History of the Royal Canadian Air Force*, vol. 1 (Toronto: University of Toronto Press in co-operation with the Department of National Defence and the Canadian Government Publishing Centre, Supply and Services Canada, 1980), 497.
7. "No. 46 Squadron, Royal Air Force, Outline of History Since Proceeding Overseas 20-10-1916," National Archives, London, file: AIR 1/692/21/20/46.
8. Wise, *Canadian Airmen and the First World War*, 501.
9. Ibid., 502.
10. Ibid., 503.
11. Taylor Downing, *Secret Warriors: Key Scientists, Code Breakers and Propagandists of the Great War* (London: Little, Brown, 2014), 94.
12. *Combats of the Air, Squadron No.46,* National Archives, London, file: AIR/1/1223/204/5/2634.
13. Wise, *Canadian Airmen and the First World War*, 509.

CHAPTER SIXTEEN: May, June, July 1918

1. Jack Herris and Rob Pearson, *Aircraft of World War I: 1914–1918* (London: Amber Books, 2010), 152.
2. Ibid., 148.
3. D.R. MacLaren, "The Last Three Months of the War in the Air," *Chambers Journal*, 7th ser., vol. 9 (1918–19), 305–9, 327–29.

4. *Combats of the Air, Squadron No.46,* National Archives, London, file: AIR/1/1223/204/5/2634.

5. Norman Franks and Greg Van Wyngarden, *Fokker DrI Aces of World War 1,* Aircraft of the Aces 40 (Oxford: Osprey, 2003), 7.

6. *Combats of the Air, Squadron No.46.*

7. RG150, National Personal Records Centre, Library and Archives Canada, Ottawa, file: 1992-93/166, Box 7015.

8. *Combats of the Air, Squadron No.46.*

9. MacLaren, "The Last Three Months," 305

10. Ibid., 305–6.

11. Herris and Pearson, *Aircraft of World War I,* 166.

12. *Combats of the Air, Squadron No.46.*

13. Herris and Pearson, *Aircraft of World War I,* 169.

14. *Combats of the Air, Squadron No.46.*

CHAPTER SEVENTEEN: Amiens

1. S.F. Wise, *Canadian Airmen and the First World War: The Official History of the Royal Canadian Air Force,* vol. 1 (Toronto: University of Toronto Press in co-operation with the Department of National Defence and the Canadian Government Publishing Centre, Supply and Services Canada, 1980), 521.

2. Ronald Dodds, *The Brave Young Wings* (Stittsville, ON: Canada's Wings, 1980), 91.

3. "No. 46 Squadron, Royal Air Force, Outline of History Since Proceeding Overseas 20-10-1916," National Archives, London, file: AIR 1/692/21/20/46.

4. Tim Cook, *Shock Troops: Canadians Fighting The Great War 1917–1918,* vol. 2 (Toronto: Penguin, 2008), 451.

5. Wise, *Canadian Airmen and the First World War,* 541.

6. MacLaren, "The Last Three Months."

7. Ibid.

8. *Combats of the Air, Squadron No.46,* National Archives, London, file: AIR/1/1223/204/5/2634.

9. MacLaren, "The Last Three Months."

10. Ibid.

11. *Combats of the Air, Squadron No.46.*

12. Wise, *Canadian Airmen and the First World War*, 558.

13. "Notes from a Speech May 1979 of D.R. MacLaren," George Metcalf Archival Collection, Canadian War Museum, Ottawa, file: 58A1 32.

14. MacLaren, "The Last Three Months," 327.

15. Ibid.

16. Ibid.

17. "Notes from a Speech May 1979."

18. MacLaren, "The Last Three Months."

19. Wise, *Canadian Airmen and the First World War*, 564.

20. MacLaren, "The Last Three Months," 328.

21. "Notes from a Speech May 1979."

22. MacLaren, "The Last Three Months."

23. Ibid.

24. "Notes from a Speech May 1979."

25. MacLaren, "The Last Three Months," 329.

26. Dodds, *The Brave Young Wings*, 92.

27. Ibid., 92.

CHAPTER EIGHTEEN: The Canadian Air Force

1. RG150, National Personal Records Centre, Library and Archives Canada, Ottawa, file: AIR/1/1223/204/5/2634.

2. Ibid.

3. S.F. Wise, *Canadian Airmen and the First World War: The Official History of the Royal Canadian Air Force*, vol. 1 (Toronto: University of Toronto Press in co-operation with the Department of National Defence and the Canadian Government Publishing Centre, Supply and Services Canada, 1980), 610.

4. Ibid., 614.

5. "Donald MacLaren," Directorate of History and Heritage, Ottawa.

CHAPTER NINETEEN: Civil Aviation

1. "Notes from a Speech May 1979 of D.R. MacLaren," George Metcalf Archival Collection, Canadian War Museum, Ottawa, file: 58A1 32.

2. Chris Weicht, *Trans Canada Airway: An Aviation History*, Air Pilot Navigator Series 4 (Roberts Creek, BC: Creekside Publications, 2007), 28 and 30.

3. Mary E. Oswald, ed., *They Led the Way: Members of Canada's Aviation Hall of Fame* (Wetaskiwin, AB: Canada's Aviation Hall of Fame, 1999), 116.

4. Weicht, *Trans Canada Airway*, 28 and 30.

5. Frank H. Ellis, *Canada's Flying Heritage* (Toronto: University of Toronto Press, 1954), 319.

6. "Donald MacLaren," Library and Archives Canada, Ottawa, File: MG 30 E 296.

7. Ibid.

8. Weicht, *Trans Canada Airway*, 33 and 34.

9. Ibid., 41.

10. "Donald MacLaren."

11. Ibid.

12. Ibid.

13. Ibid.

14. Ibid.

15. Weicht, *Trans Canada Airway*, 43

16. "Donald MacLaren."

17. Ibid.

18. Ibid.

19. Ibid.

20. Ibid.

21. Ibid.

22. Ibid.

23. Oswald, ed., *They Led the Way*, 116.

24. "Notes from a Speech May 1979."

Bibliography

BOOKS

Barker, Ralph. *The Royal Flying Corps in World War I*. London: Constable & Robinson, 2002.

Bashow, Lt. Col. David L. *Knights of the Air: Canadian Fighter Pilots in the First World War*. Toronto: McArthur & Company, 2000.

Bishop, Arthur. *True Canadian Heroes in the Air*. Toronto: Prospero Books, 2004.

Bowen, Ezra. *Knights of the Air*. Alexandria, VA: Time-Life Books, 1980.

Bowyer, Chaz. *Sopwith Camel — King of Combat*. Bourne End: Aston Publications, 1988.

———. *Bristol F2B Fighter, King of Two-Seaters*. London: Ian Allan, 1985.

Bruce, J.M. *Vintage Warbirds No. 4, The Bristol Fighter*. London: Arms and Armour Press, 1985.

Clarke, John D. *Gallantry Medals and Awards of the World*. Somerset, UK: Patrick Stephens, 1993.

Cook, Tim. *Shock Troops, Canadians Fighting the Great War 1917–1918*. Volume Two. Toronto: Penguin Group, 2008.

Cooksley, Peter. *De Havilland D.H.9 in Action.* Aircraft Number 164. Carrollton, Texas: Squadron/Signal Publications, 1996.

———. *Sopwith Fighters in Action.* Aircraft Number 110. Carrollton, TX: Squadron/Signal Publications, 1991.

Cosgrove, Edmund. *Canada's Fighting Pilots.* Toronto: Clarke, Irwin & Company, 1965.

Cross, Wilbur. *Zeppelins of World War I.* New York: Paragon House, 1991.

Dancocks, Daniel G. *Legacy of Valour: The Canadians at Passchendaele.* Edmonton: Hurtig Publishers, 1986.

Dodds, Ronald. *The Brave Young Wings.* Stittsville, ON: Canada's Wings, 1980.

Drew, George A., Lieutenant Colonel. *Canada's Fighting Airmen.* Toronto: Maclean Publishing, 1931.

Fitzsimons, Bernard, ed. *Warplanes & Air Battles of World War I.* New York: Beekman House, 1973.

Franks, Norman. *Albatros Aces of World War I.* Aircraft of the Aces 32. Oxford: Osprey Publishing, 2000.

Franks, Norman, and Greg Van Wyngarden. *Osprey Aircraft of the Aces 40 Fokker Dr 1 Aces of World War 1.* Oxford: Osprey Publishing, 2001.

———. *Sopwith Camel Aces of World War I.* Aircraft of the Aces 52. Oxford: Osprey Publishing, 2003.

Fredette, Raymond H. *The Sky on Fire: The First Battle of Britain 1917–1918.* Washington, DC: Smithsonian Institution Press, 1991.

Funderburk, Thomas R. *The Fighters: The Men and Machines of the First Air War.* New York: Grosset & Dunlap Publishers, 1965.

Gilbert, Martin. *The Battle of the Somme: The Heroism and Horror of War.* Toronto: McClelland & Stewart, 2006.

Gunn, Roger. *Raymond Collishaw and the Black Flight.* Toronto: Dundurn, 2013.

Guttman, Jon. *Osprey Aircraft of the Aces 79 Bristol F2 Fighter Aces of World War 1.* Oxford: Osprey Publishing, 2008.

Hamilton-Paterson, James. *Marked For Death: The First War in the Air.* New York: Pegasus Books, 2016.

Hart, Peter. *Aces Falling: War Above the Trenches, 1918.* London: Phoenix, 2008.

———. *Bloody April: Slaughter in the Skies Over Arras, 1917.* London: Cassell, 2006.

Herris, Jack, and Bob Pearson. *The Essential Aircraft Identification Guide Aircraft of World War 1 1914–1918.* London: Amber Books, 2014.

Hunt, C.W. *Dancing in the Sky.* Toronto: Dundurn Press, 2009.

Johnson, J.E. *Full Circle: The Tactics of Air Fighting 1914–1964.* New York: Ballentine Books, 1964.

Jones, H.A. *The War in the Air, Being the Story of the Part Played in the Great War by the Royal Air Force.* Vols. 4, 5, and 6. Uckfield, East Sussex: The Naval & Military Press, 1934.

Keegan, John. *The First World War.* Toronto: Vintage Canada, 2000.

Kilduff, Peter. *Richthofen: Beyond the Legend of the Red Baron.* New York: John Wiley & Sons, 1994.

Lee, Arthur Gould. *No Parachute: The Exploits of a Fighter Pilot in the First World War.* London: Arrow Books, 1969.

———. *Open Cockpit.* London: Grub Street, 2012.

Levine, Joshua. *On a Wing and a Prayer: The Untold Story of the Pioneering Aviation Heroes of WWI, in Their Own Words.* London: Collins, 2008.

Libby, Frederick. *Horses Don't Fly.* New York: Arcade Publishing, 2012.

Lincke, Jack R. *Jenny Was No Lady: The Story of the JN-4D.* New York: W. W. Norton & Company, 1970.

Mackay, James, and John W. Mussell. *The Medal Yearbook 2001.* Devon: Token Publishing, 2001.

Maclennan, Roderick Ward. *The Ideals and Training of a Flying Officer.* Manchester: Crecy Publishing, 2009.

Malinovska, Anna, and Mauriel Joslyn. *Voices in Flight: Conversations With Air Veterans of the Great War.* Barnsley, UK: Pen & Sword, 2006.

Manitoba Library Association. *Pioneers and Early Citizens of Manitoba, A Dictionary of Manitoba Biography from the Earliest Times to 1920.* Winnipeg: Peguis Publishers, 1971.

McCaffery, Dan. *Air Aces: The Lives and Times of Twelve Canadian Fighter Pilots.* Toronto: James Lorimer & Company, 1990.

McWillians, James, and R. James Steel. *Amiens: Dawn of Victory.* Toronto: Dundurn Press, 2001.

Morrow, John H. *The Great War in the Air: Military Aviation from 1909 to 1921.* Washington, DC: Smithsonian Institute Press, 1993.

Nowarra, H. J., and Kimbrough S. Brown. *Von Richthofen and the "Flying Circus": The Life and Death of Manfred Freiherr von Richthofen and the History of the Richthofen Jagdgeschwader.* Fallbrook, CA: Aero Publishers, 1964.

O'Connor, Mike. *Battleground Europe, Airfields and Airmen, Arras.* Barnsley, South Yorkshire: Pen & Sword Books, 2004.

O'Kiely, Elizabeth. *Gentleman Air Ace: The Duncan Bell-Irving Story.* Madeira Park, BC: Harbour Publishing, 1992.

Oswald, Mary E., ed. *They Led the Way, Members of Canada's Aviation Hall Of Fame.* Wetaskiwin, Alberta: Canada's Aviation Hall of Fame, 1999.

Pengelly, Colin. *Albert Ball VC: Fighter Pilot Hero of World War I.* Barnsley, UK: Pen & Sword, 2017.

Roberts, Leslie. *There Shall Be Wings: A History of the Royal Canadian Air Force.* Toronto: Clarke, Irwin & Company, 1959.

Robertson, Bruce, ed. *Air Aces of the 1914–1918 War.* Fallbrook, CA: Aero Publishers, 1964.

Shannon, Norm. *From Baddeck to the Yalu: Stories of Canada's Airmen at War.* Ottawa: Esprit de Corps Books, 2005.

Shores, Christopher, Norman Franks, and Russell Guest. *Above the Trenches: A Complete Record of the Fighter Aces and Units of the British Empire Air Forces 1915–1920.* Stony Creek: Fortress Publications, 1990.

Springs, Elliott White. *War Birds: The Diary of a Great War Pilot.* Barnsley, UK: Pen & Sword, 2016.

Toland, John. *No Man's Land 1918 — The Last Year of the Great War.* New York: Doubleday, 1980.

Weicht, Chris. *Trans Canada Airway.* Roberts Creek: Creekside Publications, 2007.

Whitehouse, Arch. *The Fledglin: An Autobiography.* New York: Duel, Sloan and Pearce, 1964.

Wise, S.F. *Canadian Airmen and the First World War: The Official History of the Royal Canadian Air Force*. Vol. 1. Toronto: University of Toronto Press in co-operation with the Department of National Defence and the Canadian Government Publishing Centre, Supply and Services Canada, 1980.

WEBSITES

Bruce Forsyth. "Canadian Military History." militarybruce.com/canadian-forces-base-borden.

"The Calgary Connection, Your Key to the City of Calgary, History of Calgary." incalgary.com/History_of_Calgary.htm.

Image Credits

103 (bottom)	© Imperial War Museums Q 067601
107	Department of National Defence, Directorate of History and Heritage
110	Author's collection
117	Department of National Defence, Directorate of History and Heritage
118	Department of National Defence, Directorate of History and Heritage
127	© Imperial War Museums Q 068941
129	© Imperial War Museums Q 066937
139	Canadian War Museum 20050145–002
140	Canadian War Museum 20050145–001
143	Author's collection
151	© Imperial War Museums Q 056013
152	© Imperial War Museums Q 050328
153	© Imperial War Museums Q 042283
160	© Imperial War Museums Q 107381
174 (top)	Library and Archives Canada PA-006011
174 (bottom)	Library and Archives Canada PA-006093
175 (top)	Library and Archives Canada PA-006026
175 (bottom)	Department of National Defence, Directorate of History and Heritage
181 (top & bottom)	Author's collection
183	Author's collection
184	Author's collection
200	Library and Archives Canada PA-118056
208	Library and Archives Canada C-087010
210	© Imperial War Museums Q 108869
226 (top)	Department of National Defence, Directorate of History and Heritage
226 (bottom)	Canadian War Museum 20080040–012
234 (top)	© Imperial War Museums Q 050329
234 (bottom)	© Imperial War Museums Q 058050
286	Library and Archives Canada C-087000
287 (top)	Library and Archives Canada C-087013

287 (bottom)	Library and Archives Canada C-087014
288 (top)	Department of National Defence, Directorate of History and Heritage
288 (bottom)	Library and Archives Canada PA-006023
291	Library and Archives Canada PA-118052
304	Department of National Defence, Directorate of History and Heritage

Index